To Mary —
Thanks for your
help on this —
and the cake!!!
Jerry Cook

TOWARD THE EVENING SKY

made him a
carrot cake
for birthday
2015

Helped Jerry
with critiquing
before print.

Jerry W. Cook

Jerry W. Cook

Toward The Evening Sky

Contents

Jerry W. Cook

To all the pilots and aviators
who have "flown West" from this world
into the next before me

Especially to Waymon Pearson; one of the
finest people whom I've known and finest pilots
with whom I've flown

ACKNOWLEDGEMENTS

Many are due thanks for urging me to write another book. To those who have commented after reading my first; "It ended too soon, I wanted more," or "When are you going to write another?" I thank you. You are responsible for putting the idea in my head that I could or even should, write another.

Of Susan Marchand for her encouragement and her willingness to use part of her limited spare time in an informal edit of this material.

Of Kent Shreeve and Bob Bryant for their valued review and edits of my manuscript.

Of my wife Linda; her support and her assistance as my sounding board during this project were invaluable. She sat patiently through many writings and re-writings while offering insight as to potential readers' interpretations of certain aviation and other related materials. And of course, if it had not been for her persuasion, there would not have been a first book for this one to follow.

Jerry W. Cook

INTRODUCTION

This volume is essentially a continuation of my book, "Once a Fighter Pilot". It begins the next day after "Once..." ends; and from there encompasses forty-five years of flying, mostly jets. Again it is a compilation of aviation related short stories that are arranged in the approximate order in which they occurred.

The recounted experiences within these pages include several facets of aviation with which I was personally involved; airline, military, private, charter, and corporate. Also at the end of several of these are postscripts which contain some personal observations that have been shaped by these aviation occurrences.

As in "Once..." these accounts are taken from recollections of the events and as such are as accurate as memory can make them. The statements and conversations recorded within are not represented to be word for word, but they do capture the substance of the circumstances. Although times, speeds, altitudes and places etc. may not be exact, the emotions and sensations experienced within these happenings are faithfully represented upon these pages.

As I look back on fifty-three years of flying jets, I appreciate just how privileged I was to have landed in such a wonderful and at times exciting profession.

Also, whenever I look back, I'm reminded of a common saying among pilots; "It sure beats working for a living!"

WELCOME BACK TO THE *REAL* WORLD

Offshore, South Vietnam; October, 1966

The shoreline seemed to slowly drift southwestward in the late evening haze, toward the setting sun. It seemed rather symbolic. Just yesterday morning, I had taken off on my two hundred and fifth combat mission, not realizing that it would be my last. The Twelfth Tactical Fighter Wing did not inform pilots that they were flying their final flight in the war zone and it was probably a good policy. Before it was established there had been at least one Phantom shot down after the crew had been told before takeoff that they were flying their last combat mission. Both pilots had been killed. There was certainly no implied association, but somehow it seemed even more tragic under those circumstances. The new policy had been instituted shortly after their loss.

    The noise from the C-130 Hercules' four turbo-prop engines set at climb power not only drowned out any possibility of conversation with my two fellow passengers, but seemed to effectively interfere with any extended thought processes. Regardless, my jumbled thoughts continually returned to the abrupt change of direction in my life in the last few hours. It was amazing. Suddenly the dangers of combat flying were over, but so were the possibilities of any further MiG encounters.

    I had failed in my personal campaign to find, engage and "down" enemy fighters. Unfortunately, at least from my admittedly biased point of view, the MiGs just weren't coming up to fight very often in 1966. The word had been circulating that many of the North Vietnamese pilots were still being trained, probably by Russian fighter pilots. If that was the case then I suppose that they were inclined to stay on the ground most of the time when we were in the area. I had only acquired two MiG fighters visually and a couple of "probables" on radar. In one case, the MiG had fled into the buffer zone along the Red Chinese border to safety. Our orders were very clear and very strict in that event. We were to let them go and to not encroach on the "buffer zone" under threat of all kinds of things, none of them desirable and all having to do with international politics, court martials, and the end of our military careers. The other two probable MiGs and the second "visual" had hustled back into their protective surface to air missile "rings" thereby instantly converting any offensive pursuit of glory into a defensive battle for survival against the SAMs. Some fighter pilots had been losing such battles. As well as adding an Oak Leaf Cluster to my Longevity Ribbon, perhaps the "Discretion over Valor" lessons from Aviation Cadet training had kept me from joining their number. But it was particularly difficult to break off from a possible MiG shoot-down and to not chase them all the way back to their airfield "sanctuaries".

Although air to ground held its share of excitement and reward, air to air victories have been the principal goal of fighter pilots from the inception of air combat in World War One. Since arriving in Vietnam, I had flown mostly air to ground missions. I had flown very few missions into areas where the MiGs were operating.

Therefore, early in 1966, I had requested to extend my tour in Vietnam for six months which would lengthen my personal MiG hunting season. My request had been denied for some unknown reason. That made absolutely no sense to me especially since at that time the Air Force was reportedly short of fighter pilots, particularly those with combat experience. Whatever the reason, my MiG hunting days were over. The fact that the risk involved in hunting MiGs was *also* over did not seem as significant to me as the absence of any additional opportunities for air-to-air combat. I suppose you could call that type of thought process warrior mentality or perhaps, an absence of good sense.

The engine sounds of the C-130 lessened as we leveled off for the cruise portion of the flight to Japan. I glanced out of the window. The South Vietnamese shoreline had slipped into the gathering darkness. I thought that I had probably seen it for the last time in my life. I certainly wouldn't miss it; except for the MiG hunting.

I had recently made up my mind to resign from the United States Air Force. That decision had been finalized while walking through the deep sand with my squadron commander several months before. We had been talking about how we missed being with our families. He told me that his wife back home was struggling to raise their teenage children without his help and that he hadn't gotten to be with them very much over the years. I looked over at him. He was probably ten years my senior and there he was, just as I, sweating with the effort of dragging his feet through the deep sand. I remember thinking, "Is this what I want when I'm his age?" The answer had been emphatically, "Not only no, but...*Hell no.*"

However, there was to be a slight delay of my return to the civilian world. I had been informed that my move back to the good old USA was a PCS (Permanent Change of Station) and therefore I owed the Air Force another year of active duty to pay for their expense of my return from the war. I looked down at my half full green duffel bag shoved under the seat in front of me. It didn't seem like something to have to spend another year of my life for and besides, *I* was the one lugging it. I supposed that they must have thought that eleven and one-half months of flying combat and getting shot at wasn't enough for a pre-paid return ticket home. It was an interesting personnel policy but pretty typical in that day's Air Force.

But what I thought about it really didn't matter. It was a done deal whether I liked it or not. I had been fortunate in that all I had needed "in country" was underwear, socks, and a couple of flight suits. My foot locker with the rest of my belongings in it had been PCS shipped from the states supposedly to me eleven and one-half months ago. I finally found out that it had been side-tracked to somewhere in Australia and evidently just sat there for a while. It had arrived in Vietnam only just a few months ago.

It all added up to a continuing "Snafu" (situation normal, all *fouled* up). I had not been provided with a promised "Port Call" either. That was the Air Force term for an airline ticket home. So here I was, hitchhiking to Tokyo on a C-130 and wondering how I was going to get home from there; PCS expense, *my ass*.

The war was over for me. I was alive. I was well. I was going home. But, I realized that I was also bone tired. It had been a long eleven months. I weighed one hundred and sixty-seven pounds. I was wearing the same uniform (from the recently arrived foot locker) that had fit me when I went to Vietnam weighing two hundred and seven pounds. I probably looked like they had dug me up to put it on me.

My day of good fortune continued on into a night of incredible luck. Although I had arrived in Japan without a clue as to how I was going to get the rest of the way home, here I was sitting down in the only empty seat remaining on the Airlift International DC-8. It seems that a sailor had gotten drunk while celebrating his good luck to be going home. He had partied just a little too long and had missed the plane. One of life's important lessons; in many cases one person's misfortune becomes another person's good fortune.

Anchorage, Alaska was to be the next stop on my sudden and unplanned journey back to mid-sixties America. I thought about the anti-war protesters back in the United States. If I could have foreseen the future I probably would have wondered how I would handle it if our future "Commander-in-Chief" or some other liberal protester spit on me, called me a disparaging name or tried to throw "blood" on me. I had been reading about such occurrences in news articles from the United States for some time. As it turns out he and his ilk must have been somewhere else. My thoughts returned to the present. It was hard to believe that I had flown my last combat mission just yesterday morning.

I couldn't help glancing at the stewardesses. Such is the inherent nature of most adult males, to be fascinated by the femininity of women; especially if they haven't seen one in months. The divine Creator is a master designer indeed. The attractive young women looked wonderful.

It had been a long time. I thought about almost three year old Jeff who had been so solemn and serious the day I left, and Kristin, my baby girl I'd never seen. She was four months old already. I was feeling lonely. I realized that I needed to go home. It was time.

As I closed my eyes I seemed to be able to feel the "warrior" starting to slowly, somewhat reluctantly, retreat back into the deep recesses of my mind. I wondered if I would ever again find it necessary to require "his" reappearance. I freely admit that it was satisfying for me to realize that I possessed another nature that had emerged when I needed it. My warrior identity had been tested in combat. It was a feeling impossible to fully describe but definitely satisfying. I realized how much I would miss the action, the adrenaline pumping through my body. However, I also realized that I needed to learn to live in the real world again; in its relative peace and security. The warrior part of me could rest for now, perhaps forever, but it was gratifying to know that it was there.

I was going home. It had been almost a year with a lot of close calls. The realization of just *how* close many of them actually had been became stronger as the DC-8 put more and more miles between me and the dangers of Vietnam. My regret at having been disapproved for an extension of my combat tour began to slowly dissolve. I realized that I had been more than lucky on more than one occasion. I could easily have been traveling below the passenger floor of the DC-8 in a body bag, instead of up here in a semi-comfortable seat watching the stewardesses' skirts sway back and forth as they served us snacks and drinks. I wondered if they knew how much we enjoyed watching them each time they passed. I think they must have known judging by their perceptive smiles, but they didn't seem to mind.

It had been more than eleven months since I had left home. I sat back in my seat and closed my eyes as I considered my good fortune at having completed my tour at least physically unscathed. Tens of thousands of my comrades in arms were not so lucky. Indeed, some of their bodies were perhaps traveling below the floor beneath my feet.

They had already…*gone Home.*

Postscript: President Lyndon Baines Johnson and his Secretary of Defense Robert Strange McNamara, utilizing their *infinite* wisdom combined with their *vast* combat experience, had declared Hanoi, Haiphong Harbor and the ships within it, along with several other safe zones for the enemy, off limits. Reportedly these two *military experts* were also picking our bombing targets in North Vietnam.

McNamara had essentially been a "bean counter" for General Curtis Lemay in World War Two. He evidently did so well at counting the beans that he was promoted from Captain to Lt. Colonel in just three years.

Meanwhile in 1941 while still a United States Congressman from Texas, Johnson was appointed as a Lieutenant Commander in the Naval Reserve. He was sent to the Southwest Pacific as part of a three man survey team in early 1942 purportedly because President Roosevelt wanted his own reports on conditions in that area from a "trusted" agent. I guess he didn't trust our military so he sent…*a politician!*

While there Johnson was awarded the Silver Star. According to reports he was riding as an observer on an AAF B-26 Marauder that had to turn back from a combat mission with a mechanical problem.

The Silver Star medal is defined as being awarded for "gallantry in action against an enemy" and for "showing extraordinary heroism." What possible actions Johnson could have accomplished to qualify for the Silver Star as an observer on the aircraft is simply beyond my comprehension. I guess that he "displayed gallantry in action" and "extraordinary heroism" just for riding along with the aircrew.

In fact, that is basically what his award citation states. According to the Department of the Navy's Naval Historical Center his Silver Star Citation indicates that it was awarded for *gallantry in action* for volunteering as an observer on a hazardous aerial combat mission. The citation ends with; "he evidenced marked coolness in spite of the hazards involved. His *gallant action* enabled him to obtain and return with valuable information." *What a crock....!*

Given that Johnson's *coolness* prompted *his* award, I must presume that the flight crew panicked like little schoolgirls since *none of them* got the Silver Star. In fact most accounts indicate that they didn't receive any recognition at all for that particular mission. Why would they? It wasn't even completed.

Now; "fast forward" just a few years later and we find these two self-appointed military experts selecting targets for our combat aircraft in North Vietnam. Incredibly they had declared that the MiG airfields were also off-limits to American pilots. Evidently it wasn't fair for us to destroy the North Vietnamese Air Force while they were still on the ground. Instead we had to wait for them to take off and attempt to shoot us down before we could attack them. And then after they tried to shoot us down, we had to let them escape if they got within a 10 mile buffer zone as they fled back toward their airfields. Sort of like the old kid's game "King's X".

In my view the President and his Defense Secretary were incompetent, were driven by politics, or were against us winning the war for some reason. It's still hard for me to believe that those two supposedly intelligent men in the highest positions of leadership in our country could have been that naive. I have heard some people state that they wonder if there was a hidden agenda of some sort.

What I believe is that they were unjustifiably influenced by both domestic and international politics *and* were totally unqualified to make any sort of decisions impacting tactical military operations. These factors, in concert with their refusal to utilize relevant input from the military leadership, including the Joint Chiefs of Staff, were the perfect recipe for the disaster that they created.

Whatever the case, their inane rules of engagement and appalling tactical decisions effectively kept the U. S. Air Force, Navy and Marines, from quickly gaining complete air superiority over the North Vietnamese Air Force. That would have been one of the first steps to winning, and thereby ending the war. Then the air defense network, the transportation system, petroleum and weapons storage facilities ought to have been destroyed. All military targets inside of North Vietnam should have been targeted. (We certainly dropped enough bombs to have accomplished all of this.) Closing Haiphong harbor would have been a cinch and any ships caught in it should have been sunk, period. And there should have been no bombing halts until every significant target in North Vietnam was destroyed. (And I don't mean some damned inconsequential bamboo bridge across a creek like those two tactical masterminds were picking for us.) The North Vietnamese wouldn't have been able to get to the negotiating table fast enough.

We didn't lose the Vietnam War.

Those two despicable military geniuses *gave it away.* And as you can probably tell, I'm still outraged about it.

Over 58,000 lives lost just on our side alone; and for what?!

THE AIR FORCE WAY

MacDill AFB, FL; October, 1966

I had gone immediately to the base personnel office when I got back from Vietnam. My request seemed simple and reasonable to me. It had also seemed that way to the other F-4 pilot who was involved. He and I were good friends. We were the same rank. We had been promoted the same year. We also were about the same age. We were within a few hours of each other in flying time and experience. We both had just returned from Vietnam combat tours in the F-4. We had been based at MacDill together before our deployment.

Some differences were; I was married, he was not. I owned a house in Tampa; he did not own a house anywhere. I had a family to move, he did not. I wanted to stay based at MacDill AFB, he did not. He wanted to be transferred to Homestead AFB; I did not. While still in Vietnam I had requested to return to MacDill as my base assignment while he had requested to go to Homestead. I got assigned to Homestead, he got assigned to MacDill.

We simply wanted to exchange assignments. Both of us were to fly F-4Ds, just at different bases. Everything else was basically equal. *Too damn bad.* According to the Air Force it was too late to change. It was the same answer that we had received in Vietnam several months before when we had first pursued the assignment swap. That answer was pure bull____ then and it was pure bull____ at MacDill. They just didn't want to go to the trouble. It seemed that in those days the Air Force just contained numbers, not people. It was another reason that I had elected to get out. The nonsense about the assignment trade just served to further reinforce my decision. I hoped that I would be more than an identification number in the world of civilians.

I began planning to move my family to Homestead AFB. My friend began looking for a place to live in Tampa, near MacDill. Unfortunately he didn't want to buy a house; mine included.

Jerry W. Cook

DOES HE WALK ON WATER TOO?

Homestead AFB, FL; March 1967

We finally began getting our new F-4D Phantom IIs from the McDonnell factory in Saint Louis. There was a scramble going on to get us recurrent in the brand new fighters because pilots from other aircraft types were soon to begin arriving at Homestead AFB. There they were to transition into the F-4D and learn how to employ them in combat. We were to be their flight instructors. Then, after their graduation from the fighter transition and combat course, they would be heading to other F-4 units, mostly in Southeast Asia.

Now that we were finally receiving our new F-4Ds the drill for us was a couple of practice flights to get us up to speed and then three different check rides. The first was an instrument flight check in an AT-33. The second was a tactical evaluation check in the F-4D. The third check ride was to qualify or re-qualify as an instructor in the F-4D. (One of the peculiarities and absurdities of combat flying was that while you were engaging in combat flying on a near daily basis, you very soon lost two things. One was your instrument flying currency and the other was of all things, your combat ready status.)

Although our flying proficiency was probably at its all-time high, the flight checks to confirm that were waived during our combat tours. Consequently, we came back from nearly a year of combat flying, technically unqualified for combat flying. How about that?

My re-currency flights in the Phantom had gone well. The F-4D was basically the same machine that I had been flying for several years. Although there were some very minor avionics differences from the F-4C, I felt immediately at home in the cockpit. In fact, things had progressed so rapidly that my instructor pilot decided to have me accomplish my check rides early *and* to combine them all into one flight. We were still short of F-4s and he didn't see a need to waste more flying hours and his time in any further flights. Therefore in just one extended check flight, I became both combat ready and recurrent as an F-4 instructor pilot.

The next morning in the Wing Command Post Standup Briefing for the Wing Commander, the Colonel immediately noticed my busy check flight of the previous day on the briefing slide. He studied it for a few moments and then said, "Does this guy Cook walk on water too?"

The now nervous briefing officer paused for a moment and then he grinned and answered, "I'm not sure sir, but his initials *are* J.C."

The Colonel didn't laugh.

Toward The Evening Sky

WHAT WERE THEY THINKING?

Homestead AFB, FL; 1967

As stated previously my job as an instructor at Homestead AFB was to train pilots in the F-4D before they were transferred to Vietnam or other bases in Southeast Asia to fly combat. The reason that I heard was that the Air Force didn't want their fighter pilots to have to serve multiple tours in combat. (Why did they think we had signed up to be fighter pilots in the first place? It certainly wasn't to be flight instructors.) Some of the pilots who we were tasked to train had been flying only large multi-engine aircraft for several years. And it became painfully obvious that certain of those pilots should never have been put into that situation.

One of my students was a prime example. He was a Major and had been a KC-135 pilot in the Strategic Air Command. His basic air work and instrument flying were fine but I noticed that whenever we rolled into a turn with more than thirty or thirty-five degrees of bank he would sound as if he was hyper-ventilating. I didn't think too much about it until we left the transition phase and entered the air to ground weapons deployment segment.

We were on our first high angle dive bomb demonstration with me flying the Phantom from the back seat. While I was turning onto the base leg of the bombing pattern using about ninety degrees of bank, I heard him breathing very hard. When the target approached our nine o' clock low position I pulled the fighter into a high G ninety degree left turn and then rolled it inverted and pulled the nose down. He was breathing so hard that I was not sure that he heard any of the instructions that I was giving over the interphone. As I pulled out of our steep dive using about five G's I heard him grunting very loudly and rapidly. As we turned onto our climbing downwind leg I waggled the stick and gave him control of the airplane.

We leveled at eight thousand feet and when the target was at about our seven to eight o'clock position I instructed him to turn onto our base leg. He turned using about forty degrees of bank and was breathing very loudly. I shoved the stick over until the bank was about ninety degrees and said, "Like *that.*" He was really pumping in the air now. He rolled out on the base leg for the dive bomb pass.

When we reached the proper position from the target I called, "Roll in now." He rolled into about a forty-five degree bank.

"I said *roll in!*" I repeated in a louder voice.

He replied, "I did."

I stated firmly, *"No...you didn't!"* and before we'd gone too far I grabbed the stick and rapidly rolled the Phantom into a left 135 degree bank and snatched the nose down with about 4G's until it was 45 degrees below the horizon. Then I rolled upright with the big fighter's nose pointed just below the target.

"*Now* you're rolled in." I announced, thoroughly exasperated.

I thought he would burst his lungs from his extreme breathing. It was painfully obvious. This guy was petrified. What was he going to do when the "bad guys" started shooting at him? He did *not* belong in a jet fighter.

As an example of the reason why, the very next year a friend named Dick whom I'd been stationed with at MacDill AFB was flying combat wing on another F-4 over North Vietnam. His lead aircraft was being flown by a Major. They were suddenly attacked by MiG-17s.

Dick called out his flight's call sign and; *"MiGs! Break Right!"*

The Major evidently thought that *"Break Right!"* meant 60 or 70 degrees of bank and three G's. Dick called for his lead pilot to tighten the turn because the MiG-17s were beginning to "pull lead" (aim their guns out in front of the Phantoms to shoot them down). The leader did not tighten his turn or better yet, use his Phantom's superior power to go vertical or to accelerate away from the MiG-17s.

Unfortunately, Dick stayed too long in the turn with his flight leader. A 37 millimeter cannon shell tore into his Phantom and he began losing fuel at a high rate. Now having no choice he immediately rolled upright and pulled his Phantom into a near vertical climb, leaving his attackers and the other F-4 far below.

He almost made it to the KC-135 tanker out in the Gulf of Tonkin before the last of the fuel streamed out of his severely damaged F-4. His engines flamed out. He and his back-seat pilot ejected and were plucked out of the water in a few hours. They were deposited back at Da Nang Air Base later that evening.

Of course Dick's flight leader ended up being shot down in that engagement. It is my opinion that the two pilot deaths and the *two* downed F-4s may have been the direct result of gravely flawed judgment by the officials in charge of Air Force fighter pilot staffing.

Was the Major a former student of the F-4 checkout program at Homestead Air Force Base? I don't know. But one thing is for damn certain. Any pilot who thinks a 70 degree banked 3G or 4G turn is a fighter break sure as Hell isn't a fighter pilot and absolutely does not belong in one no matter what his background may be.

To essentially end up as cannon fodder to die and kill your back-seat pilot in the process is a high price to pay for such a misguided concept; no matter whom or where it came from.

It's terrible enough when your own flawed decisions end up killing you. It seems even more tragic when someone else's do.

Toward The Evening Sky

MUCH HARDER AND MORE CRITICAL

Homestead AFB, FL; 1967

I had been serving in the Homestead Air Force Base Command Post as the Officer Duty Controller when the sergeant handed me the phone message. It was from National Airlines. They wanted me to call them.

The Wing Commander at Homestead had recently banished me to the command post when he could not persuade me to stay in Uncle Sam's Air Force. He had called me to his office when he was informed that it was my intention to resign from the USAF. He even "ran the American flag up the flag pole", so to speak, and had insinuated that the only patriotic thing for me to do was to stay. That had ticked me off somewhat because I had not been back in the States from the "Unpopular War" but a few months. Perhaps the war was *so* unpopular that flying combat in it did not count as paying any patriotic dues in his opinion. In any case when he saw that the tactic was not working, he had then opened his top desk drawer and pulled out a TWX message form. He said, "I would hate to lose you from my F-4D Wing here at Homestead Captain Cook, but I'd hate even more to lose you to the airlines. If you stay in, I'll give you this assignment, a regular commission, and a "below the zone" promotion to Major." (I remember thinking that he had just made at least two promises that he probably didn't have the "horsepower" to guarantee. The assignment he probably could have made happen if he wished.)

I looked at the message form. It was an assignment to Nellis Air Force Base, Nevada. The job was flying the F-111 "Aardvark". I laid the TWX down on the Wing Commander's desk and said, "Sir, I'm already flying twice the airplane that 'piece of crap' will ever be." (In my opinion, that the F-111 even existed was another shining example of pork politics in action. Some called it McNamara's "Baby." Others jokingly referred to it as his "Flying Edsel". But it really was no joke. McNamara had insisted on building it despite its many developmental problems. He believed that both the Navy and Air Force could be adequately served by the aircraft which was to be joint-use. Fortunately for them the Navy was finally able to drop its version in 1968 because of difficulties adapting it for Navy use. Although many in the Air Force considered the plane a failure in meeting its requirements, they took delivery. Interestingly, Aardvark means earth pig…in my opinion a very appropriate moniker.)

The full Colonel sitting in front of me did not take my remark too kindly. Now there were two of us pissed off and he had me seriously outranked. Although perhaps not very smart, it was my disposition to not back down when I knew that I was right. The F-111 was a piece of crap and I wanted no part of it.

11

"Have you ever heard the term 'furlough' Captain?" He had suddenly changed tactics again. He was of course referring to the word used when the airlines lay off some of their pilots.

"Yes sir and I've also heard the term RIF," I answered. I was referring to the term used when the Air Force initiated a "reduction in force." It meant that they thought that they had too many personnel and you were basically fired. However unlike the airline's furloughs, you had no recall rights. Your Air Force career was over.

"You're dismissed Captain," he fired back. He was really ticked off now. I saluted and quickly left. During the next few days I was transferred to the Wing Command Post as a duty officer. (I wonder *why* that happened.) I still flew the F-4D until my separation date; just not as my primary duty and not quite as often as before.

The thoughts of my final meeting with the Wing Commander quickly faded as National's Chief Pilot looked up at me. His head was big, bald and shiny as he bent over my Air Force Form 5 flying records. I was having difficulty in containing my excitement at being called for an interview with the Chief Pilot of National Airlines. I had interviewed and taken the written test for pilot employment with them about a month before but had not heard from them until that morning.

"I see here that you have just over two thousand and eight hundred hours of military flying time," he said.

"Yes sir. That is correct," I replied.

"Do you have any civilian flying hours?" he continued.

"No sir. Everything I have is Air Force," I answered.

"I see. How much of your two thousand, eight hundred hours is jet time?" he asked.

"Everything is jet except for about one hundred and thirty hours in T-34s and T-28s as a student pilot," I replied.

"Do you have any multi-engine time Captain?" he inquired. I knew what he was driving at. He wanted me to have some transport category multi-engine experience, which I did not have. I could tell that he considered that to be important, but it didn't matter. I had none.

"The only flying time I have with more than one engine is in the T-37 and the F-4," I anxiously answered. (However they are considered "center-line thrust"; not as critical with an engine failure as real multi-engine aircraft with their power-plants further apart.)

"Well Jerry, I sure wish you had some multi-engine experience. You're going to have to realize that flying for the airlines is *much harder and more critical* than what you have been doing in the Air Force," he began.

His remark caught me off guard and I had to swallow hard and bite my tongue. I regained my composure, "Well sir, I...." I was glad that he interrupted me because I didn't know what I was going to say next.

"Let me give you an example," he continued. "Let's say that you're scheduled to fly a trip in a Boeing 727 from Miami to New York with a scheduled stop in Washington D.C. The weather is beautiful in Miami, with sunny skies and seventy or eighty degrees. You take off but before you get to Washington National Airport, the weather has lowered to two hundred feet overcast and one-half mile visibility with rain. You have to perform an ILS (instrument landing system) to get on the ground."

I waited for the "kicker". I knew that there had to be a kicker, like an engine failure or fire, a hydraulic or a landing gear problem, something. I waited for the rest of the scenario. There was a long pregnant silence. When he finally looked quizzically at me for my reaction, I realized that the scene was finished. That was it…200 feet and a 1/2 mile visibility with rain and an ILS approach. He had to be kidding. I had strafed and skip-bombed in weather not a whole lot better than that; sometimes in the mountains of Laos and Vietnam. I remember thinking, "Man how naive can you get? What a dumbass." But I couldn't say it. Not if I wanted to fly for his airline, I couldn't. Instead I said, "Well sir; I guess I see what you mean. But I'm sure that I can learn to do that if you will give me the chance."

"Our policy is that we don't just hire co-pilots Jerry," he said. We hire future airline captains," he continued.

"Yes sir, I understand. That's just what I want to be," I announced.

"We'll see, we'll see," he mused. "Can you stay here another hour or so?" he asked.

"Certainly," I stated inquiringly.

"We have to see if you can actually fly," he said rather matter-of-factly. He was serious. This guy didn't have a clue and he was National's Chief Pilot. He picked up the telephone. Me? I was fuming on the inside and trying very hard to keep it on the inside.

"Bill, I've got an Air Force fighter pilot over here who thinks he can learn how to fly airliners. I'm going to send him over to see if you think that he can," the Chief Pilot said. "Yeah, he said that he could stay another hour or so. I'll send him right now," he ended and hung up the phone.

I entered the front door of the training building and followed the signs to the simulator briefing room. "Bill" proved to be a gruff and unfriendly character with glasses hanging off his nose. It seemed like it "pained" him when I stuck out my hand and introduced myself.

"Yeah, I know who you are," he said as he gave me a "dead fish" handshake. (I hate that from a man. It always makes me want to squeeze hard to the point of bone breakage, but it's usually too late by the time I realize it.) "Sit down and listen. I'm not going to say this twice." I remember thinking, "What an ass_____."

"We're going to takeoff on Runway 09 Left, then intercept and track the 348 degree radial to the Biscayne VOR, then direct to the intersection of the 165 degree radial of Biscayne and the 130 degree radial of the Miami VOR, then direct to the Miami VOR. Maintain six thousand feet and when you cross the localizer course for Runway 09L at Miami, slow to holding airspeed. Hold at the Miami VOR at six thousand. Ignore the published holding pattern. I'll give you the holding radial and the direction of turns just before we get to the VOR. I want you to tell me the type of holding entry within three seconds. We'll make a couple of turns in holding, and then execute the VOR teardrop approach to Runway 09L. We'll make a full stop landing; any questions, *Captain*?" His voice was nearly dripping with disdain as he used the word.

I wasn't about to ask this charismatic character any questions. He had talked so fast and briefed me without any warning or preparation on my part. I didn't even have a pencil or anything to write it down on if I had. I thought to myself, "This guy is either trying to shake me up or he's crazy." Either way I wasn't going to give him the satisfaction of my having to ask him a question. A couple of things were for sure. One; I was determined to show him that I could indeed fly. Two; I wasn't about to let him shake me up. I thought quickly about his abrupt "briefing" and was pleasantly surprised that I pretty much remembered everything he had said. I knew that he would have to loan me some airway and instrument approach charts. Surely he didn't expect me to have them memorized.

My next thought was, "I don't have a clue what kind of aircraft simulator we will be in." However, I wasn't about to ask this walking attitude problem. Thinking back to the National Chief Pilot's remarks about flying the 727 to Washington, I thought maybe it would be a Boeing 727, their newest equipment. At least that was a jet and I would know something about the engines anyway.

As we walked through the door into the simulator area I saw the placard, "Lockheed Electra". *"Wonderful!"* I had never flown a turbo-prop aircraft in my life. Once again I kept my thoughts inside. I would not allow this guy to see me sweat. No way.

He motioned me into the right seat of the strange machine. As I was strapping in I was wondering, "How in the world am I going to start this thing?" I was looking around the strange cockpit as stealthily as I could.

"We weigh eighty five thousand pounds. What are V1, VR and V2?" he suddenly barked.

Providence was with me. My gaze had just settled on a chart taped towards the bottom of the instrument panel. I barked back the speeds and watched as he set them on his airspeed indicator. I did the same. Heck, I barely knew what the terms *meant*. I wondered if he had really expected me to know the numbers themselves or where to find them. I figured that he was still trying to see if he could rattle me. I was determined that he was not going to do it.

He helped me to start the four turbo-prop engines. That he was willing to help that much surprised me. I guess if he had not, I would have located the checklist and done it myself. I had found Miami approach plates and the local airways chart in a side pocket.

"Do you remember what you're supposed to do, *Captain*?" he asked with what again appeared to be undisguised contempt.

"Yes I do," I replied.

"Then do it," he growled. He had taxied us onto Runway 09L at Miami International Airport and aligned the Lockheed Electra aircraft simulator with the runway centerline. I pushed the throttles up to the approximate setting which I had found on yet another placard placed perhaps providentially in my line of sight and away we went. As he bellowed out the word "Rotate," I pulled the control yoke back, lifting the nose wheel clear of the runway, and we were off.

"Gear up," I called when we were definitely airborne and climbing. I didn't have a clue about the flap retraction speed. I had not found that particular information yet so I just let the airspeed build to thirty knots above the rotate speed and called, "Flaps up." I guess it was fast enough because he raised the flaps and we didn't fall out of the sky.

I had the number two navigation receiver, after I had found it, tuned to the Runway 09L localizer frequency and followed its back course as we headed east toward Miami Beach and the Atlantic Ocean. I had tuned the number one navigation receiver to the Biscayne VOR and cross checked the number one VOR indicator needle so I could intercept the radial of the VOR station. I was amazed that I was remembering all of his briefing, but I was and the charts helped.

My "flight examiner" said nothing. He just sat and watched. The Electra turned out to be just another airplane. I had learned early in my flying that, "If you can trim them, you can fly them." I was really being smooth. However, I think it was mostly because the big turbo-prop was so much heavier on the controls than the F-4D Phantoms that I was used to and not necessarily due to any particular finesse on my part.

We were within about ten degrees of the airway course and it was time for me to begin the turn to intercept the radial southbound toward Biscayne. I set in the new inbound radial in my course indicator and re-tuned my navigation receiver to the Biscayne VOR frequency. And so it went; I tracked along the briefed radials consulting the chart on my lap while the guy in the left seat just watched. We eventually turned north and proceeded toward the Miami VOR, located to the northwest of Miami International Airport. It was where the instrument approach procedure would begin. I then re-tuned the number one navigation receiver to the Runway 09L localizer and began checking the left side course deviation indicator for movement.

As we crossed the localizer course, I pulled the throttles back and began to slow to the holding airspeed which the left seat pilot had just assigned me. (It was the first help that he had given me besides the engine starts.) We were now within about three minutes of the VOR station. We were approaching the time when he was supposed to assign me an inbound holding radial. My mind was racing to review the possible entry procedures.

"Two seven zero, right hand!" he literally yelled it out. It was *so* loud that I almost jumped out of my seat. According to his earlier briefing, I had to call out the type of entry to the holding pattern within three seconds.

"Parallel," I called out.

"Forget that," he said. Then, "Three five zero, left turns," he said loudly.

"Teardrop," I called quickly.

"Zero eight five, right turns," he called out the third consecutive holding instruction. It appeared that he was trying to keep giving them out until I made a mistake.

"Direct," I said. He seemed disappointed.

"Okay, forget all that. Hold as depicted," he finally said.

The door suddenly opened to the simulator. We were about a minute and a half from the VOR. I glanced up and over my left shoulder. There were several young men trying to squeeze into the small space behind us. I looked back at my instruments and then down at my approach chart.

"Excuse me," said one of the young men behind me. I looked at him momentarily as he leaned over my left shoulder and pointed at my RMI (Radio Magnetic Indicator).

He continued. "That little needle there; doesn't it point to the VOR station?" he asked.

"If it's selected to the VOR it does," I answered.

"When you cross over the VOR station, doesn't it swing and point toward the tail?" he said.

"Once you are out of the 'cone of confusion' directly over the station, it keeps pointing at the VOR whatever its direction from your aircraft," I answered. I was thinking that these guys must be on a high school field trip or something.

"Okay, thanks," the young man said.

"You're welcome," I answered. It was almost time for me to begin the holding pattern entry. The visitors began filing out of the simulator.

I completed the outbound turn in the entry and my curiosity finally got to me. Up to this point I hadn't said a word to the friendly soul in the left seat except "Gear up, flaps up," and when calling out the types of holding pattern entries.

"Who were those guys?" I finally asked.

"That was part of the new pilot class that we just hired," was his cryptic answer.

I couldn't believe it. The guy who had just asked me about "that little needle" had already been hired to fly for National. Meanwhile, here I was being examined by this unfriendly bastard in the left seat to "see if I could fly".

It really was unbelievable to me, almost unacceptable. It made me wonder about the thought processes going on around National Airlines those days. I didn't have time to think about it further as the timing was up and it was time to turn and intercept the holding radial. Twenty five minutes later we were back in the briefing room; just me and Mr. Personality.

"You did all right. I'll call the Chief and tell him you can fly," he said.

"All right my ass," I thought. This guy had thrown an unexpected briefing at me, thrown me into an unfamiliar airplane simulator and been as helpful as a "bump on a log". I hadn't forgotten a damn thing or made any mistakes at all that I was aware of and he certainly hadn't pointed any out to me.

"All right my ass," I thought again.

"Do you have any questions?" he asked.

"Only one," I answered. "Were those guys *really* in the new pilot class that National just hired?"

"Yeah, why?" he said.

I thought, "If you don't know, I'm not going to tell you," but I just said, "Oh, nothing."

"Bill said you did all right." I was back in the Chief Pilot's office. I thought again about the "highly qualified" new class member I had just observed and said nothing. I also thought that I was beginning to understand *why* this Chief Pilot thought airline flying was so hard. Hard is a comparative term when used in that way. Whether or not something is hard depends on one's personal capability to do it. I wished I could take this guy for a ride in an F-4D and let him show me "if he could fly". I was pretty sure that I already knew the answer. (Looking back, I believe that this experience helped to further convince me not be impressed by titles in front of, or capitalized initials behind a name until the individual proved that they deserved them.)

"What did Bill do before he started checking fighter pilots to see if they can *actually* fly?" I said with just a touch of sarcasm.

"Oh, he's a medically grounded Captain; really a nice guy. You have got to feel sorry for him," he answered.

"Yeah, right," I thought to myself. "Sorry" wasn't exactly the word I was thinking of, at least not in the same context. "Oh well. Don't screw it up now," was my next thought.

"Oh," was all I said.

Jerry W. Cook

THE WORLD'S MOST EXPERIENCED

Homestead AFB, FL; July 1967

I had been hired by National Airlines; however the telegram I had just received was not from them. National had hired me for a mid-July class as a first officer candidate in a Boeing 727. I was happy about the job but I was having mixed emotions. I knew that the best thing for my family was to leave the life of a fighter pilot and become a civilian. Since the only thing I was trained for was to fly airplanes, I thought that the airlines were my best bet for a job as a pilot. Still I had never really had much of a desire to fly for the airlines. Hauling people or boxes from point A to point B had never struck me as being a particularly rewarding experience; at least not as far as excitement and challenge. In fact, it seemed very boring. However, it had the advantage of being financially rewarding and did not involve periods of months and even years away from home. That was the main consideration, the time at home. Still, I was really going to miss flying jet fighters.

Way in the back of my mind was a possible solution to my dilemma. I had discovered the Air National Guard while at Lackland AFB when I first arrived fresh from civilian life. Several of the cadets I met there had been members of the Air Guard. I was amazed at what they had revealed to me. Instead of having to compete for the highest class standings so as to obtain a fighter assignment, they knew exactly what they would be flying and where. They got the same training that I did and then they went to check out in whatever aircraft types that their particular Air Guard unit flew. After they had finished their checkouts in the new aircraft, they reverted to civilian status and flew several times a month to fulfill their requirements and maintain their currency. (Air Guard members are responsible for the same readiness requirements as their regular Air Force counterparts. They also are required to serve at least fifteen days a year on active duty.) The rest of the time they are free to pursue any civilian careers that they wished. Most of the ones that I knew had become airline pilots; talk about "having your cake and eating it too". They were flying airliners for a living and jet fighters for the love of it. It had been too late for me by the time I found out about the Air National Guard. I was already committed to the Air Force. However had I known about it in time, I would probably have been Air Guard all the way.

My new plan of action had become; get a job with the airlines first, then join an Air Guard unit and fly fighters again, part time. I wanted a piece of the same cake that my old pilot training friends were having. I was just going to have to accomplish it in the reverse order from what they did. I thought that National Airlines had just helped me to take the first step.

However what had been an easy decision; stay in the Miami area and fly 727's with "Florida's Own Airline" had suddenly become a more difficult one. The telegram in my hand was from Pan American World Airways. I had interviewed with them several months before but had not heard a word. The Western Union message stated that they had accepted me for an August class in San Francisco. I was to be trained as a Pilot/Engineer in Boeing 707's. They wanted me to be based in San Francisco, California and "ride sideways" as an engineer on a Boeing 707 until I was senior enough to move into the first officer position. That didn't sound too bad as I had been told by Pan Am that I should move to the Captain's seat within five years.

But San Francisco was over three thousand miles away instead of just staying in the Miami area and flying for National. Additionally, I would be riding as a Pilot/Engineer in a 707 instead of actually flying a National 727 as a real pilot in the right seat. Looking back, it seems like a very, very bad decision. However, one of the reasons I had made it was National's continuing management and personnel problems. Recently, several of their unions had or were, threatening to strike. It seemed that they were always in the local papers with some sort of problem. Another factor was the less than positive impression that the National Chief Pilot had made on me. I wasn't sure that I wanted to fly for someone that ignorant.

On the other hand, in 1967 Pan American World Airways had a reputation as the number one airline in the world, even with many pilots from other airlines. It was undeniably a pioneer in the aviation industry. It was the first to fly many types of aircraft. It had designed and built many airline navigational facilities and was instrumental in the development of several of the world's airports. It was the premier "Flag Carrier" of the United States. All of its routes were international. As far as I and multitudes of others were concerned, it was the most prestigious airline in the world. I was even told, by a Captain with another airline that, "If every airline in the world folded, Pan Am is so financially and politically strong they would be the last to go." That represented the prevailing conventional wisdom. So I thought; "Why would I want to fly for 'Florida's Own Airline' instead of 'The World's Most Experienced'?" Sadly, as I soon learned, "Most Experienced" didn't necessarily translate into best managed or even the safest flight operations.

Perhaps because of the apparent disrespect and ignorance that I had received from the National Chief Pilot; instead of informing National that I wasn't going to work for them, I called another F-4 pilot friend of mine at Homestead AFB. He had interviewed with National also and had been given the same, "Let's see if you can fly" routine as I had. They had not as yet told him that he would be hired, but they had indicated that he had passed all of their tests. Like me, he was getting out of the Air Force in early July but did not yet have a job. I informed him that I was not going to accept my job with National but instead was going to Pan Am. I suggested to him that if he wanted my class slot with National, to show up in my place for the first day of class and I would not tell them that I wasn't coming. I was pretty sure that they would want to fill the class and since he had passed all of their tests that they would let him stay. That is exactly what happened. He became a 727 co-pilot for National.

I didn't feel a bit guilty for not having told them. I was still hacked off about the "Airline flying is much harder and more critical than what you've been doing in the Air Force", and the "Let's see if you can *actually* fly", remarks. I didn't particularly care if they got mad at me or not. Besides, I didn't want them to stick one of those, "Doesn't that little needle point to the VOR?" guys in the class instead of one of my friends.

Toward The Evening Sky

BIG MISTAKE

San Francisco International Airport, CA; August 1967

After packing up and bringing my family completely across the country and moving them into an apartment in Belmont, California, I found myself sitting in the Pan Am training building at San Francisco International Airport, also known to pilots as KSFO. I could hardly see around the stacks of manuals, books and checklists that had been issued to me and my classmates a few minutes before. The instructor was talking about the training course and what we would be studying. It did not seem in the least bit interesting. It sounded like we were going to be learning how to build a Boeing 707 instead of being instructed on how to operate one. Also it was becoming increasingly clear that there was an undercurrent of something unpleasant in the whole atmosphere of the place. It almost seemed that there was resentment at having to teach us the 707 systems and I silently wondered if this was another medically grounded pilot who hated his job like the one had at National. He seemed to resent any questions from the class and more than once gave the questioner the "dumbs___" treatment. Consequently, in the following days the questions became fewer and the atmosphere increasingly gloomy. I began to think that I had made a serious error in judgment in coming to Pan Am. I wished that I was back in Miami in the Boeing 727 pilot class at National. At least I would be learning how to fly one instead of how to build it.

One day in electrical class, I thought that I would lighten the atmosphere which had not improved in the few weeks that we had been in ground school. Each student had a huge chart of the entire Boeing 707 electrical system spread out on the table in front of him. Unluckily I had just been asked by the instructor if I thought that I could trace an electron from the engine number three generator all the way to its circuit breaker located on circuit breaker panel P13.

As I stared down at the huge myriad of circuits with all the diodes, resistors and relays I replied, "I'm not sure sir, but if you'll show me where the Tokyo Palace Hotel is on this map I think I can find my way to the Ginza." The whole class laughed; except for the instructor. He obviously did not think that I was nearly as funny as I did. Fortunately however, I finally did manage to trace the electron to circuit breaker panel P13.

After a few weeks of this I thought that I had figured out the reason for the dour attitude at Pilot/Engineer training. It turned out that for years Pan Am had used non-pilot flight engineers. They were referred to as "Professional Flight Engineers" versus our being "Pilot/Engineers." As a result of a Federal Aviation Agency rule change and a shortage of flight engineers, Pan Am had begun hiring pilots to fly as flight engineers until needed as co-pilots.

Pan Am had offered pilot training assistance to the professional Flight Engineers so that they could get into a pilot status, but relatively few had taken them up on the offer. I don't think they wanted to give up seniority and start over at the bottom of the pilot's seniority list. Additionally, I suspect that some of them were very unsure of how well they might do training to be a pilot so late in their careers. Consequently newly hired Pilot/Engineers would eventually be bypassing them to the First Officer (Co-pilot) position and then to the Captain's seat.

Instead, they seemed determined to prove that somehow they were not only indispensable but should be separate from the "piloting" crew. So in addition to the engineers' union and seniority list being separate and apart from the pilots, they had essentially established an "invisible" wall in the cockpit between the pilots and the flight engineers. Another apparent viewpoint of some of the professional engineers was that there wasn't any pilot smart enough to be a Flight Engineer. Perhaps that was the basis for the sour and very unaccommodating attitudes toward new pilots hired as Pilot/Engineers.

It was hard for me to believe that so many of the Professional Flight Engineers did not seem to be the least bit interested in what was going on in the pilots' seats. Indeed they had indicated to us as newly hired Pilot/Engineers that we were not to be either; not if we wanted to keep our jobs. There was very little crew concept or crew coordination between the pilots and the engineers and I believe that in some instances the checklists were separate.

In my opinion "The World's Most Experienced Airline" was being managed and operated by some individuals with very unprofessional attitudes. Much like National Airlines had in the Miami newspaper articles, they seemed to be having serious personnel problems of their own. They were using procedures that not only did not contribute to flying safety but in my opinion seriously detracted from it. I began to be more and more convinced that I should be flying National Airlines' Boeing 727s out of Miami, but it was too late.

To add to my consternation about becoming a party to the dysfunctional cockpit crew procedures at Pan Am, I had received a telegram from American Airlines requesting that I report to Dallas for processing to become a pilot for them. I had felt at the time that there was no way that I could leave and move my family to Dallas so soon after moving them to California. Besides, I would be a Captain at Pan Am in five years…yeah, *right*. Unfortunately, many times over the ensuing years I would live to regret that decision.

Instead, I would be riding sideways to the far side of the Pacific, and indeed the world, risking my job by sneaking glances at the pilots' instruments. I knew that they would have to be quick looks so the

Professional Flight Engineer wouldn't catch me. I had a strong suspicion that I would be in trouble and possibly fired if one of them did. This job did not look like it was going to be the least bit enjoyable and instead, very boring and unrewarding. My duties were going to mainly consist of maintaining proper cabin pressurization, keeping the fuel tanks in balance and trying to stay awake. And the professional engineers had tried to convince us that one had to be really smart to do this job; *"What a load of bull!"*

But probably the thing that amazed me the most was that the Professional Engineer group got away with dividing the cockpit the way that they did. I don't think that some of them that I flew with *ever* looked outside of the cockpit windows for other airplanes.

But who was I to question the world's premier airline? I was just a probationary Pilot/Engineer who would have to sneak glances at the pilots' instruments and out of the cockpit windows for other air traffic because; *no job is worth dying over….*

Jerry W. Cook

FLYING "BIG BIRD"

Stockton Metropolitan Airport, CA; September 1967

At least it was a big bird to me. It was a beautiful airplane but on the controls it felt like what I imagined an eighteen wheeler would feel like; that is if a truck could fly.

In ground school it had been difficult for me to believe that such a flight control system as the one in the Boeing 707 would actually work on anything larger than a Cessna or a Piper. But remarkably, the flight controls were moved by a cable and pulley system. The rudder was slightly more sophisticated as it also had a hydraulic boost to assist the pilot in moving it. And even more surprising, the control cables weren't actually attached to the ailerons and elevators. They moved servo tabs attached to the ailerons and elevators which "flew" those control surfaces into the positions (or fairly close to it) that were being called for by the pilots' control yoke. They reduced the effort required to move the controls because of their leveraged location near the rear of the control surface. They changed the airflow over and under the affected surface when they were moved up or down. This in turn, caused the ailerons and elevators to move in the opposite direction from the control tab, which moved the wing or tail of the plane in the desired direction. As one might imagine there was some delay between the control yoke input and the desired result.

As Pilot/Engineers we were given a short checkout in the 707. The purpose given to us was so we could fly and land it in case the pilots were both incapacitated. This was all very interesting to me especially since it was done in an airplane and not a simulator. Additionally, since we were not to receive any recurring proficiency flights, I'm not sure of how great we would have done after a year or two of not flying the plane; *probably not all that great.*

A question in my mind was, "What about all of the flights on which the engineer was not a Pilot/Engineer but a Professional Flight Engineer? What if the pilots were both incapacitated then?" I wondered, but I never asked.

There were several of us on board for the training flight. We had been round and round the traffic pattern making multiple touch and go and full stop landings. Finally the aircraft made the full stop landing that I was waiting for and taxied onto the large ramp where the trainees were swapped.

I was next. I slid into the right seat and strapped in. The instructor pilot taxied to the end of the long runway. In addition to having very little air traffic, the long runway was another reason that Pan Am used the Stockton airport. If my memory is correct, it was more than 10,000 feet long. The instructor lined up the 707 on the runway centerline and turned over the controls to me, but he would steer with the tiller located on his left console until the airspeed became fast enough for me to guide down the runway using only the rudder. We received takeoff clearance from the tower and I pushed up the throttles. The flight engineer made the final engine thrust settings and away we went with the instructor calling out the V1, VR and V2 speeds. What a handful the big bird was. At the slower speeds in the airport traffic pattern, quite a bit of muscle power and a lot of lead time was required to make the turns.

We were on the downwind leg opposite the runway for my first of three landings. It was to be a normal landing using all engines and full flaps. I wrestled the plane through the base leg turn and rolled out on final approach after calling for the landing gear and flaps at the designated places in the pattern. I was getting more used to the heavy control feel and the delays in response from the big aircraft.

This was a flying demonstration of the meaning of inertia. The big plane wanted to keep going in whatever direction it was going at the time and had to be forced to change. The control yoke was in constant motion to keep the wings where I wanted them to be and the throttles had to be frequently moved to keep the targeted airspeeds. I was sweating but I was enjoying the challenge of putting the plane where I wanted it instead of where it wanted to go. The instructor did not say much or offer any instruction. It was obvious to me that he probably wasn't really trying to give any flight instruction but was just filling the squares. He knew as well as I did that this would probably be the last time for a long time that I would get to fly the 707 again, so why bother?

The second traffic pattern that he had me to perform was with three engines and with a partial flap landing. He gave me the target speeds and we set the airspeed reminder bugs. Then he talked a little bit on the downwind about flap settings but that was all. I was surprised that he wanted me to make an engine out approach and landing because we had not had any ground school or simulator training in such maneuvers or for that matter any maneuvers. He pulled the number 4 engine to idle. All went well and it was actually much easier than I thought it would be. I primarily used engines number 2 and 3 for speed control with number 1 set at a relatively low thrust setting. I didn't move it except for very small adjustments when absolutely necessary. That effectively avoided any noticeable yaw induced rolls. It also required a lot less rudder trimming and re-trimming. We touched down and the instructor reset the flaps, trimmed the stabilizer for takeoff, the rudder back to neutral and "stood up" the four throttles until all four engines were at nearly the same RPM. That took several seconds and then he turned the throttles back over to me and said, "Push em up." I rotated when he called "VR" and up we climbed to pattern altitude for my last landing.

I assumed that my final landing would be with four engines and normal flap settings but I was wrong. The instructor looked at me and said,

"Do you want to try a two engine approach and landing?"

I answered, "I can give it a shot." I tried to mask the surprise in my voice.

He said "Okay, how do you think you would do it?"

I replied, "I would keep my speed up all the way around the pattern, ask for at least a seven mile final, lower the gear on final, and lower the flaps in increments as we got closer." I also said that I would not use full flaps for landing or pull the power back on the "good" engines until we had the landing assured.

He said "Fair enough. *Don't get slow.*"

Then he pulled back engines 3 and 4 to idle. The aircraft started to yaw to the right and I quickly trimmed in some left rudder. I was really surprised now. I had not thought that he would leave me with "good" engines on just one wing. I had expected him to leave me with number 2 and number 3; or numbers 1 and 4, which would have been much less critical. Opposing engines on each wing would cause much less of a yaw and roll tendency in case I needed to speed up and had to add power. Even asymmetrical engines on each wing would have been less critical. Like the man had said, *"Don't get slow."*

I actually enjoyed the challenge and had fun ripping around the traffic pattern at two hundred knots and then maintaining the required speed changes as we proceeded down the long final approach. I was nervous but I was determined to pull this off without his assistance. I never came close to getting too slow and maintained a cushion of speed using mainly number 2 engine. Again, that reduced any yaw tendencies and provided plenty of power, as long as I kept the speed well above the minimum for each flap setting. I was still about ten knots fast as we touched down. But like I said; it was a nice long runway.

After all these years I still wonder sometimes why he let me try that. Maybe he was bored.

Toward The Evening Sky

IN-COUNTRY

Southeast Asia; Fall-Winter 1967-68

In-Country #1: When I had flown my last combat mission in Vietnam just a little over a year before, I figured that I had seen the last of that beautiful green but war torn country. But here I was sliding down the final approach again to the runway at Cam Ranh Bay Airbase, South Vietnam.

This time however I was riding sideways on a Boeing 707-320C freighter. It was a dark night and we were lined up on the new concrete runway that they had opened since I left. I swiveled my seat around to the front and I could see the approach and runway lights dead ahead.

The hills far off to our left side as we flew up the small bay suddenly lit up with tracer fire. It was small arms stuff, likely thirty caliber. I had seen this little fireworks display before during the nearly year that I was stationed here. The "real estate" to the west of the army base at Cam Ranh belonged to the bad guys, especially at night. They were well out of range but occasionally would take pot shots at passing aircraft.

Our co-pilot was flying the approach and was supposed to make the landing. He looked over and saw the gunfire activity and yelled, "They're shooting at us." He immediately added power and pulled the nose of the 707 up.

"They're way out of range. They do this every night," I quickly said to him but it was too late. He had added go-around power and we were now well above the glide path. He then started to "jink" the big freighter (turning sharply) to the right.

Finally the Captain who had been looking out of his side window at the gunfire said, "I've got the aircraft," and took the controls. By now we were far above the glideslope and well right of the center line of the runway. (There were unlighted hills to the right of the centerline which were much more dangerous than the distant gunfire.)

I thought that the Captain would probably make a go-around and come back for another approach but nope; he attempted to salvage the approach and landing. He banked the heavily loaded airliner steeply back toward the centerline of the approach course but by now we were on a short final and still high. We were descending at a dangerous rate and when I felt I couldn't wait any longer I yelled, *"Sink-rate!"* (That callout was supposed to be the co-pilot's job.)

The Captain rotated the nose of the 707 up but the plane kept going down. I don't know what the rate of descent was when we contacted the runway but we hit hard and bounced so high that he had to land it again. Additionally, the plane was still at an angle trying to get back to the centerline of the runway that when we smacked onto the concrete we were jerked violently sideways in our seats.

The Captain pulled the engines into reverse after the second touchdown and finally got the plane back under control. We taxied to the cargo ramp without comment but as I got off the plane the Captain was talking rather vigorously to the co-pilot.

As the Air Force ground crews unloaded the freighter I walked carefully around the plane inspecting every rivet and seam that I could see. I inspected the bottoms of the engine nacelles on engines number one and four fully expecting them to be scraped and dented from contact with the runway. I didn't see how, but they were not. I could not find any popped rivets or fuel leaks anywhere. I couldn't believe that there was no damage to the plane after the hardest landing that I had ever sat through; but there was none. What an extremely tough bird. My hat is off to Boeing.

The Viet Cong didn't know it but they had almost "shot down" a B-707 without even having to hit it; thanks to a panicked co-pilot.

In-Country #2: It was a month or so later and I was crewing on a 707-320B passenger flight into Da Nang Air Base, RVN. We were carrying a load of soldiers back in-country from their "R and R". We were scheduled to unload them, then pick up one hundred and sixty-five more and take them to their Rest and Recuperation destination.

It was approaching evening as we descended over the South China Sea for our landing at Da Nang. One of our stewardesses was visibly excited as she entered the cockpit. When asked why she said the reason was that a friend of her family's was stationed at Da Nang as an F-4 fighter pilot. I asked his name and was surprised to find out that I knew him well. We had flown together at the same base a few years before. I had not known that he was flying F-4s at Da Nang.

She had come to the cockpit to ask the Captain for permission to make a quick visit to his squadron for a few minutes to perhaps say hello to him and see how he was doing. Of course the Captain granted her request. After we parked the plane she exited quickly and I saw her hitch a ride in an Air Force flight line vehicle.

We proceeded to get the plane turned around for our evening departure back to Taiwan. The soldiers were already walking across the ramp to board the plane when she returned.

I was standing in the cockpit by the open door when she reached the top of the boarding stairs.

"Did you see him?" I asked her. When she looked at me I knew something was wrong.

"No," she said.

"Why?" I asked.

"He was shot down today," was her tearful reply.

Postscript: Our friend survived but was captured and spent several years as a Prisoner of War in North Vietnam.

Jerry W. Cook

PULL UP

Darwin, Australia; Fall/Winter 1967

We had spent the night before in Tokyo. After a very early takeoff we flew down to Hong Kong and picked up a load of military personnel returning from their Rest and Recuperation leaves, then flew them to Saigon, South Vietnam. After refueling, restocking food and drinks and loading one hundred and sixty-five war-weary military members, we took off for Darwin, Australia. The soldiers, sailors and airmen were headed for their R and R's to relax and get away from the dangers of the war for a while.

Our Captain was a very nice guy, a little overweight, bald-headed, in his late fifties and approaching the then mandatory retirement age of sixty. Interestingly enough the First Officer was also in his late fifties. He was polite but very quiet and seemed somewhat reclusive. The Professional Flight Engineer had told me earlier that the First Officer had tried to check out as a Captain a few years before but could not pass the upgrade training.

So, besides sanctioning the "divided" cockpit between the pilots and flight engineers, Pan American Airways allowed something else that made me wonder about their corporate wisdom, especially in the area of flight safety. If a pilot was not skilled enough to check out as a Captain, Pan Am allowed him to return to the right seat to finish out his career as a First Officer.

Many airlines and other professional flying organizations have an up or out policy. If you can't pass the upgrade training to be a Captain, it means that it was probably a mistake to hire you in the first place. Usually you are given another chance and if you still can't hack it, you are then let go. After all, that is the pilot who has to fly the plane full of passengers if the Captain passes out or; even dies in his seat. (*It has happened.*)

Is that really who you want in the right seat flying your plane as a single pilot, a pilot who wasn't good enough to pass the check out as a Captain? It certainly made me wonder what the folks in charge at Pan Am were thinking. I was convinced, and still am, that it had a lot to do with the power of the unions.

It had been a very long day and now it was a very dark night. Because of the extra-long duty day we were flying with an augmented crew. In this case it was three pilots and two flight engineers. The Professional Flight Engineer was sound asleep with his head on the navigator's table. The additional First Officer (referred to by Pan Am as a Third Officer) was sitting back in the First Class section, also probably asleep. As we passed over the Darwin VOR at twenty thousand feet, the Captain turned to intercept the outbound course, pulled the power on all four engines toward idle and started a descent outbound over the water.

At twelve thousand feet the Captain started a right descending turn and the first officer dialed in the inbound VOR course on the pilots' horizontal situation indicators. I sneaked a peak at the instrument approach chart clipped to the First Officer's control wheel and noted that the pilot was supposed to level off from the descent at two thousand feet. *(Remember, I'm not supposed to be watching any of this.)* The power on number one and number four engines was at idle and numbers two and three were pushed forward with just enough rpm for their turbo compressors to maintain the airliner's cabin pressure. In fact that was my primary job during such a descent; to continually maintain the two inboard engines' rpm just enough above idle to keep the cabin altitude gauge, which was located on the flight engineer's panel, in a descent.

Just as we exited the bottom of the clouds an amber light on the engineer's panel attracted my attention for a few seconds. As I turned my head back toward the front of the plane I looked over the First Officer's shoulder through the front windscreen. I searched in the darkness for the Darwin airport lights. Finally I spotted the runway lights in the distance. *They appeared to be going almost flat!* I quickly looked at the Captain's altimeter. It was descending rapidly toward one thousand, five hundred feet.

"Pull up!" I yelled and at the same time I shoved all four throttles forward. The startled Captain began hauling back on the control wheel and the big airliner began to violently shutter and shake. Its nose finally began to rise above the distant lights of Darwin. The airspeed was bleeding off rapidly.

We bottomed out of the descent at around five hundred feet. The engines had finally begun producing enough thrust to stop the rapid airspeed loss. The Pratt and Whitney JT-3D jet engines were not known for their quick response times. In fact they usually took about fourteen seconds to accelerate from idle to full power. The airliner finally began to accelerate and the Captain climbed slowly back to two thousand feet. No one said a word. I looked at the First Officer. He was staring out of the windscreen and not moving a muscle.

The Professional Flight Engineer was now wide awake. His eyes were huge and his face was drained of any color. Suddenly the cockpit door opened and one of the stewardesses stared wide-eyed into the cockpit. Looking past her I could see several terrified soldiers throwing up into their Sic-Sacs. Quite a few oxygen masks had come loose and were hanging down through their open doors in the ceiling. The masks' doors had sprung open due to the violent shaking of the big airliner as it pulled out of its rapid descent just on the verge of a stall. The stewardess didn't say a word. She just stared at us for a few seconds and then closed the door as she left the cockpit.

No one said anything. After landing, except for reading the checklist, still no one said anything. During the van ride to the hotel when normally there would have been laughing and joking among the crewmembers, there was complete silence. After we reached the hotel and received our room keys, more silence. Everyone immediately scattered toward their rooms. No plans were made to meet for dinner, which was the usual routine.

Later, after having a late dinner alone, I walked out by the swimming pool. A couple of the stewardesses were sitting with their legs dangling in the water and drinks in their hands. One of them was the one who had come into the cockpit. None of the three pilots or the professional flight engineer were anywhere to be seen.

Both of the girls looked solemnly up at me.

"Did we almost die?" one of them quietly asked.

"Yes," I answered.

Toward The Evening Sky

BUSTED CHECKRIDE...*REALLY?*

San Francisco International Airport, CA; March, 1968

The first chance that I got to bid out of the San Francisco crew base; I did. I had been occupying a flight crew position known as the "Second Engineer" since completing my line check and starting to fly trips a few months before. The position was literally at the bottom of the flight crew food chain at Pan American World Airways. It was decided by seniority and it was basically an assistant to the flight engineer. The job absolutely sucked and I was earning less than half of what I had been making in the Air Force.

Not only was I assigned to fly on augmented crews all of the time, but the other engineer was usually one of the Professional Flight Engineers. It was difficult to deal with the attitudes of some of them on trips. I never could understand why many of them seemed to think that they were as important to the flight as the Captain and were definitely more important than the co-pilot. What *bunk*.

Those individuals were obviously buying what the engineers' union was trying to sell to Pan Am; their indispensability. That attitude apparently included animosity toward the Pilot/Engineers.

It had been six months since I had checked out at Pan Am and it was time for me to receive another simulator check ride. My initial flight engineer check had gone well and I had no reason to believe that this one would be any different. I felt that I had learned the aircraft systems, the checklists and procedures and I had not had any problems while flying trips.

I was confident about my performance, especially after the near accident at Darwin. The Professional Engineer who was supposed to be supervising me on that trip had never mentioned it to me. I guess he was not too upset that I had violated their *professional* guidance and looked out through the windscreen that night. Interesting enough, no one else on the crew had ever talked about it during the rest of the trip either; with the exception of the two stewardesses by the pool.

I reported to the simulator building and introduced myself to my simulator check engineer. He fit the now familiar mold; gruff and unfriendly. Then it got worse. There was an inspector from the Federal Aviation Agency with him. As luck would have it, he would be accompanying us into the simulator along with the Captain, the First Officer and their check pilot. The FAA inspector would be observing the check engineer as he administered my check ride.

One could think that might not be a bad thing. Because of the FAA observer I surmised that my check engineer would follow normal check-ride protocol and rationality as he tested my procedures and actions in the simulator cockpit.

I was wrong. It turned out that the FAA inspector and my check engineer were apparently old buddies and they had decided to make a sporting match out of my check ride. The FAA examiner used my aircraft manuals bag, which I would need several times during the check flight, as a seat (and I might add was not seat-belted). If I needed a manual or aircraft diagram, I had to ask him to please move. In the next four hours I had to do just that several times.

During the first two hours I experienced continuous failures of systems on my engineers' panel in addition to the problems that the pilots were being given by their flight examiner. Normally the check engineers would fail a system to test your knowledge of it and your correct response to it and then they would give you the system back. In other words they would "fix" the simulated failure and then they would go on to something else. My "checker" was not giving the systems back to me. Instead, he was leaving them inoperative and consequently they were multiplying rapidly. Soon there were so many of them that I was having trouble keeping track of what had failed and what was still operating.

Once again I had to ask the FAA examiner to please get off my book bag and then I took out a roll of narrow tape. I tore off pieces of the tape and stuck them on the inoperative gauges and switches that had been failed by the check engineer. It was just about then that I first realized it; the FAA inspector and my check engineer were quietly laughing and making bets on whether I would catch the next failure that he gave me.

I could not believe it. Those two heartless bastards were jeopardizing my job with their "fun" and I couldn't do a thing about it. I had heard them laughing before in the session but I had not known why. Also I noticed the examiner who was checking the Captain and First Officer looking back at them several times with a frown on his face, but he didn't say anything.

Mercifully the four hours of the simulator check were almost finished. I had so many pieces of tape and so many failure lights on my panel that I could hardly believe my eyes. And the two callous "checkers" were still snickering and making bets under their breath.

The Captain was beginning his final instrument approach. He suddenly turned around toward me and said, "Why can't I trim the pressure off the ailerons?" I looked at his control yoke and it was about twenty degrees off center to the left.

I immediately suspected a fuel imbalance and checked my fuel gauges. There it was; my check engineer had failed the valve connecting the right outboard fuel tank which allows fuel to be transferred into wing fuel tank number four. About three thousand pounds of fuel had been trapped toward the end of the right wing. If I had seen the valve failure indication, which consisted of a small white light *not* coming on momentarily and then extinguishing, I would have immediately stopped the transfer of the left outboard tank into the number one fuel tank. That would have kept the Boeing 707 in balance, but then we would have had about six thousand pounds of fuel unavailable. I had failed to see the transfer light not illuminate.

I got the FAA jerk off my book bag again and looked up the possible consequences. As it turned out, the Boeing 707-320 model did not have any restrictions on landing with a full outboard fuel tank in one wing and an empty one in the other. All that was required was just some extra trimming and a slight speed increase on final. After I briefed the Captain he said, "No problem, thanks." I felt better.

When the check ride finally ended I was soaked with sweat and thoroughly drained mentally. I counted the pieces of tape on the engineer's panel indicating failed items. There were over twenty.

The Captain thanked me for my assistance with their emergencies and left the cockpit. The check pilot stood up and looked at me and then at my panel with all of the taped failures. He just shook his head and smiled rather sadly. My two tormenters had already left the simulator.

The check pilot was debriefing the Captain and the First Officer in another room and the FAA examiner had already left. As I sat down opposite the check engineer I was feeling tired but pretty good. I had been figuratively shot at for four hours by this jerk and his FAA buddy and had only missed the fuel transfer light not coming on to indicate the failed valve. I hated that I had missed it, but with all of the other failures that he had given me I certainly wasn't surprised. Besides that, the Boeing 707-320 did not have any serious problems landing with the trapped fuel. It was in the book.

"I'm going to fail you on your check ride Cook," the check engineer said. I thought that I was hearing things.

"What did you say?" I asked.

"I'm busting you on your check ride," was his blunt answer.

"Why are you failing me?" I said.

"Because you missed the failed fuel transfer valve and that caused a dangerous situation," he answered.

"The flight manual doesn't say that is a dangerous situation and that's not what they teach in ground school," I protested.

"I don't care. *I* say it's a serious situation in older models of the 707, so *I* think that it should be a problem in *all* 707s. I am failing you. That's that." He then stood up and left.

I was stunned and I just sat there. Out of the corner of my eye I saw someone standing near the door. I looked up. It was the check pilot who had been in the simulator.

He shook his head and said, "Don't worry. I'm going to talk to the Chief Pilot and tell him what they just did to you. You'll probably have to take another check ride, but I am going to pick your check engineer and there's going to be a union representative in the cockpit too. It'll be just fine.

Don't worry." He left shaking his head and mumbling something under his breath.

Any doubts about why I bid out of the San Francisco crew base just as soon as it was possible? By the way, my re-check went great; and I didn't have to stick pieces of tape all over the flight engineer's panel.

Toward The Evening Sky

WELCOME TO DUM DUM

Los Angeles International Airport, CA; Spring 1968

I had never heard of Ojai, California before another pilot told me about it, but it was beautiful. Located to the west and north of Los Angeles, it was about an eighty-five mile drive to the Los Angeles International Airport.

I rented an attractive Spanish style house on Avila Street for the family. Orange and grapefruit groves were scattered everywhere throughout the town. The weather was just about perfect with lots of sunshine. In addition, Ojai benefited from the ocean breeze off the Pacific Ocean, which is located about fifteen miles to the southwest.

Downtown, there were artists with their easels and paints around nearly every corner. There were lots of interesting views with Spanish style buildings and beautiful trees everywhere you looked. Those pleasant scenes were the usual subjects for the artists' paintings. However some of them drew caricatures and would quickly sketch a tourist's likeness for a few dollars. What an idyllic way of life they seemed to lead.

My life; it was somewhat different. Because of my lowly position on the seniority list, the trip that was usually awarded to me in Los Angeles was the Pan American Flight One. That trip proved to be a particularly demanding one for the cockpit flight crews. The extended length flights when coupled with the constantly changing time zones were physically and mentally fatiguing. If my memory serves me, Pan Am Flight One left every day of the week westbound and was heralded as "Around the World". However, because Flight One's last flight leg was from London to New York and terminated there instead of Los Angeles, the expression "Around the World" was slightly inaccurate.

On the other hand, the last leg of the trip for the cockpit crew from London was aboard Pan Am Flight 121, a daily non-stop flight to Los Angeles. After ten and one half to occasionally more than eleven hours in the air, we would arrive in Los Angeles some ten days after we had departed there and we had essentially flown around the world.

At any rate, when a flight crew departed Los Angeles on Flight One, the first leg of the trip was to Honolulu. After arriving in Honolulu the entire flight crew including the stewardesses would be replaced by a crew that had departed Los Angeles the day before on that day's Flight One. The plane would then proceed to Tokyo. That crew in turn would be replaced by one that had landed in Tokyo the day prior.

This routine continued on as far as Hong Kong. There the exercise changed. Hong Kong was not a layover for the pilots and engineers, but it was for the stewardesses. At Hong Kong the Los Angeles based cabin crew would leave the aircraft and be replaced by stewardesses who were based in

New York. These ladies had arrived in Hong Kong a day or two prior aboard Pan Am Flight Two, an east-bound daily "Around The World" flight out of New York. These New York stewardesses would then fly back westbound on Flight One as far as London with the Los Angeles based pilots and flight engineer.

The Los Angeles based stewardesses who had worked the flight with us would change to the Flight Two after resting for a day in Hong Kong. They would end up back in Los Angeles about three days later. The Los Angeles stewardesses' schedule made more sense, was safer, and was much easier on the human body than the pilots' and engineers' schedules. They could link up somewhere over the Pacific with their body clocks and then begin unwinding as they headed eastward back toward California. On the other hand, the cockpit crew's internal clocks just wound tighter and tighter as we continued westbound on Flight One. They never got to unwind.

After the passenger stop in Hong Kong, our next destination was Bangkok, Thailand. The arrival time there was sometime in the early morning, I believe around one or two o'clock. The local time was about fourteen hours ahead of Los Angeles and our internal clocks were really screwed up by now. They were telling us that we should not be here; that instead, we should be back in California or at least somewhere in that direction. Our brain was telling us that the sun should be shining and there should be light outside, but the local sunrise was still hours away.

In addition to the growing stress on our bodies from time zone syndrome, we were just plain tired from the long day that had started in Tokyo. From Tokyo to Hong Kong is over three thousand miles. Then after the Hong Kong stop, Bangkok is about another two thousand miles. That is a total of more than 10 hours of flight time plus the time spent on the ground in Hong Kong during the passenger stop. By the time we turned Flight One over to the next crew and got to the Intercontinental Hotel, it was probably three in the morning locally, but it was approaching lunch time the day before in California.

I was hungry. I got some eggs and bacon at the 24 hour coffee shop and tried to keep my eyes open for a while longer. The sun would be coming up in a few hours in Bangkok, so I felt that I needed to delay before going to bed. Our next takeoff would be about three o'clock the next morning. We would need to get out of bed sometime before midnight in order to catch the crew bus to the airport.

Good quality crew rest was a very real problem when you were half-way around the world from where you had begun. If I went to bed and tried to get eight hours of sleep anytime soon after we arrived in Bangkok, then what would I do until eleven p. m.? If I decided to take a power nap for a couple of hours and then stay up awhile and go to bed again later, would I be able to go to sleep? If I delayed going to bed during the morning and early afternoon so as to try to get eight hours of sleep before I needed to be up, I would be delaying until about three p.m. There was no good answer.

(Adequate flight crew rest on that round-the-world trip was impossible and the situation was evidently overlooked by Pan American World Airways and the FAA. Crew fatigue at some point during this trip was a given. The Pan Am Flight One out of Bangkok was being flown by virtual zombies, some of whom had likely missed the equivalent of at least one night's sleep since leaving Los Angeles.)

Early the next morning, Flight One with our team of sleep deprived pilots lifted off from Don Muang International Airport headed for Rangoon, Burma. It was a relatively short flight across western Thailand and the Gulf of Martaban.

Following that stop, the next leg of Flight One on that particular day was to Calcutta, India. (On other days of the week it would stop in New Delhi instead of Calcutta.) It was my first trip on Flight One and my first trip to Calcutta. I remember that at the time I thought that the airport name was somewhat humorous; "Dum Dum".

I glanced out of the left cockpit window in the dim moonlight as the Captain banked the Boeing 707 into a turn to the left and then rolled out of the bank to line up with the runway. While he was making the turn in the faint light, it had appeared to me that we were *very* close to the trees below.

Pan Am 707s were equipped with barometric pressure altimeters which were the primary instruments to determine the aircraft's altitude. The elevation of the ground below the plane's position had to be known in order to determine the 707's height above it. These altimeters depended on an accurate pressure setting that the pilots had to dial into them before they would correctly measure the aircraft's height above sea level. On descent prior to approach and landing, the elevation of the airport was subtracted from the pressure altimeter's indication to determine its height above the airport.

In addition to these primary altimeters, there was a standby pressure altimeter and two additional altitude indicators called radio or radar altimeters. They did not depend on a pressure setting of any kind. Instead they sent an electronic beam from the aircraft to the ground or water and it bounced back to the aircraft. The elapsed time for the signal to return to the plane was electronically converted into distance in feet. Some limitations were that only the distance to the earth immediately below the plane was accurately measured. Rising terrain ahead of the aircraft would not be detected and if the aircraft was in a bank, the reading was inaccurate.

On the final approach I looked to check the Captain's radio altimeter but it was not indicating the distance to the ground. I then checked the First Officer's and it too was not giving any indications. I then realized that both instruments were turned off.

The Captain continued on his final approach to the runway. We landed and began to offload the few passengers who were deplaning at Calcutta.

As we finished preparing the cockpit for our next flight leg to Karachi, Pakistan, I got my chance to ask the Captain the question that was on my mind; "Why were the radio altimeters both turned off?"

His answer was one that I would never have suspected but I assume was accurate. He said that Pan Am had no operational procedures written for using them so most pilots did not turn them on. The First Officer nodded in agreement, apparently indicating that it was a normal thing to do. I could hardly believe my ears.

(In the Air Force my radar altimeter had literally kept me from crashing into the Pacific Ocean near Okinawa a few years before during a night intercept mission. I did not recall any operational procedures that were written for using it in the F-4 either, but I knew how it worked and common sense told me to turn it on. I used it as a backup to my barometric altimeter.)

In my opinion, just because someone in Pan American's operations procedures section had not written a "modus operandi" for using the radio altimeters at Calcutta or anywhere else did not seem like a valid reason for not turning them on. I've always believed that everything that is available in the cockpit to assist in safely flying the plane should be used. In my increasingly critical view, the folks who were managing; and some of them who flew for "The World's Most Experienced Airline" were looking less and less judicious.

Our flight crew completed that particular round the world trip with no difficulties apart from fatigue and time zone syndrome. I was quickly learning that those two factors were an integral part of this particular trip. I began crewing Flight One regularly about once a month as were approximately thirty other Pan Am crews with no mishaps; that is until June 12th, 1968.

Postscript #1: It is my lasting belief that on that day crew fatigue likely played a major role in what happened more than half-way round the world. Fortunately for me I wasn't part of the crew on that particular Boeing 707 named the Clipper Caribbean, as it attempted an instrument approach and landing at Calcutta's Dum Dum Airport.

The reported weather at the time was a 400 foot ceiling with less than 2 miles of visibility in rain. Flight One struck a tree and crashed a little over one-half mile short of the runway. The accident investigation stated that the pilots were 360 feet lower than they thought that they were because they had not set their barometric altimeters properly. They had adjusted them to 29.93 *inches* instead of the 993 *millibars* that the controller had relayed to them.

I suspect that a combination of jet lag and a lack of quality crew rest at their Bangkok layover perhaps contributed to the pilots' misunderstanding of the altimeter instructions by the Indian air traffic controller. Then add the cockpit "barrier" that discouraged flight engineers from operating as a member of the piloting team. Could less fatigue and more crew coordination have helped? I certainly think so.

Operating a jet aircraft not only demands piloting skills but clear thinking because of the many decisions that must be made; some of them critical. Not setting the altimeters correctly that morning was a fatal mistake that caused the death of six passengers. In addition there were numerous injuries and the complete destruction of a four year old Boeing 707.

I vaguely remember seeing a picture of the crashed airplane in a newspaper. The fuselage was burned almost completely through, but the tail section was relatively untouched by the fire. And if I remember the image correctly, on the vertical stabilizer which appeared to be almost intact, the blue Pan Am logo had been painted over in black.

Was it a feeble and disingenuous attempt to deceive the public? I certainly can't think of any other reason.

Postscript #2: Piloting an aircraft while drunk is a crime. Piloting an aircraft full of passengers while drunk is an even worse offense. In many places around the world, if as a result of a pilot being drunk, the aircraft crashes and people are killed, it is at the very least considered manslaughter.

An airline would never dream of allowing a drunken pilot to fly one of their planes. Yet every day somewhere in the world, pilots in a condition as debilitating as if they were intoxicated likely are flying aircraft.

Studies have shown that an individual who is fatigued exhibits similar characteristics to those of one who is drunk. Attentiveness, decision making, vision, mental clarity, and memory are all degraded as severely as they are in a person who is legally drunk. Long periods of duty on extended east or west international flights involving multiple time zones are especially insidious.

When an aircrew has flown for several days in a row over thousands of miles and is taking off halfway around the world and many time zones away from their normal domicile, they are in all probability becoming fatigued. Some of them even develop a rise in their body temperature as one of the common side effects. They are not able to perform their duties at anywhere near their rested level of competence. Their minds' and their bodies' abilities are being severely degraded by fatigue coupled with time zone syndrome.

No, they are not inebriated but they might as well be. Their bodies keep reminding them that they should be asleep and a constant battle is waged to try to remain alert. An additional insidious issue is that the pilots may not realize that they are not alert.

As an example; you have had a long day, and are especially tired. You are driving down a two-lane highway. You glance into the rearview mirror and there is a car in the other lane going in the opposite direction. It has obviously just driven past you but you don't remember seeing it before. You knew that you were tired and sleepy, but you thought you were doing just fine. Obviously, you were not. Pilots are no different. Sometimes they realize that they are tired and sleepy but they think that they're performing their pilot duties satisfactorily. They are not.

If they were performing at that same level because of intoxication instead of fatigue, they would be violating both the law and flying regulations. They could and should be arrested, charged and have their pilot licenses suspended or revoked. However, because according to flight regulations pertaining to crew rest, they have been provided enough hours at the hotel to rest, they are perfectly legal.

According to man's laws they are a well-rested and highly qualified flight crew. But according to nature's laws they may be severely, perhaps even fatally, handicapped. Fortunately, most of the time, nothing bad happens.

Most of the time drunks make it home too...*Most of the time*.

Toward The Evening Sky

COBRAS, CAMELS AND BIG BLACK BIRDS

Karachi, Pakistan; Spring 1968

We departed Bangkok at the usual three a.m. and after passenger stops in Rangoon and Calcutta we landed in Karachi, Pakistan. I had laid over in Karachi a few times and although I was bone-tired I was looking at the sights from the crew bus as we drove to the Intercontinental Hotel. We would be getting crew rest there for two days.

Our driver was frequently beeping his horn at the camel drivers to get them to move out of the dusty roadway. Outside of several roadside buildings there were camels tied up. It reminded me of similar scenes of horses outside a bar in an old western movie. I was thinking that this must be the Pakistani version of the Wild West.

Then I spotted the dark-skinned man with a turban on his head playing a flute. He was sitting in the dirt in front of a large basket with his legs crossed. Jutting out of the basket about two or three feet and weaving back and forth was a huge snake with his hood flattened out. It was a cobra. At times during its dance the snake would appear to strike out of the basket and then return to his swaying. There were several people standing around watching the snake. The individuals surrounding the snake were standing much closer than I would have been. I decided that this was not like the old American west after all.

The van pulled up in front of the Karachi Intercontinental Hotel. I had just learned a few months before that all of the Intercontinental Hotels were owned by Pan Am and they were very luxurious. The accommodations and the food in the hotel would make the stay in Karachi pretty relaxing as our internal body clocks tried to catch up with our location on the globe. Getting to spend two days in the same location would help the fatigue to subside somewhat.

A quirk in the crew contracts having to do with crew rest resulted in an unusual situation during the layovers in Karachi. Only the flight engineer and the six stewardesses stayed there. The Captain and First Officer did not layover until the next stop which was Beirut, Lebanon. The Karachi layover included either one non-flying day or two, depending on which day of the week that you arrived. The reason was that on alternating days Flight One would land in Tehran, Iran instead of Karachi. Then on certain days of the week it would fly to Tehran two days in a row, thus the occasional two day stay in Karachi.

In the sixties stewardesses were bound by strict weight and age limits. Consequently I don't remember there being many who appeared to be over 35 years old or over 125 pounds. I believe that if they gained a certain amount of weight over what they weighed when hired and then did not lose it; they were fired. One might say that it wasn't fair to them, but they *were* very easy on the eyes. In fact, I can't remember a Pan Am stewardess who was not attractive. (On the other hand I flew with a Pan Am Captain who had to suck in his huge gut to rotate the 707 for takeoff. That wasn't a pretty sight. It also wasn't a healthy one. It made me wonder if Pan Am didn't put more emphasis on the stewardesses' looks than on flight safety.)

We checked into the hotel and received our room keys. The sun was shining bright and hot. I walked out by the swimming pool. It looked very cool and inviting. While I stood there I noticed several very large black birds circling high above the hotel.

Since I didn't have to work again for two days I felt that I could unwind. I went to my room and changed into my swim suit and went back down by the pool. I hadn't been there very long until a couple of the stewardesses came down. They were both wearing bikinis and looked like they just stepped off the pages of a Sports Illustrated Swimsuit Issue. I held in my stomach and tried to look slimmer as they said, "Hi," and pulled a couple of lounge chairs close together.

Although I was a married man with two kids, I still didn't want my stomach to hang out; *like a married man with two kids*. The ladies were well organized and immediately made themselves right at home. It was obvious that they had been around the world a few times before and knew how to make the most out of any opportunities to relax.

I decided to relax too, except for my stomach which I was trying hard to keep pulled in. I had just stretched out on my back in the lounge chair when "it" hit me.

Remember the big black birds circling over the pool?

One of them had just welcomed me to Karachi. *"Crap!"*

You think that the stewardesses laughed don't you? *Hysterically!*

Toward The Evening Sky

NOT *EXACTLY* WHAT I WANTED TO HEAR

Beirut, Lebanon; Summer 1968

I was becoming a veteran of Pan Am's Flight One "Around the World" service with five or six global circles under my belt and as usual during these trips I was tired. As in several of our other layover cities between these flights our hotel in Beirut was one of the Intercontinental Hotels chain.

All of our crew stayed over in Beirut; however the pilots were usually pretty zonked out by the time they arrived there. They had started their flight duty day in Bangkok. I had only started mine in either Karachi or Tehran and only then after at least one non-flying day. Consequently I was not as tired as they were.

After getting to my room I looked out of the window. It overlooked the pool and the pool area seemed deserted although it was a very nice day. I looked up and didn't see any big black birds circling so I decided to go down by the pool and take in some sun.

I was almost asleep on a lounge chair when I heard some footsteps coming toward me. The footsteps stopped nearby so I opened my eyes and saw one of our stewardesses. She was one who had been working in First Class and had also been the one serving food and drinks to our cockpit crew. She was pretty with coal black hair, olive skin and large brown eyes. She was wearing a robe over her swim suit and carrying a towel and some reading material.

She smiled at me and said, "Hi, mind if I join you?" She had a heavy Spanish accent but because we had so many foreign born stewardesses I wasn't sure of her nationality.

I said "Sure, be my guest," and she rearranged a couple of lounge chairs and sat down. I shut my eyes and lay there for a minute or so. I sensed that she had not stirred from her sitting position.

I opened my eyes and looked quizzically at her. She said, "I'm sorry to bother you but may I ask you a question?" I told her that I supposed that would be all right.

"From where do you get your dark skin and hair?" she said. I answered that it was mostly from my Native American ancestors who were of the Cherokee nation.

She said "Oh, so you're not of Mexican or Spanish descent."

"Nope, not to my knowledge," I answered.

She studied me a little longer and asked, "Are you married?"

I held up my left hand with my wedding ring and said; "Yes."

"Do you have children?" she continued.

I proudly answered, "Yes I do; a boy and a little girl."

"Do you have any pictures of them with you?" she continued.

I picked up my wallet and showed her some pictures of my son and daughter, Jeff and Kristin.

"They really are beautiful kids," she exclaimed. "I thought that they would be," she smiled as she said it.

"Thanks, I think so too," I replied.

"Is your wife blond?" she inquired.

"Yes, that's where my son gets his blond hair and blue eyes; from his mother," I replied.

"Can I tell you a story?" she continued. I was beginning to wonder about all of the questions.

Before I could respond she began; "I am from Mexico City. Last Christmas while I was there I visited a friend of mine from school and her husband. He is a medical doctor and they have been married for several years. They have been trying to have children without any success for quite some time. Of course they suspected that one of them might be infertile, but they were tested and disappointed to find out that they both were unable to have children."

By now I was getting a little uneasy about this conversation.

She continued, "They really want to have children and they made me a proposition. They said that if I would have a baby for them they would pay me ten thousand dollars. I have been looking for a possible father for the baby for the last six months. I noticed you and your dark skin and hair as soon as I got on the plane in Hong Kong."

She paused and looked at me for a moment before she said very businesslike; "Would you be interested in ten percent?"

To say that I was surprised would be an understatement. At the same time I have to admit that I was also somewhat flustered.

After stuttering and stammering for a few seconds I finally recovered my composure and replied, "I guess it would be many men's fantasy for a woman to offer him money to go to bed with her." (One must remember this was in the sixties and she wasn't talking about artificial insemination.)

As I started to continue she interrupted and said, "But you would have to get me pregnant before I would pay you your share."

I thought, "This is incredible." I then thought about how to phrase what I was going to say next.

"I am surprised that you would present me with such a proposition, but I could never do such a thing. First, I am a married man and second, I simply cannot imagine siring a child that I would be giving up to someone else and would likely never see. I have to decline," I finished.

She smiled again and said, "I respect your position and your wife is fortunate to have such a husband. I guess I will have to continue looking."

I don't know if her story and the offer were real or if she was just playing a game of some sort. If it was true, I have wondered if she found a donor and then if she was able to actually give away her child.

When I got home a few days later from the trip I made a *big* mistake. I was feeling pretty good about the proposal from the stewardess and I suppose that I wanted my wife to realize how *lucky* that she was to have me so…*I told her the story.*

However, she did not seem at all pleased and immediately let me know just how lucky she felt to have me as her husband.

Her exact words as I remember them were; *"YOU'RE NOT WORTH IT!"*

"OUCH." Like I said…*"Big* mistake."

Jerry W. Cook

WAS IT A *MIRAGE*? NO; IT WAS REAL

Tehran to Beirut; December, 1968

Things had gotten very tense in the Middle East lately. In fact the Israelis had attacked the Beirut International Airport just a few days before. They had gone in at night and blown up about fourteen aircraft belonging to three different airlines. Middle East Airlines based in Beirut had lost nine airliners including one brand new Boeing 707. Airline service into the airport had been disrupted for a time but that was where we were headed as we took off from Tehran.

We were climbing through about eight thousand feet when the anxious sounding call came from our Pan American Operations (PanOps) office at the Tehran International Airport. We immediately went from being a rather relaxed flight crew to one in a state of high anxiety.

The message stated that a very agitated man had turned away from the boarding gate of our flight at the last minute and then hurried away. The problem was; his luggage was on board the aircraft and they were concerned that there might possibly be a bomb in it. (*They thought that they were concerned! They should have been in that cockpit with us!*) Justly alarmed, the Captain asked whether we had any ideas about how to deal with the possible bomb.

The First Officer did not say anything so I spoke up; "We could level off and not climb anymore."

The Captain asked me why and I told him; "If there is really a bomb there is a chance that it could be one with an aneroid type fuse. That type arms when it ascends through a preset altitude and then detonates the bomb when it descends back down through another pre-programmed altitude."

He immediately leveled off the plane. We were about ten thousand feet.

We began discussing our situation. Finally I said, "We could slowly depressurize the plane at this altitude and then I can go down below the cockpit and get into the forward luggage compartment. If I can get the baggage door open I'll throw every damn bag out."

"You can do that?" he asked.

"I think that I can get into the forward baggage compartment," I said. "I'm not sure about opening the baggage door from the inside if I can get in. But I can go down and try."

"What about the bags in the rear compartment?" he asked.

"I don't think that I can get back there," I answered.

The Captain got on the radio to relay our plan to Pan Ops and asked them if they knew which compartment the passenger's luggage had been loaded into. Pan Ops said that they would check on the baggage. They also said that they didn't have any better ideas, but were trying to locate the passenger who had turned back at the gate and to, "Stand by".

I said that I really didn't want to stand by because a bomb could also be on a timer. The Captain agreed. I made the adjustment to raise the cabin altitude to ten thousand feet. I unfastened the fire axe and got a flashlight, pliers and a screwdriver out of my flight bag. Things were very tense in the cockpit as I lifted the grill that led down into the "Lower 41" area as it was labeled.

Pan Ops called again just as I was starting down the short ladder, "Captain, we have just located and talked to the passenger who did not board. He is at the hospital. He was paged immediately before departure with the information that his son had just been involved in an automobile accident. Also, our information is that the gentleman is a respected businessman here in Tehran and that he travels with us back and forth to London quite often."

"You are sure that this information is all correct and that he is at the hospital with his son?" the Captain earnestly queried the Pan Ops Manager.

"Yes sir Captain, it is all correct. He asked if we could please return his baggage on the next flight back from Beirut."

The Captain thought for a minute and then answered, "All right thank you. We will proceed to Beirut and keep our fingers crossed. You contact us immediately if any of this information changes."

I closed the grill and sat back down in my seat. As I put my flashlight and tools back into my bag I was thinking that I had not been that nervous flying combat in Vietnam.

The rest of that flight was one of the quietest that I had been a part of with Pan Am. We didn't say it but none of us was completely convinced that there was no bomb on board. But we knew that if there was one that we would never know it. It was time to descend....

I don't think anyone from the cockpit began to breathe normally again until we were in the crew bus going to the hotel in Beirut. The stewardesses were laughing and talking as usual. They had not been informed as we had seen no reason to upset them. I think under certain circumstances it may be better to *not* know what is going on.

Although we had said at stressful moments in Vietnam, "Relax damn it. Why die all tensed up?" *It's much easier said than done.*

The next day, I was preflighting the Flight One plane before our departure to Istanbul. There were several burned out hulks of airliners scattered around the ramp. Most of them had been Middle East Airlines' planes. And while walking around the plane I noticed numerous bullet holes in the sides of the airport terminal building.

Suddenly in my peripheral vision I saw something moving low and fast. I quickly turned my head to look and saw the Israeli Mirage jet fighter as it flashed across the airport. It was about 100 feet in the air and probably moving at six hundred miles per hour. The sound was trailing it by several thousand feet. As it left the airport boundary and swept out over the Mediterranean the pilot raised the nose of the fighter a few degrees and performed a couple of quick "victory" rolls. He then broke hard left and headed south.

I looked back at a couple of the gun positions which now encircled the airport. The soldiers manning the guns didn't appear to have moved at all except for their heads. They were looking in the direction where the Israeli jet had disappeared.

I wondered if they appeared surprised in the pictures that the Mirage had just taken of them.

I expect that I did.

Toward The Evening Sky

TAHITI, FRAULEINS AND RACE QUEENS

South Pacific Ocean; October 1968

It was late Friday afternoon when our home phone rang. I figured it was probably Pan American Scheduling. One of my trips had canceled and I was short of my minimum guarantee for that month by several flight hours. I dreaded picking up the phone because of the kind of trip I would likely be assigned. Junior pilots at Pan Am did not usually do very well on trip assignments.

"Is this Jerry Cook?" the male voice on the phone said.

I told him, "That is me," and he announced, "This is Pan Am scheduling and I have a trip for you."

"Here it comes," I thought as I grabbed a pad and pencil to write down the details.

"Ready," I said and he began to give me the particulars of the trip. When he had finished I said, "You're kidding, right?"

He said "Nope, you got lucky. I wish that I was going with you."

"I can understand that," I said and thanked him.

I reread what I just had written and I still had trouble believing it. The trip was to leave Los Angeles Saturday night around midnight and arrive early Sunday morning in Tahiti. Not only that, the next flight out of Papeete was the following Thursday morning. After our four days in Tahiti we were to fly to Auckland, New Zealand and lay over for a day. Then; on to Hawaii for still another layover.

It was probably one of, if not the most senior trip in Pan Am. The old saying, "It's a tough job but someone has to do it," came to mind as I smiled in disbelief. And not only was it a great trip but the flying time involved brought me to just under my maximum which meant some extra money that month. One thing for sure, I wasn't about to call the scheduler back and ask him if it might all be a mistake.

Saturday arrived and as I drove my blue Volkswagen bug airport car the eighty-five miles to LAX I was still having trouble believing my good fortune. I checked in at Pan Ops and met the Captain and the First Officer. The most senior stewardess, referred to by Pan Am as the Purser, was there. She was from Denmark and spoke with a distinctive accent. She was probably around thirty and was one of the older flight attendants with whom I had flown. As I mentioned, this trip was usually bid for and awarded to the most senior crewmembers.

We lifted off from KLAX on time and headed southwest for about four thousand miles. The Boeing 707 was full of happy passengers headed to the island paradise. The crew members were in very good spirits also. Looking toward four days in Tahiti can do that to you.

One of the stewardesses was an attractive brunette. She was a rarity, one of those young women who seem totally unaware of their good looks. Additionally she was one whose personality proved to be as pleasing as her appearance. That she was so unpretentious and friendly to everyone around her added to her charm. She was also the flight attendant who was assigned to take care of the cockpit crew so we got to observe firsthand her attention to her job.

Unfortunately on some prior trips it had appeared that the stewardesses assigned to the cockpit duty either resented it or just ignored it. This young lady did neither and kept the coffee, meals and snacks coming; always with a generous smile.

The Captain was an outgoing and optimistic fifty-year old named Bob. It was likely that he had been hired relatively young at Pan Am or he would not have been awarded such a trip. The first officer was probably ten years younger than the Captain and had been flying in the right seat for quite some time. From their discussions I learned that they both had flown this trip several times before.

The First Officer was approaching his chance to upgrade to the left seat. If there was any drawback to upgrading it was that he would immediately be junior on the seniority list again and therefore unable to bid and receive such good trips as this one. Although that was a consideration for him, the approximately sixty-seven percent pay raise was just too great to pass up. At that time a First Officer's salary was about sixty percent of a Captain's.

Our flight was just over eight hours long and the arrival at the Papeete airport was in the early morning. The Captain made a nice landing to end the very pleasant flight. The guy had been awake all night but as we left the plane he did not appear to be at all tired. In fact, he got the crew together and announced that anyone who wished; could go with him by ferry to the island of Moorea, which was about nine miles away. He said that he knew the manager at the Club Med and could get some rooms for us there instead of in Papeete. Two stewardesses said that they wanted to stay in Papeete and shop.

The rest of us headed for the dock. I could not resist the opportunity to see Cook's Bay
and stay at a Club Med. I figured it was a once in a lifetime chance. I had always marveled at the accomplishments of the famous explorer Captain James Cook with whom I shared a last name. I was fascinated that he had sailed to these islands some two hundred years before.

Moorea turned out to be a truly beautiful place. Reportedly it was formed as the top of a volcano about two million years ago. When we checked in at Club Med the Captain introduced us to his friend the manager. She was a tall German fraulein with the typical blonde hair and blue eyes. Just as he had promised she booked us into individual huts. It appeared likely that he had done this before. I seem to remember that the huts were built from wood with what appeared to be thatched roofs. They were scattered among the palm trees and faced the beach. I don't remember that they had screens on the windows and there was no air conditioning except for the constant ocean breezes. Who cared? Wow, what a place. Another interesting thing was at check-in we exchanged money for colored beads which snapped together. We then wore them around our neck and anything that we bought was purchased with beads. I thought that was really cool and made it easy to carry "money" the next few days for snacks and drinks.

I was really tired and decided to take a nap. But before I lay down I looked out toward the beach. There was the Captain running into the water for a swim. I was impressed that a fifty year old man could fly all night and then go for a swim. I was almost twenty years younger than he was but me; *I* was going for a nap. I remember thinking that I was going to use his fitness as goal when I got to the ripe old age of fifty. But I would start later, after a nap.

I enjoyed the stay on Moorea very much. The inhabitants were gracious hosts and the scenery was breathtaking. The pretty brunette was one of the four stewardesses who came to Club Med and I saw her with the other three a few times as they passed by on their way to the beach. Almost every time that I saw the Captain he was running, playing volleyball or swimming. He seemed to know everyone there and he was one of the most active guys of any age that I had ever seen.

Wednesday came too soon and it was time to go to the ferry. We had to return to Papeete and stay at the crew hotel that night because of our early Thursday morning takeoff.

It was October 17th and my thirty-first birthday when we lifted from the runway at Papeete. After we climbed to about fifteen hundred feet the Captain pulled the power back and set it to maintain two hundred and fifty knots. I didn't know what was going on but he just smiled and said, "We're going to take the passengers on a little tour."

He then got on the public address system and welcomed the passengers on board. As he did so he turned and pointed the nose of the 707 toward the island where we had just spent three days. He told the passengers that Moorea would be coming up on the left side of the plane very shortly if anyone wanted to get a look at the island, the barrier reef, and Cook's Bay.

We headed toward the southeast side of the island and then flew around it counter-clockwise just off the beach. He then announced that we were coming up on Club Med. (I wondered if the plug might be part of the deal he had with the manager.) I was standing up and looking out of the forward windscreen. I saw someone on the beach waving something as we approached. As we got closer I saw that the individual was waving her sarong over her head and evidently that was everything that she had been wearing. Suddenly the Captain saw her too and said, "Oh crap. I wish she wouldn't do that." It was his fraulein friend the manager. He banked to the right and then began our climb for Auckland. That guy was one of the fittest pilots that I ever flew with at Pan Am. And he was obviously "living the life".

Auckland New Zealand is twenty five hundred miles southwest of Tahiti and almost a six hour flight. About two-thirds of the way is the International Date Line where you immediately lose twenty-four hours when heading westbound. As we crossed, it was suddenly October 18th and no longer my birthday. (A twelve hour long birthday just didn't seem fair but how could I complain after four days in Tahiti? I didn't. I just don't count that birthday.)

New Zealand was a very interesting place. The people were friendly and rather laid back. To me it was like stepping back into the 40's and 50's in America. I remember thinking at the time that if I was ever going to live in another country New Zealand would deserve some serious consideration. I really liked what I saw but the time spent there was too short to see very much.

The next day, October 19th, we were on our way to Honolulu. The flight to Hawaii was about forty-four hundred miles; or about nine hours over lots of water. Once again the pretty and vibrant brunette was assigned to the cockpit duty and again she did a great job of taking care of our flight crew. She never seemed to get tired although the stewardesses were on their feet so much that it was as if they walked all the way to Hawaii. We regained our lost day as we crossed the International Date Line and we were back to October 18th.

We were to lay over in Honolulu until the next evening before we took off for Los Angeles. Later I was walking down one of the streets near Waikiki Beach. In the distance and strolling toward me I recognized a world famous sports celebrity. There was a young lady walking along with him. As they drew a little closer I also recognized her.

Just the previous day she had been serving me coffee and a crew meal.

Postscript: Fast forward to September 1971. I was sitting with some other Air National Guard pilots on the front row in the grandstand at the Reno Air Races. It was the opening ceremony and they had just announced that the Reno Air Race Queen would be passing in front of the grandstand. We could see her convertible approaching from our left.

There was a very pretty brunette sitting up on the back of the car; smiling and waving at the crowd as she approached where we were sitting. *Guess who?*

I would tell you that she saw me, called out my name and waved even bigger; but you probably wouldn't believe it. The other pilots sitting with me didn't want to believe it either!

Toward The Evening Sky

THE "PRATTLE" OF MIDWAY

Tokyo to Honolulu, 1969

Another trip I once received in my monthly bidding that was not an around the world was a Los Angeles to Honolulu; Honolulu to Tokyo; Tokyo to Honolulu and finally Honolulu back to Los Angeles. It was a four day trip with two layovers in Honolulu and one in Tokyo. Compared to the monthly round the world trips that I usually crewed, it was a breeze.

If memory serves me, our crew layover hotel was called the Tokyo Palace. There were usually several airline crews staying there at the same time including some from Northwest Airlines. Because of the varying flight schedules, there was nearly always someone from an airline crew in the twenty-four hour coffee shop. I did not frequent the upscale hotel restaurant because Pan Am paid our expenses by per diem. The daily amount would not allow for fancier meals unless one wanted to add their own money and I didn't have very much of that.

I had not seen anyone that I had flown with in the Air Force since I joined Pan Am. This was surprising in light of the fact that there were quite a few of my former pilot friends who had taken jobs with various airlines including Pan Am.

I was hungry by the time I checked into the hotel and got to my room. I changed into my "civvies" and headed downstairs. When I walked into the coffee shop I saw a Northwest pilot sitting alone at a small table. He was in uniform and his flight bag and luggage were beside the table. I recognized him as one of the F-4 pilots that I had flown with in the 558th Fighter Squadron at Cam Ranh Bay Air Base, Vietnam. I called, "Hey Jim," and he looked up from his food.

He smiled and said, "Jerry Cook, what are you doing here in Tokyo?" and stood up to shake my hand. I sat down at his table and we began to catch up on our activities since leaving the Air Force and finally we got around to talking about the airlines.

The same as I, he was riding sideways in a 707 and detesting it. He talked a little about how poorly he thought Northwest treated their passengers and said that it really bothered him.

He then asked me, "Do your passengers dislike Pan Am?"

I told him that I had not personally witnessed anything that would make me think that, but at times we certainly had some passengers who were not all that happy with us. I then added that I didn't think you could always please everyone.

He looked at me, shook his head sadly and said, "Our passengers hate us." He then added, "I made a big mistake coming to Northwest. In fact, I probably made a mistake by getting out of the Air Force."

It reminded me of someone that I knew; the same guy that I saw in the mirror while shaving every morning. We both agreed that flying for the airlines wasn't "all that it was cracked up to be". We then agreed on the accuracy of the "grass is greener" syndrome.

He looked down at his big Seiko and announced, "I've got to go catch the crew bus; I'm heading back to Seattle." We shook hands and wished each other good luck in our airline careers. He was the only former Vietnam buddy that I ever saw during my Pan Am travels.

The next afternoon I was back in the coffee shop, this time in my uniform. I had finished my lunch and was about to leave when she walked in. She was quite a beauty and might have even rated a "ten" if she had not been wearing just a little too much makeup. She was dressed in her blue Pan Am stewardess uniform and sat down across the room with a couple of other Pan Am stewardesses.

She was really a pretty woman. Unfortunately it seemed that she thought so too. That was too bad. Few things are more unattractive than someone who clearly thinks that they are attractive. Whatever the case, because the stewardesses were preparing to leave also I assumed that we were probably on the same flight crew. I stood and picked up my bags and walked into the lobby to wait for the crew bus.

We departed from Tokyo in the late afternoon and before long flew rapidly into the shadow of the earth and toward the approaching night. We were at our assigned cruising altitude of 39,000 feet. It was a dark night and we seemed to be all alone in that part of the Pacific. We had not heard any other air traffic for an hour or so and were appreciating the solitude.

The Captain was a personable guy and the co-pilot was single and exhibited a keen sense of humor. The very pretty stewardess and her friends in the coffee shop were indeed part of our cabin crew. Her attractiveness had been briefly mentioned by our single co-pilot along with his impression that she seemed to think that she was pretty special. We all agreed that appeared to be the case.

About two thirds of the way to Honolulu our filed route took us over the top of Midway Island. At that time the island was home to a U. S. Navy base. As we passed over Midway it was procedure to report our position to a radio operator on the island for relay to Air Traffic Control and to our company. We were about one hundred and twenty miles northwest of the island when the cockpit door opened. We could smell her perfume before we could see her in the darkened cockpit. It was the pretty young subject of our earlier observations.

After saying "Hi" to each one of us she said, "Captain, don't we pass right over Midway Island on the way to Hawaii?" She had a lovely voice too.

"Yes we do. We should be overhead the island in just a few minutes," he answered.

"Isn't there a military base on the island?" she continued.

"Yes ma'am. There's a U.S. Navy base located there," he said.

"I thought that there was. You know I can't help feeling sorry for those boys stationed way out here in the middle of the ocean. I know that they must get very lonely," she stated rather sadly.

"Yeah; probably so," the Captain answered.

She continued, "I was wondering if they might like to hear a feminine voice like mine since they most likely haven't heard one in a while. Do you think that they would?"

The co-pilot turned toward her and quickly answered before the Captain had a chance to say anything; "Why yes. I know that they would like to hear a voice like yours after all this time. I'm sure it would make their day. I know that it would mine." He then turned to me and said, "Jerry, why don't you fix this pretty young lady up with a headset and microphone and then connect her to the interphone."

With that he turned back around to face the front while I got an extra headset and microphone for the now visibly excited young lady.

I positioned the switches and said, "Okay, you're all set."

She giggled and said, "What should I say?"

The co-pilot turned around toward her and told her to say, "Midway Island, Midway Island, this is Pan Am Clipper 009, over."

She took a deep breath, which the co-pilot seemed to immensely enjoy observing, and then said in a very sultry voice; "Midway Island, Midway Island, this is Pan Am Clipper 009, over," and then she waited expectantly for an answer. None came.

The co-pilot turned toward her and said, "Try it again."

I looked at the Captain. He was looking straight ahead and shaking his head slightly. I could tell that there was a grin on his face. She tried again, with just a little more urgent sound to her voice this time. Still there was no reply.

The co-pilot appeared to be looking out of his side window. "Try again," he said; "Third time's a charm, you know."

She tried again. Suddenly out of the dark night came an excited sounding male voice with a distinctly southern accent, "Why, hello there Pan Am 009. This is Midway Island. Where are you at, Honey?"

"He answered me, he just answered me," the thrilled stewardess exclaimed excitedly. I looked at the co-pilot. He appeared to still be looking at something out of his window. I knew that there was nothing out there to see and I observed in the dim cockpit lights that his shoulders were quivering just slightly.

"Why don't you answer the poor guy," the co-pilot finally said.

"What should I say?" the stewardess asked.

"I don't know. Tell him about yourself. I bet he'd like to know all about you," he added.

That was all the encouragement she needed to start telling the guy that she had thought that he would like to hear a feminine voice after all that time on the island with all those other boys. And that she just thought that she could make him feel better by calling up and talking to him.

The "Midway boy" started gushing back at her, expressing how much he appreciated hearing such beautiful voice after all this time and how he wished that he could meet her when he got back to the States. He told her how he could tell that she was a gorgeous woman just by listening to her. He was pretty slick.

Although she was a little hesitant at first, she ended up giving him her name, age, height, measurements, marital status (single), and finally, her telephone number.

Suddenly the guy said, "Say Honey, where are you at right now?"

Evidently not realizing that we could hear every word, she lowered her microphone and said, "That Midway boy wants to know where we are."

The co-pilot said, "Tell him we're about twenty miles northwest of the island at thirty-nine thousand feet."

She quickly relayed that information to the "Midway boy".

"Quick, tell your pilots to turn on their landing lights and I'll run outside and maybe I can see you," the voice said excitedly.

She lowered her microphone and eagerly relayed the request.

The Captain could barely contain himself as he reached up and turned on the landing lights.

"Tell him they're on," the Captain told her, joining in the banter for the first time.

She eagerly relayed his message.

The co-pilot was still hunkered over looking out of his window into the dark sky.

Suddenly the breathless sounding message came; "I see you. I see you Honey." The guy sounded really thrilled.

"He sees us," the stewardess giggled as she said it.

The co-pilot turned to face her and said, "Good, but you'd better say your goodbyes now. We've got to give our position report." His voice sounded a little strained and there appeared to be some remnants of tears in his eyes.

The Captain now was looking out of his side window. I was biting my tongue, hard. It almost wasn't enough.

The pretty little stewardess said her sweet goodbye to her "Midway boy" and said, "Maybe I will see you when you get back to the States."

"Midway boy" replied, "You can bet on that. I'll call you as soon as I get back."

She handed the microphone back to me and stood up. She thanked the Captain for letting her brighten that lonely boy's night on Midway. Then she left the cockpit with a big sigh and a self-satisfied smile.

We all cracked up with laughter as soon as the door closed behind her, although I felt just a little sorry for her. After the cackling subsided somewhat the Captain looked over at the co-pilot and said, "You ought to be ashamed of yourself."

The co-pilot replied, "Me? You're the one who turned on the landing lights for that poor lonely boy down on Midway. Besides, I got her number didn't I?" He grinned as he said it.

I don't know if she ever figured out that her "Midway boy" that she was making so happy that night was actually the co-pilot talking to her on the cockpit *interphone*. She had just assumed that she was talking on the aircraft *radio*.

Perhaps she realized what had happened back home in the States when the co-pilot called her.

If she did; "Good luck on getting that date, 'Midway boy'."

Jerry W. Cook

WHERE ARE WE?

Taipei to Seattle; 1969

"I hate to wake up and find my co-pilot asleep." So goes the old Captain's joke. My ex-fighter pilot friend who I saw at the beginning of the previous story had related an incident that happened to him at Northwest Airlines.

He was the flight engineer on a Boeing 707 freighter. The crew had arrived the day before in Taiwan and had minimum crew rest before heading out early the next morning for Seattle. The scheduled takeoff time was very early in the morning; sometime around 2 a.m.

They got airborne on time and headed northeast on a great circle route. Their routing took them fairly close to Russian claimed airspace but if it was adhered to it would keep them well clear. In those days the relationship between Russia and the United States was not that friendly and it was extremely important to steer clear of their territory, including their claimed airspace.

The Northwest crew was well into their flight and it was still several hours before sunrise when the Captain asked the co-pilot if he felt okay. The co-pilot assured him that he did. The Captain then told him and my friend at the flight engineer's station that he was going to put his head back for a few minutes and rest his eyes.

My engineer friend said that sometime later he was really having trouble keeping his eyes open. He said that he was staring at something on the engineer's panel and remembered thinking that he would shut his eyes for just a minute.

Suddenly he opened his eyes with the co-pilot tugging on his shirt sleeve. He started to say something but the co-pilot shushed him and pointed toward the left seat. He looked over at the Captain who was still sound asleep and snoring away. Then he looked back at the co-pilot as he tried to blink himself awake.

"I went to sleep and I don't know exactly for how long," whispered the co-pilot.

"The dopplers are both pegged at their maximum distance so we're more than 99 miles north of course. Turn us south with the autopilot turn knob while I try to figure out where in the hell we are before the Captain wakes up," he quietly but urgently instructed.

"And keep your eyes peeled for MiGs. We may be in Russian airspace," he said in a low anxious voice.

My friend said that statement really got his attention. He turned the 707 due south and then stood up from time to time to look out of the cockpit side windows for "unfriendlys".

The co-pilot was working feverishly with their Loran C equipment to locate their position as the jet raced southward. Finally he turned around and whispered that they were out of Russian airspace.

Sometime later they had just turned the 707 back on course and the bright sun was starting to stream into the cockpit. It started shining in the Captain's face and he began to stir. Finally he opened his eyes and looked over at the co-pilot.

"How are we doing guys?" he said sleepily as he stretched his arms over his head.

"Fine Captain, we are doing *just* fine. We're a little behind on time but we're right on course," the co-pilot replied.

Postscript: As it turns out, the co-pilot's concern for the possibility of MiGs intercepting them was not so far-fetched.

About fourteen years later on September 1, 1983, a Korean Air Boeing 747 that had strayed into Russian airspace was shot down by a Russian interceptor after being misidentified as a spy plane.

Jerry W. Cook

CALCUTTA SUNRISE

Calcutta, India; 1969

We were still in the turn toward our final approach for landing when we saw something suddenly appear out of the landing lights' illumination and flash by the left side of the plane. No one in the cockpit was sure of what it was, but we surmised it must have been a bird. I wondered what a bird was doing flying at this time of night.

As I walked around the 707 during the pre-flight inspection before the next leg of Flight One, I arrived at the left flap area. As I moved the flashlight beam along the forward edge of the flaps where they met the cove lip doors I spotted some damage. Something had impacted toward the forward edge of a fowler flap and torn about a four inch hole into it. I remembered the object that had flashed past our cockpit window and decided that it had not been alone. There was a large amount of blood, guts and black feathers still imbedded in the torn metal at the rear of the hole.

I went back up to the cockpit and informed the Captain. He returned with me and by now the station manager was looking up at the hole along with a member of his ground crew.

After the Captain had examined the damage he looked at me and said, "What do you think?"

I replied, "I think we could 'speed tape' the torn area closed and continue the trip."

Then the station manager spoke up and said, "Oh no Captain. I can't dispatch you like that without checking with New York first."

That was it then. It was the station manager's plane while it was on the ground. What I thought didn't make any difference.

The Captain shrugged and said to the Calcutta station manager, "How long will it take to get an answer from New York?"

The manager said, "I'm not sure Captain."

In a few minutes the answer came back. New York said it had to be fixed before we could fly it again. It was the middle of the night and there was no estimate of how long that might take.

The Captain and the station manager made the decision together; unload the passengers and find them a place to stay in Calcutta.

But first; we had to get them through Indian Customs. The biggest obstacle was that we had several Pakistani passengers. Those two countries were not the best of friends in the late sixties and the station manager had his hands full getting them past the big Indian Customs Guards with their rifles in hand. Finally, sometime in the early morning, our passengers were headed for a hotel.

It must have been after five a.m. when our crew bus finally stopped in front of our hotel. As we stepped onto the sidewalk the Captain said, "If any of you have never been to downtown Calcutta at sunrise there's something you need to see."

I asked, "What is it?"

He replied "I don't want to tell you. You have to see it yourself to believe it; but I promise you'll never forget it for the rest of your lives. If anyone is interested, meet me in front of the hotel at six a. m."

Two of the stewardesses and I said we'd be there. I could not imagine what could be such an amazing sight that I'd never forget it.

It was six a.m. and just before sunrise when the Captain walked up to the three of us and said, "Let's walk down this way."

We went about a half block and turned the corner. I heard the engine of a truck coming in the distance. It seemed to be starting and stopping every few yards. Suddenly walking towards us we saw two large uniformed men on each side of the street. They were walking down the sidewalks and stopping occasionally. Every time they stopped the one nearest the buildings seemed to be kicking at something.

The Captain stopped and said, "Watch."

Suddenly the two men bent over and picked something up between them. The truck which we could now see had stopped just past their position. They carried the sagging object to the rear of the stake truck and swung it up and onto the back. Then they returned to the sidewalk and continued their stopping and kicking.

We started walking toward them again when suddenly one of the stewardesses quietly said, "Oh no."

The truck was now close enough for us to see the pile of objects on its flatbed. They were the bodies of Calcutta's poor who slept in the city's doorways and alleys. They were the ones who had starved to death or died of some disease during the night. The uniformed men had been kicking their feet. When they didn't wake up they joined the others in the back of the truck.

Now both girls were crying and I was feeling sick at my stomach.

The Captain's eyes were moist as he said, "There are trucks all over the city every morning at sunrise. They take the bodies out of the city and burn them. That's what I wanted you to see." The Captain was right. I'll never forget it.

Postscript: It was about thirty minutes later and I had just turned out the bedside lamp in the 200 year old hotel room when the phone rang. "Jerry, this is Captain _____. I just got a call from the airport. They said New York called again and had changed their mind."

He continued; "The message said, speed tape the hole in the fowler flap, remove the cove lip door and put it in the baggage compartment, restrict the speed to Mach .76, and bring the plane on to New York. Are you willing to go back to the airport and work the flight to Karachi? I realize that you will be close on your maximum duty day."

I couldn't wait to leave Calcutta. "What time is pickup? I'll be there," I quickly answered.

"I thought that you might feel that way. I'll see you downstairs in thirty minutes," he replied.

It was mid-morning by the time we were finally airborne and in a climbing turn over the outskirts of the sprawling city.

In the distance I could see the rising smoke from a big fire.

HOW ARE YOU GUYS NAVIGATING OUT HERE?

Honolulu to Los Angeles; 1969

It was the last leg of my "Honolulu Shuttle" that month. That was the nickname which we gave to the trips that just went to and from Hawaii. We would fly to Honolulu, lay over about twenty-two hours and then back to Los Angeles. The trip "lines" that included a round the world flight usually added some shuttles to put the pilots' flight hours above the minimum required. If you did not reach your minimum flight hours, you were subject to being called for additional trips until you reached the minimum.

It had just become dark and we were about half way back to Los Angeles when the Purser came to the cockpit; "Captain, we have a VIP on board today."

"Oh, who is it?" he asked.

"He is _____, the astronaut," she said.

"Where is he sitting?" asked the Captain.

"He's in first class," she replied. "Do you want me to ask him if he wants to come up to the cockpit for a visit?" she continued. (In those days cockpit visits were allowed.)

"Sure, go ahead," he answered.

In a few minutes the cockpit door opened again and the famous gentleman entered. We shook hands all around and the well-known astronaut settled into the jump seat which was located behind the Captain. He had been into space and of course that was the main topic of conversation. We were all interested in talking to a guy who had literally been "out of this world". We felt privileged to get a chance to ask him some questions about the space program.

The thing that his answers did most for me was to reinforce my feelings about being an astronaut. Although I had not possessed even close to the right qualifications to be an astronaut, I had never wanted to be one. They were famous and they were considered by many to be "heroes", but I never felt that what they did was desirable to me as a professional pilot. Personally, flying a hot jet fighter seemed a lot more satisfying than sitting strapped into a capsule wearing a spacesuit with someone in Houston responsible for where it went. No thanks. (But that is just me and many people would disagree.)

In any case the gentleman looked intently around the cockpit and then asked, "How are you guys navigating out here?"

The first officer showed him the dual Dopplers and explained how they worked by bouncing radar beams off the ocean and back to the aircraft. This information was automatically converted into groundspeed and drift. He then showed the astronaut how he backed-up the Doppler information by using Loran C (a low frequency radio navigation system initially designed for ships).

Our visitor then, both by his remarks and his manner, made me think that he was not all that impressed with our means of navigation. He then proceeded to tell us that he had also been responsible for navigation during one space mission.

He went on to explain in quite some detail and for a rather long time that their main means of navigation had been inertial navigation systems. (These systems sense, by means of accelerometers, every change in motion of their host vehicle. These movements are then converted by the systems' computers into speed, drift, etc....)

The gentleman was obviously intelligent and I might add; very courageous to strap on a rocket and then be blasted into space. Perhaps it was because of his manner, but his lengthy review of his astronaut duties seemed to go on and on. Then, he gave me an opening.

He said, "I was also the one responsible for backing-up the inertial navigation systems by using a sextant to take celestial readings."

I immediately spoke up and said, "Sir, I'll tell you what. We still use Navigators on some of our polar flights. Let me get out the sextant that's stowed beneath the Navigator's table right behind you. I'll set it up and then you can take a few star shots and tell us how we're doing with our Dopplers and Loran; how about that?"

The astronaut looked at me in surprise and like I might be crazy.

He then looked at his watch before he said, "You know what? I've been up here quite a while. I'd probably better get back to my seat."

He then stood up, shook hands all around and left the cockpit.

The Captain turned, looked back at me and said, "Cook, why did you do that?"

"Do what?" I said.

Then he grinned and said, "Thanks."

Postscript: To the astronaut; if you happen to read this and recognize this account, I offer you my apology for my actions that day. In my defense I had been hearing rumors of a possible furlough, besides detesting riding sideways as an engineer while someone else got to fly the plane; therefore I most likely wasn't in a very good mood. I sincerely hope that you are in good health and are enjoying life.

And; from one old fighter pilot to another; "Check six!"

HAPPY BIRTHDAY; MY ASS

Tehran, Iran; October 17, 1969

I was in Tehran, Iran again. Yesterday, Pan Am Flight One had picked up my replacement flight engineer and dropped me off for a scheduled full day of crew rest there in the heart of Persia. If I remember it correctly, unlike Karachi, only the flight engineer laid over in Tehran. The rest of the crew stayed on the plane and flew to Beirut before their next layover. The hotel where Pan Am lodged us was the very nice Tehran Hilton. It was located on a hill overlooking the city. However, it was quite a long taxi ride from the airport.

Tehran seemed like a different world than Karachi. It appeared much more modern and up to date and I had not seen a single camel or a cobra the few times that I had been here. I had slept well and was now sitting in the coffee shop getting ready to treat myself to a big breakfast to celebrate my 32nd birthday. I was looking forward to a full day without sitting sideways on an airplane and flying through a bunch of time zones. I should be able to catch up somewhat on my rest with the day off.

I had picked up an English language newspaper in the lobby and was beginning to catch up on the world news. It was hard to get used to not being at home on holidays and birthdays. But it was the way of life for "junior" on an airline seniority list and I was still very much that. Pan Am had 3,747 pilots on their list and I only had 350 pilots below me. Of course junior ended up with what was left after the more senior pilots had selected their trips each month.

Honestly speaking, that was likely the fairest way of assigning flights for an airline. But it left pilots like me on trips on most holidays and sometimes on family birthdays, if you didn't get lucky. But at least I had an airline career which I thought at the time was the pinnacle of aviation jobs. *Ri…ght!*

I turned to the business section of the newspaper while I waited for my birthday eggs. I glanced at the big headline at the top of the page; "PAN AMERICAN WORLD AIRWAYS TO FURLOUGH 450 PILOTS!"

I closed my mouth and read it again, but it didn't change a bit. I immediately wondered if Pan Am had timed the news so they could give it to me on my birthday. Airlines were not known to be sentimental about sending out furlough notices. My next thought was that I was probably going to receive my official layoff notice as a Christmas gift. That prediction turned out to be correct. (Speaking of correct; unfortunately the Colonel back at Homestead Air Force Base had also been correct when he warned me about the airlines.)

"Happy birthday; my ass," was all I could think. I wasn't hungry anymore. By now my eggs were likely almost as cold as my sentiments toward Pan American World Airways.

Three days later I was high over northern Canada, not too far south of the Arctic Circle. I was flight-engineering Pan Am Flight 121 from London to Los Angeles; the last leg of my round the world trip. The conversation in the cockpit had naturally turned to the impending furloughs. The First Officer (who was senior enough to avoid the cutback) had brought it up with a question to me. The question was, "Jerry, are you going to get caught in the furlough?"

I answered, "If they lay off 450 pilots I will."

"What are you going to do?" he continued.

"I don't know," I said, "But obviously I made a big mistake coming to the 'World's Most Experienced Airline'. I should have gone to American when they contacted me while I was in ground school with Pan Am; or stayed in Florida and flown for National Airlines. I talked to every airline pilot that I could while I was still in the Air Force and they all told me basically the same thing, 'Go to Pan Am if you have a choice.'"

(Their message essentially had been, "If every airline in the world folded, Pan Am would be the last to go." *What a crock.* I suppose that I should have known better, but I didn't.)

"Are you in the Air Guard or Reserves?" was his next question.

"No. I've been trying to locate a unit to join but they're all either fully manned or they require you to already be current in whatever plane they're flying," I replied.

He continued, "I fly RF-101 Voodoos in the Nevada Air National Guard in Reno. We have a sister unit in Little Rock, Arkansas and they also fly Voodoos. I heard at my last Guard drill that a couple of their pilots are planning to get out of the unit. You might give them a call. You never know." I mulled that over and thought, "Arkansas? I don't want to move to Arkansas!"

I felt sick with the worry and stress as I wondered how I would support my family. I now had another child to provide for. Pretty little Tiffany had been born in the Ojai Valley hospital in August.

Then I reflected, "High performance fighters again. But what would I do for a living? Air Guard pilots are usually part-timers meaning just part-time pay." I couldn't support my family on that. Then I supposed that I might as well forget it anyway. I had never flown Voodoos so they probably wouldn't talk to me even if I tried.

I was really depressed as we continued on toward Los Angeles. Flight engineering on a Boeing 707, in spite of the bull____ that the professional engineers tried to sell, was basically sitting on your butt staring at the engineer's panel and trying to stay awake. Consequently I had plenty of time to feel sorry for myself and to regret over and over my decision to go to Pan Am.

"Happy Birthday; my ass!"

Jerry W. Cook

COLONEL "DOC" SAVAGE

Little Rock AFB, AR; November 1969

After I returned from my Happy Birthday trip, I spent several weeks trying to figure out how I was going to pay the bills and support my family after my impending furlough. Of course I wanted to find a job flying airplanes since that was all I had done for a living since I was nineteen years old.

I investigated Air National Guard units in California, Oregon, Washington State, Arizona, and Nevada. I was looking for anything as near to where I presently lived as possible.

Unfortunately, so were about four hundred and forty-nine other Pan Am pilots who were about to be furloughed. Besides that, no one really wanted to hire somebody who would probably go back to the airline when a recall came; and you couldn't blame them. As I had told the First Officer on the London to Los Angeles flight, all of the Air Guard and Air Reserve units anywhere in the surrounding states were either fully manned, or were requiring a pilot to be already flying the same kind of planes that the unit had, before they would even talk to you. I didn't blame them for that either; but it sure didn't make me feel any better about my situation. I thought again about the Arkansas Air National Guard and what the first officer had said....

"Hello, this is Colonel Byrd," said the voice on the phone.

"Hello sir, my name is Jerry Cook. I'm trying to get in touch with Colonel Savage," I said.

"He's presently away on a cross country flight. I'm his Group Operations Officer. Can I help you?" Byrd asked.

"Perhaps sir, I am looking for a pilot position with your unit and was told that I needed to talk to him," I replied.

"Yes, that's correct," Byrd confirmed.

"Can you tell me when he will return?" I asked.

"He should be back in the office tomorrow," Byrd offered.

"I'll be there tomorrow then," I quickly replied.

"You'd better call first," the Colonel stated.

I thanked Colonel Byrd and hung up the phone. There was no way I was going to call first. Colonel Savage might turn me down for an appointment over the phone. I wanted to talk to him face to face.

Early the next morning I was on a Delta DC-8 non-stop from Los Angeles to Dallas. From Dallas I got a seat on a DC-9 to Little Rock. It was cold and raining in Little Rock when we landed. I was glad that I had checked the forecast before leaving Ojai early that morning and had grabbed my Pan Am raincoat before I left the house.

There were no boarding jet-ways at the old Little Rock airline terminal at Adams Field so I hurried across the wet ramp and into the terminal building. I located the passenger information counter and was in the process of asking the attendant about Little Rock AFB.

A friendly thirty-something blonde-haired gentleman walked up next to me and said, "Did I hear that you're trying to get to the Air Force base?" he asked.

"I am," I replied; "Do you know how I can get there?"

He grinned and said, "I sure do. In fact, that's where I'm headed. Want a ride?"

I couldn't believe my luck. "My name is Jerry Cook," I said and stuck out my hand.

He said, "Lynn Scott," as we shook hands.

We ran through the rain to his car and quickly got in, tossing our bags in the back seat.

"Where are you headed on base," he asked?

"I'm going to see Colonel Savage at the Air Guard," I answered.

"You mean 'Doc' Savage?" he inquired.

"Is he the Air Group Commander?" I said.

"Yes he is and the Air Guard unit just happens to be where I'm going," Scott said. As it turned out, Scott was a pilot for American Airlines and also an RF-101 pilot in the Air National Guard unit.

"Man; what great luck I am having so far today," I thought.

Scott told me a little about flying in the Air National Guard while on the way to the Air Base. It sounded just like what my friends in pilot training had told me years before. He delivered me right to the front door of the Group Headquarters building and told me how to find Colonel Savage's office.

I thanked Scott and said, "Maybe I'll be seeing you around here soon."

Scott replied, "Yeah, maybe so. Good luck with Doc Savage. I think you'll like him."

Then he drove down the hill toward the 154th Recon Fighter Squadron Operations.

As I walked toward the Headquarters' front door I looked down the hill to the flight line and could see some RF-101 Voodoos sitting on the ramp in the rain. I wondered if it was possible that I could be flying them soon. I sure hoped that would be the case, but I realized that a lot of things would have to happen before I could even dream of strapping into one of those sleek looking fighters.

At the moment it seemed like it was really a long shot. After all, I had never flown an RF-101 and never flown any kind of photo reconnaissance missions. The only type of "recce" missions I had flown was armed reconnaissance in the F-4 while searching for possible targets visually along the Ho Chi Minh trail in North Vietnam and Laos. It was a long shot; but it was one I had to take.

I had just removed my raincoat in the small foyer and turned left down the hallway toward where Lynn Scott had told me Colonel Savage's office was located. Someone in a flight suit came out of a doorway near the end of the hallway and walked toward me. He was a trim, good-looking older gentleman with short cropped silver hair. The collar of his flight suit was turned up in the back and as he got closer I could see the Lieutenant Colonel's insignia on his shoulders. He was carrying a cup of coffee with "154th Tac Recon Sq" and the profile of an RF-101 Voodoo on it. This guy was really cool and exactly what you would imagine a fighter pilot Group Commander would look like in the movies. His nametag simply said, "Savage."

"Colonel Savage," I said.

The older pilot stopped, smiled broadly and said, "That's me; what can I do for you?"

I stood at attention and said, "Sir, my name is Jerry Cook and I just flew in from California to get a job with your unit."

He looked at me for a second or two and then said, "What kind of a job?"

"As an RF-101 pilot," I replied.

The amiable Colonel looked at me with his steel-blue eyes and said, "How do you drink your coffee?" Then he stuck out his hand.

As I followed him into his office which overlooked the flight line I looked longingly again at the four rows of Voodoos sitting in the rain. Once again I wondered if there was a "Snowball's Chance in Hell" that I'd ever get to fly them.

I was still standing at near-attention when Colonel Savage handed me a steaming cup of black coffee in the same kind of cup that he had. He grinned again and said, "Relax, have a seat," and motioned me into a chair facing his desk.

I thanked him but remained standing until he took a seat behind his desk. It was out of respect for his rank and my training in ten years in the Air Force.

He leaned back in his big leather chair and said, "Jerry is it? Tell me about yourself."

I quickly gave him a review of my ten years of Air Force experience and talked briefly about my upcoming furlough. The Colonel quietly listened, just nodding from time to time.

When I was finished he said, "Is that your AF Form 5 that you have with you?" and nodded toward a folder that I had in my lap.

I said, "Yes sir," and handed it to him.

I sipped the hot coffee while he spent a few minutes looking through my Air Force flight records.

Then he looked up and said, "How much combat did you fly in Vietnam?"

I replied, "Two hundred and five missions, sir; four hundred and twenty hours."

He nodded again and said, "And you were also an instructor pilot in the F-4?"

I said "Yes sir," and told him how many flight hours that had involved.

"I saw where you checked out in F-86s right out of Pilot Training," he stated.

"Yes sir. I had just turned twenty-one. I thought that I was the luckiest guy in the world," I answered.

He smiled broadly and said, "I bet you did."

He continued, "And you also were an instructor in jets for four years in the Air Training Command?"

"Yes I was, Colonel," I replied.

He closed my Form 5, folded his hands and looked at me.

"Well Jerry, if you can fly combat in an F-4 and aim a gun, you sure as heck can fly an RF-101 and aim a camera," he exclaimed.

He continued, "If I gave you a job flying Voodoos, what would you do for a living? It is a part-time position with part-time pay and I doubt that you could support a family on that."

"Sir, I will pump gas, drive a cab, sell real-estate; anything I have to do," I said.

He nodded his head then looked seriously at me and asked, "Did you know that we are looking for two full-time instructor pilots to instruct in the RF-101?" I knew that he could tell from the look on my face that I did not.

"No sir, I didn't know that," I replied after I took a deep breath and mentally crossed my fingers.

"I didn't think so," he said.

He then continued, "It's a GS-13 Civil Service position, but you would be wearing your military flight suit. The pay is pretty good and coupled with your Air Guard military pay I doubt that you'd have any problems at all supporting your family."

He then asked the question that I hoped would come next; "Would you be interested?"

It wasn't a difficult question to answer and it took me about half a second.

I could not believe how this day was progressing. I finished all of the required paperwork to apply for the two positions. Colonel Savage had agreed that I would start as soon as possible in my RF-101 checkout while I was still flying for Pan Am and then begin the full time GS-13 position the next day after my furlough from Pan Am was effective.

As you can probably imagine, Colonel "Doc" Savage had just become one of the favorite and most important people in my life.

Toward The Evening Sky

VOODOO DANCE

Little Rock AFB, AR; March 25, 1970

It had taken a few months to get all of the paperwork filed and to become reinstated as a military pilot. But now, I was strapping into the front seat of one of the three F-101B/F former Air Defense Command Interceptors that the 189th Tactical Reconnaissance Group used for the first couple of flights during the checkout of pilots who were new to the Voodoo. These two-seated F-101B/F flights were in addition to several "flights" in a simulator. The simulator was a single-seater like the RF-101 reconnaissance models and it had a cockpit arrangement very similar to the actual airplane.

However the three F-101B/F Voodoos were very different than the sixteen or so single-seat reconnaissance versions that the unit operated. They had been designed for a completely different mission and it was obvious in the cockpit arrangement. After spending a few minutes looking around the unfamiliar cockpit and locating the "shiny switches", I was ready to fire up the engines on this big gray beast.

My instructor that day, a full time pilot in the unit, was a former Marine fighter pilot named Charley Wood. He climbed into the back seat and strapped in. The big J57-P-55's roared into life and seemed to be rumbling impatiently while I completed the "Before Taxi" checklist. When the ground controller issued our taxi instructions, we moved out of the parking area toward the runway. On the way I experimented with the nose-wheel steering and the brake pedal pressures. I was absolutely elated to be buckled into one of these supersonic machines and I couldn't wait to get back in the air as a fighter pilot, instead of riding around sideways and being referred to as a Pilot/Engineer. Once again I could hardly believe that I was so lucky.

As we taxied onto the northeast end of the 12,000 foot long concrete slab, my instructor reminded me to raise the landing gear and rotate to about forty-five degrees of nose up pitch as soon as possible after takeoff. This former interceptor had bigger and more powerful engines than the single seat Voodoos and therefore would accelerate even more rapidly than the RF-101s, particularly on such a cold day.

I had already seen a single seat Voodoo hang its nose gear after takeoff while we were accomplishing the pre-flight inspection on our plane. The nose gear on the Voodoos retracted toward the nose of the plane, unlike on the Phantom, which retracted to the rear. They could accelerate so fast in afterburner, that if you did not climb steeply enough before the aircraft's speed passed through two hundred and fifty knots (287 miles per hour), the air pressure on the front of the nose gear would overpower the hydraulic powered retraction piston and the nose gear would hang in the down position. It would stay there until you slowed down to below two hundred and fifty knots again. Therefore, if the pilot was using his engine afterburners during cold weather takeoffs, it made for some interesting roller coaster type flight paths. Sometimes you would see a pilot rotate, but not enough; hang the nose-wheel down and then; pull the nose up to a very steep angle while reducing the afterburners' thrust until the nose gear finally clunked up, and then push the nose down to a more normal climb angle.

The tower cleared us for an unrestricted climb to seventeen thousand feet. I had been holding the brakes with the engine power at eighty-five percent while the tower operator had checked with the Little Rock Approach Controller for any conflicting air traffic on our departure. With more than eighty-five percent of power on the two big engines, one of two things would happen, either the tires would skid on the concrete or worse, the tires would rotate on the rims.

I released the brakes, pushed the throttles up to military power, and then selected full afterburners. The big gray Voodoo jumped forward like it was shot out of a cannon and I was pressed back in my seat. We had no external fuel tanks for this flight so the plane was relatively light. It felt to me like maybe this F-101F was accelerating as fast; perhaps even faster than a Phantom. I knew that it had to have been longer, but it only seemed like about four or five seconds since I had stoked the afterburners and we were already passing 175, now 185 knots.

I rotated the plane rapidly to 45 degrees of nose up pitch while I raised the landing gear handle and then quickly raised the flap handle. We shot up like a rocket. I hoped the nose gear would retract in time. It clunked into the up and locked position while the flaps were still moving. At this tremendous climb rate it was already time to think about leveling off at seventeen thousand feet. But first, I had to find the altimeter amid the extremely busy cluster of gauges scattered all around the instrument panel. Because of the radar scope they were not necessarily located where they would normally be.

By now we were climbing at almost four hundred knots indicated airspeed and the vertical speed indicator was pegged at its maximum reading of six thousand feet per minute. I located the altimeter. It was spinning upward fast and we were already ripping through fifteen thousand feet.

I yanked the throttles out of afterburner while quickly rolling the big interceptor upside down and pulled the nose down hard to keep from overshooting seventeen thousand. I think we pulled about three inverted G's and we still overshot. Charley was laughing and telling me, "Get your ass back down to seventeen before somebody notices." I guess we did, because Little Rock Departure Control didn't say anything about it.

I know that I must have been grinning like an idiot in my oxygen mask as I was thinking, "Man this thing will go." I was absolutely having a ball and; getting paid to do it.

I remember thinking, "How could there be any better way to make a living than this?"

Jerry W. Cook

PITCH-UP

Little Rock AFB, AR; March 27, 1970

My Voodoo checkout continued and I was now making all of my flights in the RF-101 "Recce Bird". I loved the single-seater partly because no one else's little pink butt was in the plane to worry about except yours. The Voodoo was a fast airplane but; it did not like to turn. It would go like "a bat out of hell" in a straight line but, when it came time to make a high G turn or pull out of a dive in a Voodoo watch out; be very careful. If the pilot hauled back too hard on a Voodoo control stick, the plane would protest and sometimes violently.

It definitely had a serious flight control problem when the plane was pulled into a critical angle of attack. The problem was labeled a "pitch-up". At one time the Air Force had even delayed deliveries of the aircraft while the manufacturer tried to solve the problem. They never did completely rid the Voodoo of its pitch-up tendencies but the Air Force finally resumed its deliveries anyway.

In their efforts to help prevent the pilot from pitching-up out of control, McDonnell installed an active inhibitor system. An instrument was installed in the cockpit and wired to an angle of attack vane located on the side of the fuselage. The cockpit instrument had a small needle which moved around a round scale. Located near the top of the scale were a yellow band and a red band. When the plane was pulled into a hard turn or pull-up, the needle would move around the scale toward the yellow band. When the needle touched the bottom of the yellow band, a warning tone was intended to sound inside the pilot's helmet earphones. At that point the pilot was supposed to release some back pressure on the control stick. If the pilot continued to pull the Voodoo still harder into the critical angle of attack range, the needle moved into the red band. At that point the system was designed to move the control stick forward using hydraulic pressure. That movement was supposed to lower the angle of attack to below the critical pitch-up zone. If I remember correctly, the system exerted about seventy pounds of forward force on the control stick. If the pilot overrode the inhibitor system or if it was inaccurate or inoperative, the aircraft would depart from controlled flight; i.e. *pitch-up*. If a pilot entered into a pitch-up below fifteen thousand feet above the ground, it would usually result in one of two things; ejection or death; maybe both.

One of the things that I found interesting and exciting during my Voodoo transition was the fact that in spite of its demonstrated flight control problems, when approaching the airbase for landing, we flew the "101" down the initial toward the runway and on the way to the "fighter break" at 1500 feet above the ground and at 350 knots indicated airspeed. Then when we were over the end of the runway, we would rack the big "One-O-Wonder" into a nearly ninety degree banked, one hundred and eighty degree turn. Leaving the throttles where they were so we wouldn't slow down too rapidly, we would keep pulling the control stick further and further back until the angle of attack indicator was just below the yellow band. Occasionally, if the air was not smooth, we would hear the pitch-up warning horn sounding intermittently in our helmet. As the airspeed quickly bled off we gradually eased off the stick to stay out of the pitch-up zone. Then, we had to begin rolling out increments of bank angle to keep from falling out of the sky; and to maintain our altitude at fifteen hundred feet above the ground. The heavy recce fighter would shutter and shake around the break, slowing down very rapidly toward two hundred and fifty knots. At that point we would then add in enough power to hold the two hundred and fifty knots and quickly lower the landing gear and flaps. We flew around the final turn at two hundred and twenty to two hundred and thirty knots; slowing on final approach to the Voodoo's normal approach speed of one hundred seventy five to one hundred and eighty five knots (between two hundred and two hundred and thirteen miles per hour).

(So you're thinking that doing a fighter break before landing in a plane with flight control issues like the Voodoo doesn't sound very smart? As I indicated in the book, "Once a Fighter Pilot", you don't necessarily have to be that smart to fly a fighter. As a much older aviation axiom states; "You can always tell a fighter pilot, but you can't tell him much.")

No, it probably wasn't that smart to do a fighter break on the verge of a pitch-up, but it sure was exciting.

Jerry W. Cook

TEACH A 'KID' WITH 230 HOURS TOTAL FLYING TIME TO DO *WHAT?*

Little Rock AFB, AR; August 1970

"Fly a single seat jet fighter at 550 miles per hour, 100 to 500 feet above the earth, navigate visually by comparing actual topographical features on the ground with a map clipped to your kneeboard, locate the target, photograph it, and then escape the area by using high speed and 'terrain masking' at very low altitudes." That was the primary mission of the pilots of the 154th Tactical Reconnaissance Squadron.

But in addition, the unit had been selected to conduct an RF-101 Replacement Training Unit or "RTU" because the Air Force was getting out of the RF-101 business. Selected flight instructors were to be responsible for new Pilot Training Graduates. These new pilots had a total of approximately 230 flight hours. The RTU mission was to instruct them on how to perform the above mission while flying one of the most unforgiving jet fighter aircraft ever built. That was my new full-time job.

I remembered from my Air Force days that USAF assignments to the RF-101 had been restricted to pilots with at least 1000 hours of jet fighter or fighter type experience. That rule was established because of the aforementioned flight control problems of the Voodoo. The United States Air Force's policy was to limit pitch-up accidents in the plane by allowing only jet fighter/fighter type experienced pilots to fly them. However, because of the totally different organizational structure of the Air National Guard, there were no experienced fighter/fighter type pilots from which to choose. We had to somehow overcome our student pilot's serious lack of flight experience, keep these new guys alive in the Voodoo, and teach them how to perform a very hazardous mission. *No problem....!*

He was a second lieutenant and my first student. He was a big six foot personable young bachelor with likely a whole string of lovely ladies waiting back in his home state. If he was nervous about his upcoming checkout in the Voodoo, he didn't show it. He seemed like a cool customer. That I was a little uneasy about his upcoming checkout in the Voodoo, I tried to hide. But the responsibility I felt for this young pilot weighed heavily. I knew that any failure on my part could mean a sudden and violent death for him.

We proceeded rapidly through the ground training phase which was individual instruction between the instructor and student. There was no formal classroom work, because there were usually just one or two students entering the course at any one time. After teaching him during ground training and then spending several days with the student flying the simulator while learning some basic characteristics of the 101, we proceeded to the flight phase. It began with several sorties with him flying in the front seat and me instructing from the back of one of the two-seater F-101B/Fs.

Those flights went well and it was time for his RF-101 single-seat checkout. During the first few missions I would be flying chase in another RF-101. I would be maintaining a position slightly behind my student's plane and just off to one side. In that way I would know his flight conditions at all times, because I would be matching them in my Voodoo. When necessary I would instruct the student by utilizing our aircraft radios which were tuned to a designated squadron frequency.

The first single-seater sortie called for mostly airwork which would consist of hard level turns, some rolls and a few other aerobatic maneuvers such as "Lazy 8s". The Voodoo required so much sky to do a loop, Split S, Immelman Turn or any kind of vertical maneuver; that we were going to concentrate on semi-horizontal air-work on this first mission. On later flights we would be using the Shirley MOA (Military Operating Area) over Greer's Ferry Lake for some of the altitude-eating vertical maneuvers.

His hard turns went okay as he got used to high angle of attack maneuvering similar to what he would be employing for the fighter break for landing. We then proceeded to aileron rolls which he accomplished with no problems. I hadn't expected any because the aileron roll is an extremely easy maneuver in a jet fighter. All you have to do is pull the nose a few degrees above the horizon, remove all back pressure from the stick and push the stick straight to the side and presto, the roll is done. On the other hand, the barrel-roll is not so simple.

The object is to pick a distant point far out on the horizon such as a cloud to use as a center reference; then scribe an imaginary circle completely around that point using the nose of the aircraft. The pilot is to begin by pulling the nose 30 degrees to the side of the center point. Then from a nose and wings-level aircraft attitude he is to smoothly begin a slow pull-up and simultaneous roll to reach a position with the plane's nose thirty degrees directly above the center point and the wings of the plane in a ninety degree vertical bank. All during the maneuver three degrees of roll are added for every degree of nose travel. The slow, coordinated roll and pull continues toward a spot thirty degrees on the opposite of the center point with the aircraft nose on the horizon and with the plane upside down. At this point much of the back pressure on the stick is released because gravity is assisting in pulling the nose of the plane downward. However, the constant roll is continued until the aircraft nose is thirty degrees directly below the center point. The aircraft's wings should now be vertical again. Steadily increasing back pressure on the stick must be added while continuing the roll until the aircraft is back to the original starting point with the nose and wings level. When done correctly the maneuver is a smooth, coordinated and beautiful maneuver. When it was not done correctly, at least in a Voodoo, it could spell disaster.

The student started the maneuver properly and things were going well, until he arrived at the wings inverted position. I was still in the chase position with my Voodoo also upside down, to the side and slightly behind his. At that point for some reason he stopped rolling the plane, but he kept pulling back on the stick.

As the noses of our two inverted Voodoos continued tracking downward I called him, "Demon 11, stop pulling back on the stick and keep your roll going." However he kept pulling the nose toward the ground. I called him again to stop pulling and to roll the aircraft back upright. He continued his pull; this was getting serious. I knew that there wasn't enough altitude between us and the Ouachita Mountains below to complete a pullout if he got his nose pointed vertically at the ground.

Using his first name this time instead of his call-sign, I yelled over the radio, "R__! Quit pulling the damn stick back and roll the plane upright. *Roll…Roll…Roll!!*"

As I was yelling at him, I began to roll my Voodoo toward upright while releasing back pressure but keeping him in sight. I just couldn't think of any good reason for both of us to die that day.

Finally…his Voodoo snapped over one hundred and eighty degrees to upright and the young pilot began pulling out of his dive, which was now approaching sixty degrees. Condensation was tearing away from the top of his wings. Now I was hoping that he wouldn't pull too hard, and pitch-up the RF-101. He pulled out a couple of thousand feet above the trees. I started to breathe again.

As I joined back in the chase position on the young second lieutenant's wing I called him again, *"Now Demon 11; go back up and…do it right this time!"*

He did. And less than thirty years later he was a Major General.

Toward The Evening Sky

AERO CLUB

Little Rock AFB, AR; Early 1970s

Anytime our Voodoos were flying, one of the several additional duties of an Arkansas Air Guard RF-101 pilot was to man a small mobile control unit otherwise known as "Demon Mobile". It was a blue Chevy pickup truck equipped with two Ultra High Frequency radios, binoculars, flare gun, flashlight, fire extinguisher, and various other paraphernalia. It served as an emergency back-up to the regular airbase control tower.

We would drive it out to a position near the runway where our planes would begin their takeoff roll; or where they would be touching down during their landing. Part of the equipment in the truck was a complete set of aircraft checklists and a RF-101 "Dash-One"; which was the flight operating manual for the aircraft. It contained all normal, abnormal and emergency procedures for the Voodoo. The mobile officer was to use them to assist a pilot who might be having difficulties with his plane. Flying a single-seat high performance fighter did not allow the pilot the opportunity to read a Dash-One at the same time. In the case of an aircraft emergency involving one of our planes, "Demon Mobile" would assist the airbase control tower with aircraft specific knowledge and procedures.

Also located on the airbase was an Aero Club. The club was open to military members who had, or who wanted to obtain a civilian pilot license. It possessed a few small training aircraft and anyone who was a member of the club could take flight instruction, or just rent an aircraft if they were already qualified.

The bright summer day was very hot and it was about lunch time. I was the pilot in Demon Mobile that particular day and the traffic pattern was full of C-130s practicing all kinds of approaches and landings. That was not unusual because one of the airbase functions was as the School House for most Air Force pilots who were transitioning into the C-130 Hercules. Our RF-101s were not due back from their flights for several more minutes, but I was already in place in case one of them had to return early. I was monitoring both of the UHF radios. One of them was turned to the control tower's frequency and the other to our "squadron common" frequency. Both of the radio units also included a backup receiver which was always tuned to the military UHF emergency frequency referred to as "Guard" (sometimes jokingly referred to by the Air Force as "Navy common").

I had parked the mobile truck between two taxiways leading to the runway and about fifteen hundred feet down from the end of the runway. I glanced over my shoulder back toward the huge aircraft parking ramp to my left and saw one of the air base flying club's Cessna 152s taxiing down the parallel taxiway. I remember thinking that someone was probably trying to get in a quick flight during their lunch break. I then looked back toward the full traffic pattern and thought, "Good luck with that." The little orange and white Cessna turned left onto the taxiway near me, stopped and then began his engine run-up.

I did not hear the aero club plane's pilot on the radio when he had called the tower ground controller for taxi instructions or when he had checked in with the tower flight controller after he had stopped on the taxiway near me. The reason was, that like almost all civilian aircraft, the plane's radio used a completely different frequency band than did the military's UHF. It was called VHF (very-high frequency). The airbase control tower utilized both UHF and VHF radios.

The orange and white Cessna finished his engine run-up and taxied up to the runway hold-short line. The C-130s kept going round and round the traffic pattern. The black smoke from their big tires and the smell of the hot rubber continually drifted across my truck and the Cessna. It seemed to be getting hotter by the minute and the little add-on aftermarket air-conditioner in the truck was on max; but it was losing its battle with the Arkansas summer heat and humidity. The Cessna pilot had both of his side windows pushed open as far as they would go. I knew that he must be burning up with no air-conditioner. I knew that I was; even though I supposedly had one.

He sat there watching the C-130s go round and round as his lunch hour ticked away. At least thirty minutes had passed since he had stopped for his engine run-up. Finally the little airplane began to move and then turned sharply around and started taxiing rapidly back toward the parking ramp. Of course I had not heard any of his conversations with the tower. But just before he had given up and turned around, I had heard some background laughter from the tower on my UHF radio as the tower operator was issuing still another landing clearance for one of the circling C-130s. Finally my curiosity got the best of me and I called the tower to find out the cause of the laughter.

The controller said, "I told the Cessna 152 pilot that I could possibly get him on the runway if he could wait another five minutes. He answered that, no he needed to taxi back to the ramp because his pilot medical certificate had expired while he was sitting there waiting."

A third class flight medical expires after two years. It probably did seem almost that long.

Toward The Evening Sky

HAULIN' ASS; IN THE GRASS

Northern Louisiana; Early 1970s

As a requirement for maintaining a combat-ready status, each RF-101 pilot had to fly an annual "Tac-Eval Check" flight. It was a simulated combat mission similar to what would be flown in actual wartime. Targets were assigned which the pilot would have to find and photograph during a high-low-high flight. The entire flight was flown with a check pilot in another RF-101 flying in the chase position. The check pilot's job was to evaluate the entire flight from takeoff to landing. The photos would be downloaded from the plane and processed. The resulting pictures were part of the pilot's scoring. In actual wartime these target photos would be a vital part of strike mission planning for both fighter and bomber aircraft.

Even the Group Commander was not exempt from these Tac-Eval check flights. It was time for Colonel Savage's annual check-ride and I was the chosen one to chase and evaluate his prowess. I had recently been selected as one of the Group's Standardization-Evaluation pilots and as the most junior pilot in the section, I drew the assignment of evaluating the Colonel. It is not really an enviable position for a check pilot to be in; that of testing his big boss. (i.e., what do you do if he screws it up?)

The targets that had been assigned to Col. Savage by the intelligence section were located on a low-level route in Louisiana. I remember thinking that I had not flown that route before. I don't remember whether the Colonel indicated that he had flown that particular low level either. Consequently it would be a true test of low level navigation expertise to keep the aircraft within the parameters of the prescribed route. Part of my job was to ensure that happened.

We took off in a two-ship formation with me as the Colonel's wingman. The takeoff, climb-out and high-level portion of the flight went as planned. At the specified point on our flight plan, Colonel Savage requested a descent from our Memphis Center controller and then he canceled the radar-followed instrument flight rules part of his flight plan. We would be too low for any radar to track us anyway. We arrived over the entry point of the low-level route at our preplanned five hundred feet, four hundred and eighty knots and on the planned heading; so far so good. I was flying about one-half mile back of the lead Voodoo and approximately thirty degrees to the left.

According to the map on my kneeboard we were on course when we passed over our second checkpoint. The Colonel racked his Voodoo up onto its right wing over the checkpoint and rolled out on his next heading toward the southwest with me following. His heading checked but from that point forward I could not locate anything on the ground that resembled anything on my map. Colonel Savage was proceeding exactly on the prescribed heading and I started thinking that perhaps it was just me who was lost. I anxiously scanned the surrounding terrain especially further out in front; but I still recognized nothing from the map.

I was supposed to be keeping track of where we were and I didn't have a clue. It was like we had suddenly flown into another dimension or something. Everything looked unfamiliar. My next thought was, "I hope that I recognize something soon," and suddenly, I did.

It was a Delta DC-9 pulling into position for takeoff on the northeast end of the Monroe Louisiana airport's northeast/southwest runway. I didn't know if the Colonel had seen the airport as we passed just about a mile south of it. We were traveling so fast and so low that we were in sight of the airport for just a few seconds.

I wondered if anyone at the airport had seen us. The answer to that question didn't take long to come. Our backup emergency radio Guard frequency came alive; "Two Air Force jet fighters that just passed one mile south of the Monroe, Louisiana Regional Airport; say your call sign *immediately*." It took a couple of seconds for the Colonel to change his radio transmitter to the Guard frequency. Then came his factual reply, "I may be lost; but I *ain't* stupid."

The next day we finished his check flight on a different route; in a different state and far away from the Monroe, Louisiana Regional Airport.

He passed.

Toward The Evening Sky

GUESS YOU'LL HAVE TO STOP ME

Little Rock AFB, AR; Early 1970s

It was summer camp time; the time when the 154th Tactical Reconnaissance Squadron would take most of their combat ready RF-101s and fly them to one of two bases that were used for our two-week annual training exercise. The bases were set up with buildings and other facilities that could be quickly opened and activated to support a squadron of fighters, or as in our case reconnaissance fighters, for extended flight operations. They were operated much like a forward operating base would be in a unit deployment to an actual combat area of operations.

If I remember correctly, that particular year our forward operating base was located at Hunter Army Airfield at Savannah, Georgia. A deployment of sixteen RF-101s requires weeks of preparation and dealing with numerous agencies. The planning by the flying squadron involved the selection of the pilots, flight planning for the route, weather forecasts and close coordination with all of the air traffic facilities involved along the route. Of course the first ATC facility after takeoff was the Little Rock Arrival and Departure Control which deals with aircraft within about thirty miles of Little Rock. The normal procedure for aircraft departing the airbase is for the Little Rock Air Force Base control tower to control the aircraft until it departs the traffic pattern area at the airbase and then handoff the plane to the Departure Control when that controller has the departing traffic on his radar screen. Little Rock Departure Control then issues instructions and monitors the aircraft until turning it over to Memphis Center who then controls it outside of thirty miles from Little Rock until they turn it over to another Air Traffic Control Center and so on to the destination.

A single aircraft departing the airbase or even a flight of two has no problem complying with instructions from an air traffic controller. However, four flights of four aircraft each taking off a few seconds apart and then joining up into a flight of sixteen aircraft is quite a different story. That is the reason for the intense and extensive meetings and coordination between the flying squadron and the affected air traffic control agencies. The leader of a sixteen plane formation cannot maneuver as quickly with his formation as can a single or a two plane formation. The departure of a sixteen plane flight has to be carefully planned and executed. From start engine times to taxi times to runway line-up to the detailed instructions for the multi-formation join-ups after takeoff; the plan needs to be followed by everyone to avoid a potential disaster.

Everything had been thought of. Every "i" was dotted and every "t" was crossed. We were ready to go. Our Group Commander, Colonel Doc Savage, was leading the first four-ship and after the carefully choreographed formation join-up of all four four-ship formations; he would be leading the sixteen-ship formation all the way to Savannah. It would be simulating the way it would be done if hostilities somewhere in the world required us to deploy the squadron *en masse*.

Things were going according to plan. All sixteen Voodoos were lined up on the runway with two spare Voodoos holding short of the runway and ready to launch if anyone aborted their takeoff. Colonel Savage and his wingman released their brakes and ten seconds later the second two-ship started their takeoff roll. The takeoffs were going according to plan and aircraft five and six were about to liftoff when the call from Little Rock Departure Control came; "Demon 11, we have some air traffic coming in from the west. Please start your right turn to heading three six zero now." Colonel Savage replied, "Demon 11 unable. We need to continue straight ahead for another two miles before we can start the turn to join up our formations."

I don't know what the controller must have been thinking but this is what he said; "Demon 11, I need you to start your turn now or...*I'll have to stop you.*"

Colonel Savage who was by now smoking along at over four hundred miles per hour immediately replied; "Well then I guess you'll just have to stop me."

After a very long silence a new voice came on the radio from Little Rock Departure Control, "Demon 11, continue your flight as planned. We will turn the other traffic to the south."

I guess the first controller couldn't figure out how to stop Colonel Doc and his sixteen Voodoos.

Toward The Evening Sky

VACATION BIBLE SCHOOL

Gulfport Air National Guard Base, MS; Early 1970s

It had been constructed in 1942 as a training field and was known as Gulfport Army Airfield. In 1949 it was declared excess and turned over to the city of Gulfport for use as a joint use airport. After activation in 1951 and then deactivation in 1957 as an Air Force Base, the military area ended up assigned to the Mississippi Air National Guard. It is used as an Air Guard and Air Force Reserve Training Base by over twenty thousand personnel each year. The fifteen days of Annual Training at Gulfport were irreverently referred to in those days as "Vacation Bible School". (It wasn't.)

Every military flying outfit (or civilian for that matter) has its unforgettable characters. In our case they were; "The Six Hundred Dollar Man"; and "Baby Huey". "Six Hundred" was a full-time Air Guard instructor pilot and "Baby" was one of our Voodoo pilots and also an airline pilot in the civilian domain. I was somewhat in awe of them not because I admired their antics, but by the fact that they could stay alive (and out of handcuffs) while undertaking them. I figured that if a lesser mortal, such as me, attempted to match them, I would certainly die or at least end up in jail. It amazed me and many others that they didn't.

Flying was finished for the day and I was back in the barracks that we would call home for two weeks. The base housing was located among the pine trees on the military side of the runways. Located along the street outside our quarters was a large drainage ditch. I had just finished showering and was getting dressed to go to dinner when I heard the awful roaring of an automobile engine at high rpm. Accompanying the roar was a familiar sounding voice yelling, "Hit it again Pat! Hit it again!"

I walked to the door of my barracks and looked out. I don't have any idea how he had managed it but Pat, the Six Hundred Dollar Man, had planted his old Lincoln Continental four door hardtop with suicide doors across the drainage ditch. The front end was suspended on the far bank toward the street and the rear end was hanging by its bumper from the near bank. All four wheels were suspended in mid-air and the right rear tire was spinning furiously as Baby Huey yelled at the Six Hundred Dollar Man, "Hit it again Pat! Hit it again!" Baby Huey had the right front door open and was hanging out of the Lincoln watching the rear wheel spin in mid-air while it was touching nothing. Just as I walked out of the building, Baby Huey fell out of the car and landed in the ditch on his back. He just lay there laughing and looking up at the small crowd that had gathered by now.

Finally, we got through to the Six Hundred Dollar Man that his "co-pilot" had been ejected and that his big white Lincoln land yacht wasn't going anywhere anytime soon.

Postscript #1: The Six Hundred Dollar Man was one of the best pilots with whom I have flown. He was also a carefree bachelor and when he wasn't flying, he really liked to party. One evening he was enjoying one of these parties in the Officers' Club Bar and decided that he would demonstrate how to do a handstand. Just doing a normal handstand in his present condition would have been quite a feat. However he was going to do it on top of two Martini glasses. There was one problem however. Both glasses broke and a stem pierced one wrist doing quite a lot of damage. His part of the medical bill was six hundred dollars; hence the nickname, "The Six-Hundred Dollar Man".

Postscript #2: A few years later, I ended up as these two clowns' Group Commander. One Saturday morning during Guard Drill I went down to the flight operations building for a meeting. As I entered the lobby area I saw Captain "Baby Huey" walking toward me in his flight suit. I noticed that every time he took a step with his right foot, I saw a flash of white.

As he passed me he nodded and stated, "Good morning Colonel."

I said, "Good morning Huey; hold up a second Captain." He stopped and turned to face me.

"Pull up your right flight suit leg," I said.

He hesitated but finally reached down and pulled it up. There instead of a black boot tongue behind the laces there was just his white sock filling the space.

"What happened to your flight boot?" I asked.

"I tripped over a log while I was hunting and tore the tongue off," he replied.

After reminding him that he wasn't supposed to be hunting in his flight boots, I told him to go to supply and get some new ones.

"Yes sir," he replied.

Sunday afternoon I was back in the flight operations building and again I saw Baby Huey coming toward me. This time I didn't see any flashes of white when he walked, but for some reason I decided to stop him again.

"Let me see your new boots Captain," I said.

He finally pulled up his flight suit legs. There were no new boots. Instead, he had spray-painted his white sock black...with his foot still in it.

I marched him over to Supply myself.

BACKING A VOODOO

Shirley Military Operating Area, AR; Early 1970s

In addition to chasing students, flight checking other Voodoo pilots, and maintaining my own combat ready status, I had been awarded another duty. I was now one of the designated maintenance test pilots. As such I was tasked to fly Voodoos which had just been worked on by our aircraft maintenance section. Simply put, it was my job to fly the aircraft to ascertain if the maintenance had been successful before it would be scheduled to be flown by the other squadron pilots. I didn't mind the extra duty; in fact I enjoyed being able to go up and workout the planes. Sometimes we got to fly the aircraft with no external fuel tanks. I called them Voodoo lites. Voodoo lites were definitely more fun and easier to fly because they would accelerate and turn much better than ones with the external tanks attached; especially if they still contained fuel.

If a major inspection had just been completed on the aircraft, I would take it up and comply with a comprehensive flight test checklist. The checklist covered virtually every system on the aircraft and it took quite some time to accomplish. Single purpose maintenance flights were much quicker as they were performed to check only a single system which had been "squawked" (written up) by the pilot on a previous flight.

In this particular case the earlier pilot had noted that the pitch-up warning system did not seem to be calibrated properly. He had not gotten the pitch-up warning horn when the needle had momentarily entered the yellow band on the gauge as he entered a hard turn during his flight. It shook him up a little because he felt like he had almost pitched the Voodoo up and there had been no warning. That was a very valid reason to be shaken up.

Maintenance worked the problem and announced the plane ready for a test hop. The bird wasn't a Voodoo lite but at least the external fuel tanks did not have any fuel in them. I filed a flight plan with Memphis Center and requested to enter the Shirley (MOA) with a block altitude assignment of between flight level 200 and 400 (twenty to forty thousand feet).

I planned to be at forty thousand feet to begin the test because I wanted plenty of altitude below me. According to the RF-101 flight manual, if Voodoos pitched up, they required about fifteen thousand feet of altitude to recover; *if* they recovered.

Memphis Center cleared me directly into the MOA and I lit the afterburners for the climb to forty thousand. I did not want to waste time while climbing up to the test altitude and I also wanted to burn a little extra fuel. That way the plane would be lighter during the test than it would have been had I used a normal climb without afterburners.

At forty thousand feet I leveled off toward the western end of the MOA and turned back toward the east. The flight test profile called for me to roll into a high G turn and then pull back on the control stick until the Voodoo's angle of attack moved into the yellow band (where the pitch-up warning horn should sound) and then harder; into the red band (where the stick pusher was supposed to automatically actuate). As stated previously, it was designed to direct seventy pounds of hydraulic force to move the control stick forward, thereby lowering the angle of attack of the aircraft to below the danger zone.

I added power and accelerated toward four hundred knots. I made sure that my seat belt was tight and locked my shoulder harness. At 400 knots I visually cleared the area to the north and flipped the Voodoo onto its left wing tip and pulled. As the plane's path curved toward the north I focused on the angle of attack indicator. It was moving upward toward the yellow band where the warning tone should start to sound in my helmet earphones. I added more back pressure and the airspeed began to decrease rapidly. I added full military power and pulled harder; the nose came around faster.

I was grunting with the G load and the indicator was approaching the yellow band. I could feel my adrenalin pumping hard as I listened for the warning tone; just a little more back pressure.

I still had not reached the indicator's yellow band when the nose of the Voodoo pitched straight up and then the jet snap-rolled over onto its back. I pulled the throttles to idle power. My helmet was bouncing off both sides of the canopy. Although my shoulder harness was locked, my head was jerking back and forth. The ride was so violent that I couldn't focus my eyes on the instruments.

Suddenly I saw a heavy white trail of jet fuel streaming by. It was flowing from behind me, up and over the canopy, and then off into space in front of the Voodoo's nose. The big jet was going backwards through the air. The fuel must have been coming from the large fuel vent located just below the rudder.

Without warning the Voodoo flipped again and ended with its nose pointed nearly straight down at Greer's Ferry Lake below. I found the altimeter and it was rapidly spinning downward through about thirty-three thousand feet. I had already tumbled more than a mile. I quickly checked the engines to see if they had kept running during the wild gyrations. Fortunately they had.

My left hand was on the drag chute handle which was part of the pitch-up recovery procedure; but now with the nose pointed straight down the airspeed started building. I let go of the drag chute handle and added power. When I reached three hundred and fifty knots, I began to raise the nose of the jet. I wanted to stay in the altitude block that Memphis Center had cleared me for, if I could. I pulled back a little harder and leveled off at twenty thousand.

I flew straight back to the air base and parked the jet. As I climbed out I gave maintenance the message; *"It ain't fixed yet."*

Then, I went to my locker; and changed my underwear

Jerry W. Cook

THEY WON'T LAST ANOTHER MONTH

Little Rock AFB, AR; 1971

It was about noon. I was sitting around a table with several squadron pilots. We were eating lunch that we had either brought from home or the flight line snack bar over in base operations. We were all laughing and telling bad jokes between bites.

We had almost finished our lunch when a well-dressed gentlemen who appeared to be in his fifties walked through the door. Everyone at the table seemed to know him except me. They all stood up to say hello and shake his hand. One of the other pilots introduced him to me and said that he had been a fighter pilot in the Air Force and the Air National Guard. He had retired from the Air Guard Bureau at the Pentagon as a Brigadier General. His name was Fred Hook.

As it turned out, General Hook was on a "mission". His stepson, Fred Smith, was in the process of forming an air cargo company called "Federal Express". He had bought into an aircraft refurbishing and sales company at Little Rock Airport and was in the process of modifying several Falcon 20 aircraft to install cargo doors. His idea was to haul small packages at night to a central point and then sort and route them to several large cities where he would provide his service. His plan was to deliver the packages by the next day after they were shipped.

General Hook had come to our Air Guard unit to recruit pilots. Federal Express already had several Falcon 20 planes but they needed to hire pilots to fly them. The General had presumed that if the Air Guard pilots could fly Voodoos, then we should have no trouble flying a Falcon.

The famous and comical baseball player, manager and philosopher Yogi Berra is credited with many humorous sayings. One of them is, "When you come to a fork in the road, take it." Looking back on that day, I was definitely at a fork in my road. I took it, but it was definitely the wrong fork; if one is talking about choosing which airline to fly for.

Unfortunately, not too long before General Hook's visit, a Little Rock newspaper had published a critical article about Fred Smith and his quest to start his package delivery airline. It was definitely not a news story that instilled a lot of confidence in a successful future for Federal Express.

Although we were told that any takers among the pilots sitting around the table that day would be in the very first class of Federal Express Captains, none of us decided to quit our day jobs. Not one of us wanted to fly for a fly-by-night (literally) start-up package carrier that might not last another month. The newspaper article had certainly influenced my decision.

But I was slightly curious so I had asked General Hook a question; "If I were to go to work for Federal Express would I have to give up my seniority number with Pan Am?"

His answer was, "Yes. You would have to sign a document stating that you would not accept a recall and that you would give up your airline seniority number."

Did they really think that I was stupid enough to give up my seniority number and recall rights with Pan Am, "The World's Most Experienced Airline", to fly for a little unknown outfit with a questionable business plan called Federal Express? (I can still remember that Pan Am seniority number; #03527.)

Surely they didn't think that anyone would give up such a valuable property as a Pan Am seniority number to fly a Falcon 20 at night hauling packages around. *Yeah...right.*

I figured that Fred Smith's new venture would probably fold before the first pilot class even finished ground school. Then where would I be?

Postscript: Sure enough, my valuable and prized Pan Am seniority number got me recalled from furlough in 1973. I resigned from my GS-13 Civil Service position. I would be reporting to Miami, Florida for training in the Boeing 727.

It was my thirty-sixth birthday, October 17th, and I had just begun the Pan Am ground school at Miami International Airport learning the major systems of the 727 when the news came....

OPEC had just met that very day and decided to immediately embargo all oil shipments to the United States.

The rest of the good news came shortly thereafter on that same day. I and my fellow recalled pilots were to be furloughed; again.

Pan Am had just got me for a second time on my birthday. Happy Birthday...no job again.

If I had wanted to be an airline pilot, I guess I should have listened to Yogi. Better yet; I should have listened to General Hook.

But thank God I did not resign from the Air National Guard altogether to return to Pan Am; just the full-time part. Joining the Arkansas Air National Guard was one of the best decisions that I ever made in my aviation career.

Joining Pan Am was, without any question, the worst.

Jerry W. Cook

ATP WRITTEN...*CRAP!*

Little Rock Adams Field, AR; 1971

It had been almost three years since I had taken the dreaded Airline Transport Pilot written exam. When I graduated from Air Force pilot training I had passed the written tests and received my civilian Commercial and Instrument Pilot Certificate. That license allows a pilot to fly for hire (and be hired by an airline), but the Airline Transport Pilot (ATP) rating is required before one can become a Captain on an airline.

Of course, that was the plan when I hired on at Pan Am; to become a Captain on the airline. The expectation then had been that I and my fellow new hires would be senior enough to be a Captain in five years and would need the ATP certificate at that point.

Therefore when Pan Am had offered an Airline Transport Pilot preparation course for that very extensive written exam, I had jumped at the chance to get that career hurdle out of the way. Shortly after finishing the course, I had taken and passed the exam. The next step to securing the certificate was a flight check which had to be accomplished within three years from the date of the written. If the flight check was not accomplished within that time frame, the written was invalid and had to be taken again.

"ATP written...Crap!" was the first thought that hit me when I woke up one morning.

"The three years are almost up," was my second.

"What am I going to do?" was my third.

One thing was for certain that I did not want to do; I did not want to take that test again. I didn't know why I had awakened that particular morning with the ATP written test on my mind but I was thankful that I had.

One of the most foolish things among the many that I have done in my life was to buy a fifty percent interest in a V-Tailed Bonanza. It was a pretty little green and white plane and for some unfathomable reason I thought that it was a good idea to buy it.

Looking back to that time, I have no earthly idea why I thought that. However, it did give me a potential way out of my ATP written quandary. The Federal Aviation Agency did not specify or care what kind of aircraft that you used for your ATP flight check. All that was necessary was that all required equipment be installed on the plane to accomplish the mandatory procedures on the flight check. I wanted to use a Bonanza for two reasons. I had been flying ours and was fairly proficient and it was relatively cheap to fly. The one rub was that our plane did not have an ILS glide slope receiver installed and of course that was one of the requirements for the ATP flight check.

Toward The Evening Sky

Central Flying Service at the Little Rock Airport held the answer. They had several Bonanzas for rent. I went to the airport and arranged to rent a plane for my ATP flight check. But first I flew a quick checkout flight with a Central instructor, to confirm that all of the equipment was working properly and to get familiar with the different brand of radios that were installed in the rental plane.

Next, I called and scheduled my flight check with an examiner at the local FAA field office. Then I began to sweat the check ride. (If you ever meet a pilot who says he enjoys receiving flight checks from the FAA you might want to avoid them. There's something wrong with them.) No matter how good you are, or think you are, the FAA is not there to help you to meet the requirements for a flight check. And no matter if you think that you know all of the answers to their questions, you do not. They will find something to critique. It is their job.

The day of my ATP flight check finally arrived. It was hot and it was very windy. *Perfect...!* A V-Tail Bonanza tends to hunt (i.e. yaw) even in relatively smooth air. This was going to be interesting to say the least. First I accomplished the air-work; steep turns, slow flight, approach to stalls, basic airmanship stuff, and then we proceeded into the instruments portion.

Following his instructions I tracked down the airway toward Hot Springs and he then cleared me to hold at the intersection of two airways. I configured the dual VOR navigational receivers to properly indicate the airways and entered holding upon arriving at the intersection. Of course, shortly after entering the holding pattern, the examiner informed me that one of my navigational receivers had "failed" as he reached up and turned it off. Of course it had.

Between trying to dampen out the yawing of the little plane in the unstable air, the constant tuning and re-tuning of the remaining "operative" navigation radio and alternately dialing in the two different courses required to stay in the holding pattern, I was a very busy person. The flight examiner just sat there, watched my actions, and silently wrote on his notepad.

Finally, he gave me a new clearance to proceed down the original airway toward the Arkadelphia airport for an NDB (radio beacon) approach. Fortunately I immediately spotted his little trick and refused the clearance. I then asked for a higher altitude along the airway. He had initially cleared me for an altitude that was below the minimum height for that sector of the airway. He grinned, wrote something on his notepad, and then re-cleared me at my requested altitude. I exited the holding pattern and intercepted the airway.

The NDB approach went pretty well in spite of the strong wind out of the north. Following the approach and full stop landing at Arkadelphia, he issued me a clearance back to Little Rock. The little plane was not air conditioned and we were both sweating profusely at our cruise altitude of five thousand feet as we proceeded back toward Little Rock. We arrived back in the Little Rock Approach Control area and the flight examiner told me to request a full stop ILS approach to Runway 04 and that would be the last item that I would have to accomplish for my check ride.

We descended to two thousand feet and the wind became stronger and gustier as we progressed nearer to the ground. The little Bonanza constantly bounced and fishtailed around the radar pattern as the approach controller vectored us for the final approach course. I was working my butt off to keep the plane's heading and altitude within ATP check limits. Thank goodness we were almost to the end of this trial.

We yawed and bumped down the final approach to the runway in the gusting thirty to forty degree left crosswind. The airspeed needle was bouncing up and down and the heading was constantly trying to change. My hands and feet were in continuous motion and sweat was running down my face. As we reached the flare point, I took out the crab angle and put the left wing low enough to keep the plane from drifting across the runway. We were down and I managed to keep it on the center line. As we turned off the runway, I thought, "What a work-out."

I parked the Bonanza next to the old airline terminal building where the FAA office was located at that time and shut it down. The examiner said, "See you inside," and got out of the Bonanza. I locked the controls and when I got out made sure extra chocks were in place against the main landing gear tires. Because the little plane was still rocking and yawing in the strong wind, I wasn't sure that just the chocks at the nose wheel would be enough.

I did not have a clue what the check pilot thought about the flight, but I didn't think that I had exceeded any required parameters. However, I was completely worn out from the strain of keeping the little light plane where I needed it to be for the last two hours.

He was sitting behind his desk writing when I walked in. He told me to sit down. As I did I mentally crossed my fingers. Finally he looked up and began his critique of the flight. As he continued I began thinking, "So far, so good; he has covered almost all of the flight and nothing negative yet."

"Now, let's talk a little about that ILS," he said.

"It seemed to me that you were working awfully hard as we came down the final approach. You were using a lot of control movements, don't you think?" he finished.

"Yes sir, there were a lot of control inputs but may I ask you a question?" I said.

"Certainly," he replied.

"Sir, is it true that for an ATP type rating that both the glideslope and the course needles have to be kept within the small circle on the ILS instrument to score satisfactorily on the approach?" I asked.

"That is correct," he said.

"Did I keep them in the circle?" I said.

"Yes, you did," he answered.

But then he continued, "I have a good friend who is a Delta DC-9 Captain and he says that if you trim your aircraft properly before you pass the final approach fix (where the glide path begins) you should scarcely have to move your controls again before flaring for landing."

I was having trouble keeping my cool by this point. I mulled over his statement while he looked expectantly at me for my reaction. Finally I said, "Did I pass the check flight?"

"Oh yes, you passed," he said and held out my ATP certificate toward me.

I stood up and took the paper, looked at it and then I said; "Sir, I have a message for your Delta Captain friend. You tell him that Jerry Cook said, 'Bull____!' and if he has any questions to give me a call."

I walked out of the General Aviation District Office with a new appreciation for the naiveté of some of the FAA's pilot examiners.

The Delta Captain never called. That's too bad. I wanted him to demonstrate an ILS for me in a V-tail Bonanza on a windy, gusty day.

Postscript: During my aforementioned Bonanza check out with the Central Flying Service instructor pilot, we were about 15 miles southeast of the Little Rock airport around five thousand feet. The young instructor pilot asked me if I had ever rolled my Bonanza. I told him that I had not.

He said, "They roll real nice. Let me show you," and took the control wheel. Wearing a big grin he pulled the nose up five or ten degrees and did an aileron roll.

As I took the control wheel back I thought, "I'll have a little fun of my own," so I said, "I wonder how Little Rock Approach Control liked your roll?"

He gave me a startled look and said, "What do you mean?"

I replied, "I mean since Bonanzas are not certified for aerobatics and "approach" is the FAA; I wonder what they thought when they saw our radar return do a roll on their scope."

"Oh well, maybe they didn't see it," I finished.

"They can see us do a roll on their radar scope?" he looked worried as he said it.

"I don't know why not," was all I said. Now he really looked worried.

The young instructor pilot might not have been sure about the return on the radar scope, but he was a lot smarter than I was when Fed Ex asked him if he wanted to come to work for them. In the ensuing years he became a senior MD-11 Captain for Federal Express.

(Don't worry Terry C. I won't tell anyone it was you.)

Jerry W. Cook

SO EASY AN 8 YEAR OLD CAN DO IT

Little Rock to Laredo to Little Rock; 1971

I didn't realize just how carefully he watched me when I was flying or listened to me after he would ask me a question about flying the Bonanza. During the relatively few flights we had taken together in the little green and white plane, I wouldn't have thought that he had picked up that much; especially at eight years old but....

Jeff, my eight year old son, was sitting up front in the right seat and appeared to watch every move I made. We were making a weekend trip to Laredo, Texas. I had filed IFR (instrument flight rules) along Victor Airways. Jeff wanted to keep the low altitude airways map in his lap. From time to time he would ask me a question about it and where we were in relation to the airway and the VOR stations along them. He also asked me a lot of questions about the flight controls and he even noticed when I was using the trim wheel and asked me what it was. I explained the purpose of the trim to him and demonstrated how it helped make the airplane easier to fly.

I talked to him about using very small control movements to make heading and altitude corrections. After still another question about the airways I showed him how I was tracking the airway and then how I turned over a VOR station to intercept an airway outbound. I talked to him a little bit about the indications of VOR station passage. He would sit there looking at me with those intent blue eyes and shaking his head "Yes," when I would ask him if he understood. Because he was only eight, I was surprised that he was so interested and also at the relevance of his questions.

On Sunday morning we took off from Laredo and headed toward San Antonio about one hundred and twenty-five air miles to the northeast. It was the first VOR station on the airways that I had filed back to Little Rock. During the climb it was a little bumpy with small cumulous clouds scattered around. As I had hoped the air smoothed out above five thousand feet and we leveled at nine thousand feet. Jeff was riding in the front with me again. We had done a lot of walking around Nuevo Laredo the day before and he was pretty tired. He dozed off before we reached San Antonio.

It was over two hours later with Shreveport behind us and approaching Texarkana when Jeff unexpectedly said, "Where are we?"

I hadn't realized that he was awake. I had laid the airways map up on the glare shield so I could refer to it when setting my outbound and inbound VOR radials for the airways. I took it down and pointed to our position a few miles south of Texarkana. He nodded and then looked out of the window at the ground.

Suddenly he looked back up at me and said, "Can I fly?"

I looked down into his serious blue eyes and then I asked him, "Do you remember what I told you Friday about using the controls and the trim?"

He replied, "Do you mean use little movements and always trim off any pressure that you feel?"

"That's it," I said. I looked down at his solemn upturned face. "Okay, you can give it a try," I said.

I rotated the single control wheel up out of the way and then turned and lifted Jeff onto my lap. With the control wheel back down in front of him I said, "Very gently now, put both hands on the wheel." Jeff raised his hands and placed them on the controls. Now I began to talk to him again about controlling the plane with small movements. He flew along for a while making small movements when the altitude or heading would start to change and was doing a pretty good job with the plane in trim. I told him that I was going to move the trim wheel a little bit which would make the Bonanza feel out of balance.

Jeff said, "Okay," and I moved the trim slightly forward to make the nose feel heavier. He pulled back on the wheel and stopped the descent. Then he took his right hand from the control wheel and rolled the trim back to relieve the pressure. He raised the nose slightly and climbed back up the fifty feet or so of altitude that he had lost. Then he re-trimmed the little ship again. It took him a bit of rolling the wheel back and forth until he had the trim near-neutral. I asked him if the plane was in trim. He said, "I think so."

I told him to let go of the control wheel and although he seemed a little hesitant he finally let it go. The nose started to rise slightly. I had him put his hands back on the wheel, level off, and trim it again. This time the nose hardly moved up or down at all when he let go. I was impressed. Here he was doing about as well at eight as I did on my first flight in Aviation Cadets at nineteen.

By now we were approaching the Texarkana VOR and the course needle was starting to oscillate back and forth slightly. At first he wanted to chase after it but then I reminded him about the indications of VOR station passage and what to do about it. He held the nose of the plane fairly close to its original heading as we passed over the top of the VOR. Finally the "To/From" indicator changed to a steady "From" and the course needle stabilized to the right side of the VOR course deviation indicator.

Jeff said, "Dad, I think we've passed the VOR station."

I said, "Okay, what should we do now?"

He picked up the map off the right seat and found Texarkana. Then he located the airway toward Little Rock. The nose of the Bonanza wandered somewhat while he searched the map but not much.

He said, "We gotta go over and get on that airway."

I said, "Remember what I told you Friday about how to do that?"

"I think so," he replied.

"Okay, go ahead and try it," I replied. Jeff quickly picked up the map again and checked the airway's course and set it in the VOR course window. Then he turned the little plane to the right until he was on the same heading as the course. While he was turning, the Bonanza's nose dropped slightly. He stopped it and quickly reached up and trimmed a little more nose up. He stayed pretty close to our assigned altitude of nine thousand feet as he turned. As Jeff rolled out of the turn, the nose started to rise again. He ran the trim wheel forward and the plane porpoised slightly as he did so.

"Dad how long should I wait to go over to the airway?" he asked.

"The VOR needle is pretty steady so I'd go ahead now," I replied.

Jeff turned the Bonanza to the right and intercepted the airway just like I'd described to him two days before. He overshot the outbound course slightly but then corrected back. I was impressed. I would not have thought that an eight year old kid would even concentrate on something that long, much less retain it and be able to apply it so well.

During our descent, as the speed built up, the nose wanted to rise and the plane required some "nose-down" trim. After he finally got it trimmed, Jeff flew the first part of the descent. As he did so I talked to him about why the nose wanted to rise when the speed got higher and why the nose wanted to go down when he slowed down or banked the plane to turn. He seemed to get it and shook his head "Yes," when I asked if he understood.

It was time for me to takeover to fly into the Little Rock area and Jeff climbed back over into his seat.

As he buckled his seat belt, I said, "Son, always remember, one of the most important lessons about flying is this; 'If you can trim it, you can fly it.'"

Jeff is now a Boeing 737 Captain for Southwest Airlines.

I'll wager that he keeps it in trim.

Toward The Evening Sky

EJECT! DID YOU SAY EJECT?

Little Rock AFB, AR; Early 1970s

He was a Captain who had just recently transferred into our flying squadron. He was relatively new to the Voodoo and had just a few hours logged in it. It is a requirement for all military pilots to fly a certain number of hours at night every year. This was one of his nights.

I on the other hand was the lucky winner that evening and was going to be manning the little blue Chevy pickup truck that we called Demon Mobile. As mentioned in a previous story, the purpose for requiring a Voodoo pilot to staff the mobile truck was to assist the airbase control tower operators in any unusual situations involving our squadron's airplanes.

It had been a warm but very nice day and was turning into a perfect night for flying. The mosquitos evidently thought so too because, since the sun had gone down an hour ago, they were taking off in large numbers and forming up in attack formations. As usual the little air conditioner in the truck wasn't cooling very well so I had rolled the truck windows down to catch whatever breezes that I could. I seemed to be catching more mosquitos than breezes and I was in the process of deciding whether to "sweat or swat" when the call came in on our squadron frequency.

"Demon Mobile this is Demon 21," came the call from the obviously concerned pilot.

"Go ahead 21, Demon Mobile," I replied.

"Mobile, I was entering the ILS pattern and when I lowered my landing gear handle the left main showed unsafe. I want you to relay to me the radial and distance from the airbase Tacan that depicts the point for me to eject."

Now that got my attention. I forgot about the mosquitoes.

"Did you say *eject?*" I replied, hoping I had heard it wrong.

"Roger, I don't want to land this thing with an unsafe main gear," he said.

Well I couldn't blame him for that because our normal touchdown speed in the Voodoo was over two hundred miles per hour. But wait just a damn minute..."Eject?"

"Demon 21, did you recycle the landing gear?" I inquired.

"Yes I did, and it still shows unsafe," he said.

"Where are you now?" I asked.

"I'm about fifteen miles north of the base at ten thousand feet," he replied.

"Exactly what are your indications on the landing gear?" I said.

"Right main and nose gear have a green light and left main gear has no green light," he answered.

"Are your flaps down?" I asked.

"Yes, they are down," Demon 21 replied.

"And you received no gear warning horn when they came down?" I asked him.

"No warning horn," he said.

"If you pull your throttles to idle, do you get a warning horn?" I asked. He tried pulling the throttles back and then called, "No warning horn."

"Do you have a red landing gear warning light?" I said.

"No red light," 21 replied.   "Have you tested the gear warning system?" I asked.

"Yes, and the left main gear light does not come on," he said.

"Okay, have you pressed to test the left gear light itself?" I asked.

"Just a minute," he said. Then he answered, "The light does not come on when I press it."

"Demon 21, except for the left main green light, all other indications are that your landing gear are all down and locked. The left one is probably just a burned out light bulb," I relayed to Demon 21's obviously skeptical pilot.

"Are you sure?" he said.

"Let's put it this way Demon 21. If it were me, I would bring it in right now and land it with absolutely no fear of the landing gear folding," I said.

I continued, "Or you could fumble around in the dark with a flashlight and try to install another bulb and the light might come on; but it could also be a bad socket."

"Look 21; you have no red light and no warning horn with the flaps down or the throttles pulled back and the warning system checks okay, except for the light bulb. All of that indicates your landing gear is down and locked. However, if you wish, you can bring it over Demon Mobile at a couple of hundred feet and I'll be able to see your landing gear in the lights from the parking ramp," I said.

"If I see the left main down, will you come back and land the plane then?" I continued.

"Okay," he replied, but he still didn't sound all that convinced.

I coordinated the low pass over my mobile control truck with the control tower and then had Demon 21 change his radio to the tower frequency. A few minutes later I saw his landing lights approaching from the northeast and stepped outside with my mosquito friends to look over the Voodoo's landing gear with the binoculars. As he passed above mobile I could see in the bright yellow lights from the huge aircraft parking ramp that all three of the Voodoo's landing gear looked down and locked.

"They all look down and locked Demon 21. Bring it around and land it," I said cheerfully.

After a long pause; "Okay," he replied. He sounded a little better than he had before, but I don't think I had completely convinced him. After he landed, I had him stop straight ahead on the runway while our maintenance folks installed the landing gear down locks before he taxied to the Air Guard ramp.

"Another day, another dollar," and lots of mosquito bites…but *no ejections*.

"Eject! Did you say *Eject?!"*

Jerry W. Cook

CLOSE FORMATION

Over El Paso Texas; Early 1970s

We were trading our RF-101Gs for slightly newer RF-101C models. The Gs we had been flying for several years were basically a modified fighter version; essentially they were A models that had been converted for the reconnaissance mission. As I stated before, the Air Force was getting out of the RF-101 business and all of their RF-101Cs were being transferred into the Air Guard. Our RF-101G's were all destined to head west to the Aircraft Boneyard located near Tucson at Davis-Monthan AFB. We were flying them to their final destination in Arizona as we received our replacement Cs.

I was leading the four-ship of Voodoos headed westward on their last flight. Major Hall was flying on my left wing in the number two position, with formation aircraft numbers three and four flying off my right wing. We were spread out into route formation which is flown when on longer flights, weather permitting. In this formation the wingmen move out several plane widths to the side, but in the same relative position to the lead aircraft. The extra distance between the aircraft makes the wingmen's job much easier and more relaxed than when flying in the normal closer formation position.

I had filed a southern route to Tucson which would take us across the heart of Texas, over El Paso, along the border of New Mexico with Old Mexico ; then on into Tucson and Davis-Monthan Air Force Base.

I and the other pilots felt sad about this being the last flight for these four RF-101s. Although the first ones had been delivered in 1956 to the Air Force as A models, 29 of them had been converted to RF101Gs in 1966. They were still very capable of doing the reconnaissance mission, although they had been in service for quite some time. Admittedly, so had the RF-101Cs we were receiving. The first ones had been delivered to the Air Force in 1958. However the C models were built specifically for reconnaissance and had several improvements over the Gs in mission capability. Meanwhile, the Air Force was in the process of receiving RF-4C Phantoms to replace them.

I had my Voodoo trimmed up nicely and was enjoying the view of the Franklin Mountains at The Pass in the far distance. Although the Voodoo wasn't a particularly stable aircraft and the control stick had to be continually moved to keep the plane's attitude where you wished, the stick pressures were normally light.

Unexpectedly, I had to hold some left stick pressure to keep the left wing down and to keep the plane going straight. I put in some left aileron trim as I wondered why I suddenly had to re-trim. Just as quickly the left wing dropped and I corrected back to level. I looked toward my left wing and saw the cause of the mis-trim. The pilot in the Voodoo flying on my left had moved in very close to my wingtip and the air rushing over the top of his canopy was what had pushed my wing upwards. Then, after I had lowered the wing back to level, he knew that I was either holding against the pressure or had re-trimmed the ailerons. Then he had quickly dropped downward a few feet to remove the air pressure so as to cause the wing to drop. As I looked at him he moved back into his previous wing-lifting position and once again I was out of trim.

He appeared to be having a good time messing with my plane's trim and also seemed to be enjoying the fact that I had to work harder to keep the plane on its intended heading. I flashed him the universal visual signal with my left hand and then I quit looking at him. I thought maybe it would discourage his clowning around.

Nope. My left wing would start to raise and then start to lower as he moved up and down. I guess that he was bored; but suddenly the boredom ended. I felt a jolt and a shudder go through my plane. I quickly looked in my left wingman's direction. All I saw was the bottom of his Voodoo as he sharply pulled away from me. I knew that he had run into my left wing, but my plane seemed to be flying normally. He quickly returned to his route formation position; perhaps even a little further away than normal. His plane seemed to be flying okay, however he didn't come anywhere near me again until just before we landed in Tucson.

After we parked the Voodoos on the ramp at the Aircraft Boneyard, I got out and walked around to the left wing. Sure enough, the wingtip light had been completely knocked off and the bottom part of the wingtip itself was dented and the paint was scraped. I saw Major Hall who had been my left wingman standing on the right side of his plane and looking up at the canopy. I walked over to see where he was looking. There was a long deep scratch in the Plexiglas. It started just aft of the metal frame that formed the leading edge of the canopy where it joined the windscreen structure when closed. The metal frame was dented and scraped. Now that was *close* formation.

Practically speaking though, if he was ever going to run his plane into mine; he picked the perfect flight. Neither one of us had to report the damage or even write it up in the maintenance log books. The Boneyard wasn't that particular. They were to eventually end up destroying the aircraft for parts and scrap metal anyway.

What a shame. But even supersonic jets get old.

Jerry W. Cook

QUICK…TURN OFF ALL THE LIGHTS

Little Rock AFB, AR; Early 1970s

I was leading the second element of RF-101s. The first element had rolled just fifteen seconds ago. I moved my head forward from the seat headrest. That motion was a signal to my wingman to release his brakes and rapidly increase his engines' thrust from eighty-five to one hundred percent. My next head forward movement meant, "Light the afterburners". Seconds later at one hundred and eighty five knots, we rotated and lifted off the runway. The time was official sunset and we were headed for a rendezvous at twenty-five thousand feet with a KC-135 air refueling tanker. It was once again time to practice a night air refueling, a recurring requirement every six months.

After our landing gear and flaps had retracted, I looked up and to my right to locate the first two planes. We were to fly with them in fingertip formation until we joined with the tanker. I spotted them at our two o'clock high position and banked sharply to cut inside of their wide turn to the north. We caught up with Demon 51 and 52 in short order and slid into fingertip formation for the relatively short trip to the air refueling track, which began almost due north of Little Rock in southern Missouri. The track from that point proceeded east-northeast into southern Illinois.

Our flight leader leveled off the flight at twenty-five thousand feet and called for a level-off and fuel check. After Demon 54 had checked in with "Check complete" and his remaining fuel total, the leader left our Memphis Center radio frequency to make initial contact with our tanker. In a minute or so he was back with the news that the tanker was on station and orbiting near the northeast end of the track.

We were about 10 miles from the refueling track entry point when our flight lead requested permission from Memphis Center to change to the air refueling frequency. The Memphis Controller gave the clearance with instructions to change to our air refueling radio frequency and to begin MARSA (Military Accepts Responsibility for Separation of Aircraft). It was getting darker as our flight leader changed our flight over to the refueling radio frequency and we checked in: "Demon 51; 2; 3; 4."

Although it was now becoming dark on the ground, there was still some remaining light at our altitude. However, depth perception was waning and shapes were becoming harder to distinguish. Demon 52 and I as Demon 53 were employing the wingtip lights and the formation lights on Demon 51's forward fuselage to maintain our correct position on the lead Voodoo. Demon 54 conversely was using my aircraft lights to fly his correct formation position on my wing.

We had already checked in on the radio with our tanker and he began heading down track toward us for the rendezvous. He was one thousand feet above us at twenty-six thousand. At the prescribed twenty-six mile separation point between us, the KC-135 began a left 180 degree turn. The turn was designed to place the tanker about a mile or so in front of our flight.

Suddenly our flight leader called, "Demon 51 has the tanker in sight". The KC-135 should have been about half way through his turn by that time. I was impressed that the flight leader had already spotted our tanker especially under the existing light conditions. The tanker "Rogered" lead's call and continued his turn toward the refueling heading.

Quite unexpectedly, I felt that we were descending. I took a quick glance at my altimeter and confirmed that my feeling was indeed correct. Any descent could take us out of our assigned refueling block altitudes. I called, "Demon 51, check your altitude." He did not respond and the descent continued. It was now accompanied by a very slight right turn. I was about to punch the mic button to call again when the pilot of Demon 52 said, "Demon 51, where are you going?" The perturbed sounding flight leader answered, "I'm going for the tanker. He's at our 12 o'clock." I widened my distance slightly from 51's left wingtip and took a quick look.

I spotted what appeared to be an airliner on our nose and moving to our right. About that time, it looked like they turned on every light on their airplane. I assumed they probably saw our four jet fighters headed toward them and thought perhaps we hadn't seen them. We were still several miles away from the airliner. He was moving toward the south and seemed to be in a descent; possibly going into Memphis. We were still turning toward him when suddenly most of the lights on the now recognizable DC-9 went out. About that same time, our tanker called and stated that they did not have us in sight and asked where we were.

"That is not our tanker, Demon 51. It is an airliner and we are now below our refueling block." I recognized the voice as Demon 52.

He sounded incredulous which was exactly what I was feeling. Without saying a word, Demon 51 suddenly added power and started a left climbing turn back toward the refueling track and our KC-135. Finally, we caught the tanker about ten minutes later. We eventually got our air refuelings accomplished and returned to Little Rock AFB without any further excursions.

I cannot explain why our flight leader that evening deviated from our assigned altitude block and from the air refueling track. Even though he obviously thought that he had spotted the tanker, he should never have departed our assigned altitude block. The only plausible explanation is that he had his head "up and locked".... And provided you don't already know what that means, if you give it some thought you can probably guess.

After we landed, I and the Demon 52 and 54 pilots jokingly discussed whether the airliner crew had initially turned on all of their lights so we could see and avoid them. Then when they saw us continue to head toward them they turned off their lights to evade us.

If so, it actually worked because we lost sight of them at that point. We all figured that they were glad to get to Memphis.

We never did get to discuss the flight with Demon 51. He went straight to his office and completely skipped the flight de-briefing. We did not wonder why.

Toward The Evening Sky

WHAT THE...!

Little Rock AFB, AR; Early 1970s

We had some unique characters flying Voodoos in our Air Guard unit, and more likely than not, these characters were also airline pilots. (I think it might have been because they didn't have to work at a *real* job.) But for whatever reason, the combination of Airline/Air Guard fighter pilot seemed to produce some comedians.

Bill H. was a great pilot and also a good friend. (He was Demon 52 in the preceding story.) He was also one of the funniest and most clever people I have known. In addition to being a Voodoo pilot with our Air Guard unit, he also flew with Braniff International Airways. He had not been with the airline long enough to advance to the right seat and was still flying as a flight engineer on Boeing 727s. His experience as a pilot being utilized as a flight engineer evidently was similar to mine with Pan Am; i.e. he didn't enjoy it very much and found it to be very boring.

It was a dark winter night across the northern tier of the United States and now it was raining at the airport where they had landed a few minutes prior. Fortunately, the local temperature was above freezing which certainly made things easier. Bill had been flying with the same crew all month and the co-pilot was a relaxed, easy-going guy; but the Captain was a different story. He was a very uptight sort with no apparent sense of humor.

Bill and the other pilot had tried to joke with him a few times during the month but to no avail. He didn't seem to think anything was funny. Either that or he just didn't *get* it. Additionally, and Bill and the co-pilot made fun of this behind his back, the Captain would don a pair of expensive leather Ferrari driving gloves whenever he was to accomplish the takeoff or landing. The gloves were the kind made of soft supple leather with the holes and stitching placed at strategic points. According to Bill, the guy would make a ritual of donning them; as if he was about to drive a high performance race car. Every time he did it, Bill and the co-pilot would get tickled and almost burst a blood vessel trying to keep from laughing. They had nicknamed him "The Little Dandy".

It was the Captain's time to make the takeoff. Just before pushback from the gate, he began his elaborate glove-donning procedure. Bill could see the co-pilot trying to maintain his composure while looking out of his side window. To hide his own amusement, Bill turned his face toward the rear of the cockpit.

Aft of the engineer's station, he saw the fire axe in its holder mounted on the rear wall and right beside it, glowing in the eerie red cockpit lights that were utilized in those days, hung the huge gray asbestos firefighting gloves. He turned his eyes away as he fought the urge but his mind kept coming back to the big gray gloves.

The pushback was complete and the Captain called for the checklist as they taxied through the rain toward the runway. With the "Taxi" and "Before Takeoff" checklists complete, Bill turned and looked at the giant gray gloves again. He couldn't help himself…it was his nature. He grabbed one of them and pulled it onto his left hand as the Boeing 727 turned onto the runway. Bill looked down at the glove. It looked huge and it seemed to emit an ominous looking red glow in the dimmed cockpit lights. The tower cleared them for takeoff.

Captain "Little Dandy" pushed up the power on the three jet engines and called, "Set takeoff power." (At Braniff that was the Flight Engineer's job.) Bill raised the big glove high in the space between the pilots and then slapped it down on top of the throttles.

The Captain spotted the huge reddish/gray "hand" in his peripheral vision and yelled; *"What the…!"* as he instinctively leaned to his left to get away.

Captain "Little Dandy" did not think that it was funny. He declared that it startled him so badly that he almost aborted the takeoff. Bill said that the guy never got the significance of the glove but that the co-pilot thought it was hilarious.

I believe that, after they returned from the trip, Bill got an invitation to go to Braniff's headquarters in Dallas and have a little talk with Braniff's Chief Pilot.

He said it was a good thing that he wasn't still on probation.

Toward The Evening Sky

WE *ALMOST* MADE IT

Little Rock AFB, AR; February 1973

We almost made it. We almost made it through several years of training new and inexperienced pilots in one of the "diciest" aircraft and demanding missions in military aviation without a student getting killed…*almost*.

I remember that he was from one of our sister RF-101 units in another state and that he was a student pilot in our RTU. He was not my student. However, the word among the instructors was that he was a very talented young pilot. He was not having any difficulties at all in the training program.

A lot of the advanced missions that the students flew were solo without an instructor chasing them in another RF-101. They were assigned to fly low-level missions which included several targets along the route to photograph. The flights were pre-briefed with an instructor. Later, the returned photos were the proof of whether the sortie was successful or not. The student and instructor would debrief by utilizing the prepared low-level map and the photographs as criteria for grading the training sortie.

Usually the low-level route would be several hundred miles away from Little Rock AFB. That required what we called a High-Low-High flight profile. The pilot would file an IFR flight plan to cover the high altitude portions of the mission. Then if the local weather permitted when he returned to the Little Rock AFB area, he would usually accomplish a visual approach and landing.

However, if the weather required or the pilot wanted to practice, he would perform what is referred to as a Jet Penetration. That is a descent from about twenty thousand feet while utilizing his cockpit flight instruments and adhering to a published instrument approach procedure. The procedure was designed along a prescribed route to descend to an altitude below the clouds for a visual landing. However if the cloud base was too low, the pilot would then proceed to his landing utilizing the instrument landing system or a ground controlled approach (GCA) which utilized ground based radar guidance with a controller directing the pilot's headings and altitudes.

That day, the weather was too low for a visual traffic pattern and landing. The young pilot was flying the published jet penetration procedure and had been in the clouds most of the way down from his initial altitude. He probably felt pretty relaxed during the descent because the bases of the clouds were reported as several thousand feet above the ground. He should "break out" of the cloud bases in plenty of time to see the runway and complete the last portion of his approach in essentially visual conditions.

His eyes were likely scanning his instruments in the prescribed manner and paying particular attention to his altimeter and vertical velocity indicator for the prescribed level-off. According to his altimeter, there were still several thousand feet to descend before the level off altitude would be reached.

Suddenly and unexpectedly, the Voodoo came roaring out of the bottom of the clouds. The nose was still lowered to maintain the four thousand feet per minute rate of descent and three hundred and fifty knots of airspeed. I am sure that the young pilot reacted as swiftly as humanly possible; but the odds were stacked against him. There wasn't enough distance remaining between the plane and the ground. The big Voodoo couldn't make the pull out.

Yes, he was a good pilot, but that day it didn't matter. Even a good pilot has to have accurate information. In this case he needed correct data from his flight instruments, particularly the altimeter. However, he didn't get it. His altimeter had lied to him. It had indicated that his aircraft was much higher than it actually was. Somehow, somewhere, water had gotten into the Voodoo's altitude indicating system. It had most likely frozen at altitude during the high portion of his return. The resulting restriction in the pressure sensing line had caused the inaccurate altimeter indications.

The accident report revealed that when it impacted the ground, the RF-101's altimeter indicated that there were still several thousand feet remaining before the level off altitude.

Yes, we almost made it without a student pilot dying.

But we didn't.

Toward The Evening Sky

RAPIDLY APPROACHING EVENTS

Little Rock AFB, AR; 1973

As briefly described in the previous story, the jet penetration used by jet fighters (and in some locations multi-engine jets) to descend from altitude to a point on an instrument approach for a landing normally begins with the aircraft at about twenty thousand feet. It follows a prescribed track across the ground which is designed to avoid obstacles such as mountains or towers, etc. or in other cases conflicting airspace. It may prescribe a relatively straight course or when restrictions require, a teardrop shape. The teardrop penetration is also dictated when there is no way to measure distance from the final approach fix.

In the jet fighters that I flew, the indicated airspeed was usually three hundred or three hundred and fifty knots. The resulting rate of descent was between four and five thousand feet per minute. The time of descent was normally between four to five minutes.

It was a night refueling mission and the four RF-101s in my flight were recovering in two flights of two aircraft each. The sky condition at Little Rock AFB was overcast, requiring us to accomplish a jet penetration followed by a GCA or ILS. The pilot in the Voodoo on which I was flying wing (my element leader) was one of the "best sticks" (outstanding piloting skills) with whom I'd ever flown. He was an aggressive pilot but a very smooth flight leader and it was easy to fly on his wing.

We had departed twenty thousand feet and were in dense clouds. I was concentrating on his right wingtip light and the light green formation lights located on his forward fuselage. The formation lights had recently been added to all of our planes and made maintaining the proper wingman position easier than before. As we descended rapidly through the clouds, the air was becoming rougher. Consequently, our Voodoos were bouncing and rolling quite a lot which required my full attention.

Suddenly I developed an uneasy feeling. We had been descending for several minutes and I sensed that a level-off at the final approach fix altitude should be coming at any moment. I couldn't resist the feeling, so I stole a quick glance at my altimeter.

I immediately punched the microphone button and shouted, *"Altitude!"*

My flight leader instantly pulled back on his control stick and although I attempted to stay up on his wing, my Voodoo dropped below the normal position. I realized that I was holding my breath as I pulled back up into the proper position. (Maybe I thought if I held my breath it wouldn't hurt as much if I hit the ground.) I glanced quickly at my altimeter again. We had "bottomed out" about five hundred feet below the charted level-off altitude.

My element leader climbed back to the minimum altitude for the FAF (final approach fix), about fifteen hundred feet above the ground. We configured for the approach (landing gear and flaps down) at the FAF and descended down the ILS glideslope. We broke out of the clouds about five hundred feet above the ground and I landed on the element leader's wing.

During the walk from the jets to the flight operations building, my flight leader stopped and turned to me; "Jerry; you probably kept us out of the trees tonight. I don't know what in the Hell I was thinking."

(Hugh Harrison Hurt, Jr. stated in his book "Aerodynamics for Naval Aviators"; August 1959: "The majority of aircraft accidents are due to some type of error of the pilot. This fact has been true in the past and, unfortunately, most probably will be true in the future.")

I have never flown with a better pilot than my flight leader that night. Unlike the student pilot who crashed on the same approach a few months before, my flight lead's instruments were all giving him correct indications. Obviously that was not the cause of our near collision with the ground. I believe that he unintentionally but correctly stated the reason for our near accident when he had said; "I don't know what in the Hell I was thinking."

Perhaps in aviation more than in any other endeavor; *"One's immediate thoughts must be determined by rapidly approaching events."*

Or as I used to tell my pilot students; "Stay ahead of the aircraft. The faster the plane, the further ahead of it your brain must be."

Toward The Evening Sky

DEMON 91, CAN YOU TIGHTEN UP YOUR PATTERN?

Little Rock AFB, AR; May 17, 1974

To fulfill our military flight requirements, full time Air National Guard instructor pilots occasionally would have to fly additional flights outside of our normal work hours. Many of the flight hours that we accrued flying with our students did not count toward our own minimum flight requisites. Consequently, sometimes we would takeoff on a flight after our work day ended and usually return early the next morning before our regular work hours began.

We would typically fly a high altitude navigational leg and then descend so as to join a low level route which had been pre-selected by our Intelligence Section. While on the low level route we located and took photos of assigned targets. Afterwards we would climb back up to a higher altitude and proceed to some other Air Force Base located in a nearby state. After arriving there, we would usually practice an instrument approach before landing. The next morning we would reverse the process, ending back at Little Rock AFB.

None of the pilots seemed to mind this necessity of the job. In fact most of us enjoyed the loner aspects of these cross country flights and they more approximated the real missions that we would have to fly if we were in actual combat. It was a reality that in combat, reconnaissance pilots usually flew alone and not in formations with other aircraft. In fact, the motto for Reconnaissance pilots was "Alone, Unarmed, and Unafraid." *Yeah…Sure…!*

Lieutenant Colonel Bobby Hall had flown his training flight the evening before and had landed at McConnell AFB at Wichita, Kansas to spend the night. It was the next morning and he was on his cross-country leg back to Little Rock. Having finished his scheduled requirements, he was approaching Little Rock Air Force Base from the west and descending at three hundred and fifty knots. It was a beautiful spring morning. The Little Rock Approach Controller handed him off to the air base control tower operator about fifteen miles to the west of the base.

The air base tower controller advised Demon 91 that the base air traffic was landing on runway 24 and to please call when turning a three mile initial. The Voodoo pilot turned briskly onto the initial leg three miles out from the northeast end of the runway at the prescribed fifteen hundred feet above the ground. He made the "three mile initial" call. The tower informed him that he was number one for landing.

Fighter pilots enjoy the next part of the visual overhead landing pattern. Flipping a jet fighter from that era (high wing loading and no flight control computers) into a near ninety degree banked fighter "break" and then hauling the big jet around the one hundred and eighty degree turn to the downwind required some critical energy management skills. That was because of the rapidly slowing airspeed, varying bank angle, and in the Voodoo keeping the angle of attack of the big fighter just below the pitch-up warning horn. It was always exciting; being right on the outer edge of the 101's flight envelope. You couldn't help but grin (and sweat) under your oxygen mask from the challenge the heavy fighter threw at you every time you did this. It was like riding a semi-wild stallion that you knew always wanted to throw you.

Lieutenant Colonel Hall was just seconds away from racking the Voodoo up on its right wing and pulling; almost home.

"Demon 91; can you tighten up your pattern? We have a T-37 on a ten mile straight-in final approach. If not, you'll have to break out of the traffic pattern and re-enter," was the call from the control tower operator.

I don't know what the pilot answered or what went through his mind. What I do know is that sometime during the fighter break the Voodoo suddenly pitched-up out of control and began a violent roll. The pilot did the right thing and the only thing that he could do to try to survive. He pulled the ejection seat handles. The ejection seat fired and left the jet with the pilot attached just as designed; however he had pulled the handles just a fraction too late. The jet was nearly inverted and less than fifteen hundred feet above the ground.

One of my thoughts when I heard the sad and tragic news was; "It wasn't all that long ago that Bobby and I had stood together at the Aircraft Boneyard, looking up at the dents and scratches in his canopy and laughing at our good fortune."

Postscript: Lynn Scott (who had given me the ride to Little Rock Air Force Base back in 1969) was not only a nice guy; he was a very good pilot. After I was hired into the unit in 1970 I was privileged to fly in formations with him for the next four years. I'm not sure what Scott had flown in the military but I would guess it had been jet fighters.

In any case, there was an Air Reserve unit at Tinker AFB, Oklahoma which had recently been equipped with F-105 "Thunderchiefs". One drill weekend, Lynn gave us the news that he was transferring to that unit. He was going to be flying the F-105s out of Tinker.

Since he lived in the Dallas area and could cockpit-pass on an airline to Oklahoma City, it was likely an easier commute for him than to Little Rock. And besides, he wanted to aim the Gatling gun in Thunderchiefs instead of the cameras in Voodoos.

It was July 17, 1974 when someone came in with the news; Lynn Scott had just died in an F-105D crash.

It was just two months to the day since we'd lost Bobby Hall.

Toward The Evening Sky

RRRR...EAR JET

Little Rock Adams Field, AR; Mid 1970s

I wasn't so lucky the second time that Pan Am furloughed me. My GS-13 Voodoo instructor job had been snapped up as soon as I had resigned from it. Thank goodness I had not given up my part-time pilot's position. I was actively flying the Voodoos as often as I could, but that did not provide enough money to support the family.

The mortgage, food, insurance and all of the other miscellaneous expenses involved in providing for a family of five meant that I was searching desperately for a way to pay the bills. One of my attempts was at real estate sales; but shortly after obtaining my license, I realized that as a real estate salesman, I was a good pilot. After several months and selling just one house with no prospects for more, I decided to try to get a job flying charters at Central Flying Service. I had been told that they had added a Learjet and were going to put it in their Charter fleet.

I met and talked with Mr. Claude Holbert, the owner and founder of Central. Since most of my flight experience was in jets, Mr. Holbert suggested that I obtain a Learjet type rating and then I could fly theirs as a Captain. At the time, they did not have any other pilots with very much jet experience, so it sounded like it would be mutually beneficial. Besides that, the little Lear looked like it would be fun to fly. Pilots who had flown it said that it flew like a small jet fighter. (Reportedly it was adapted from a Swiss single seat strike fighter design that was never produced.) That information set the hook for me and I signed up under my G.I. bill for the Learjet Type Rating course. The Learjet type rating course was run by Central Flying Service at their facility.

I finished the ground school for the Learjet and began the short aircraft flight checkout. The checkout instructor was none other than Mr. Claude Holbert, the owner of Central. Along with another fledgling Lear pilot, I was scheduled for my first training flight early one morning. The plan after takeoff was to perform some basic airwork to the east of the Little Rock airport and then proceed to Memphis International Airport for an approach and landing.

As stated, Mr. Holbert was the instructor pilot in the right seat and the other pilot was to fly the first half of the training mission in the Captain's seat. He was also ex-military with some jet experience and he had no problem flying the plane. He completed the airwork and then headed for Memphis. Memphis Approach Control cleared us to enter their airspace, assigned us a new IFF "squawk" (identification code) and then vectored us for an ILS and landing. The student Lear pilot had no problems with any of these elements even though it was his first time in the aircraft; so far, so good.

I was sitting on the side-facing seat opposite the entry door of the plane. From there, by leaning forward and looking to my right, I could observe the activities in the cockpit. As we proceeded down the taxiway toward the parking area I noticed that the nose of the plane was rapidly moving from side to side and the movements were rocking me back and forth in my seat. I heard Mr. Holbert quietly talking to the other pilot about the ultra-sensitivity of the Lear 24's nose wheel steering system. The soon to be new Learjet pilot nodded his head in agreement but there was no noticeable reduction in the jet's excursions. I continued to be rocked back and forth in my side facing seat. The departures of the aircraft's nose from straight ahead were quite noticeable and it seemed that the harder the pilot tried to lessen them, the more pronounced they got. I was wondering to myself if I would have as much difficulty in steering the plane. The other pilot was getting more and more frustrated as we proceeded northbound up the taxiway toward the Memphis Aero fixed base operations.

We turned onto the aircraft parking ramp. It was early and there was only one other plane parked there. It was a little Piper Cherokee 140. I looked over the pilot's shoulder through our windscreen and saw an FBO line service employee hurry out and pick up some chocks and a red carpet. He ran around the front of the other plane to direct us into the parking space next to the Cherokee. He dropped the chocks and carpet and began to try to give hand signals to our pilot indicating for him to straighten up the Learjet as it approached alongside the other plane.

The Learjet's nose was still twitching from side to side several degrees and now it was joined by some rather erratic brake applications. I was being rocked fore and aft and back and forth at the same time. The poor confused line service guy was moving his hands all over the place trying to keep up with the nose of the Learjet, but he was always about a half second behind. Mr. Holbert was rocking in his seat as he calmly continued to give the by now stressed-out pilot some more taxiing advice.

Our fledgling Learjet pilot and the line service guy looked equally bewildered. Finally we stopped. The Learjet was to some degree in the parking space, but pointed about twenty degrees in the direction of the Cherokee. I was trying hard not to chuckle but I was having difficulty suppressing it. Besides that, I had not tried to taxi the Lear yet and therefore assumed that I might not do any better on my first try. Finally the engines were shut down and the trainee pilot and Mr. Holbert were finishing the shutdown checklist. Through the left cockpit windscreen I saw the line service guy moving toward the chocks and red carpet.

I asked if the other two pilots were ready for me to open the aircraft entry door which was a somewhat tricky procedure in itself. The door consisted of upper and lower halves which were locked together by steel hooks. The hooks were powered by an electric motor with a switch located nearby.

The pilot in the left seat said, "No, let me do it. I need the practice." He got out of the cockpit and I moved my knees out of his way as he actuated the door latch hooks. Finally he got the correct sequence and when it was unhooked he raised the upper half of the door. The gentleman who had unsuccessfully attempted to guide the pilot in parking straight was standing there with a huge smile on his face. He was of Oriental ancestry.

Our fledgling Lear pilot gave him a cheery, "Good morning."

The mirthful gentleman beamed an even bigger smile and said, "*Ahhhhhh…. Good morning sirrrr…. First time Rrrr…ear-jet??*"

From behind him I could see the pilot's ears turn a bright red.

I tried hard to not laugh…without much success.

Jerry W. Cook

THE "GOV"

Little Rock Adams Field, AR; Mid 1970s

As I stated in a book a few years ago, I probably learned the most valuable lessons about flying from instructing students. Running a close second was flying military, pilot service and charters in at least thirteen different kinds of aircraft ranging from three versions of the F/RF-101 Voodoo down to a Beechcraft Musketeer; all during the same time period. (What was I thinking? Evidently not much except that I needed to pay the bills.)

There was no way on God's green earth for anyone to keep up-to-date with all of those different types of planes. Different is an understatement. For instance, the Voodoo's touchdown speed during landings was faster than the maximum cruising speeds of most of the other planes that I was flying.

Then, throw in several different brands and types of radios and navigation equipment in some planes, even of the same type, and you're really having some fun. Let's see; there was the F-101B, F-101F, RF101C, Lear 24, King Air, Queen Air, Duke, Baron 55, Baron 58, Bonanza, Debonair, Cessna 182, and the mighty Musketeer. (Yep, and it was all legal.)

Occasionally during those stressful days of flying charters and trying to pay the bills, a trip would not turn out exactly as planned. He happened to be the Governor of Arkansas and his office had chartered one of Central's Barons to go to Nashville. We lifted off at the scheduled time and had been airborne for about forty minutes. He was sitting beside me in the front seat. I guess I must have looked trustworthy because there were no security personnel riding with us that particular day.

We were just crossing the Mississippi River south of Memphis when he looked up from the papers he had been reading.

"Is that the Mississippi River?" he inquired.

"Yes sir it is," I assured him.

"We don't cross the Mississippi on the way to Nashville," he stated rather emphatically.

"Oh yes sir, we do," I answered while thinking, "Everybody ought to know that."

"Arkansas?" he said.

"Arkansas what?" I inquired.

He replied, "Nashville, Arkansas. That's where we're supposed to be going." (I don't think I even knew at the time that there was a Nashville, Arkansas.)

After I rolled out from the one hundred and eighty degree turn I had just made over the Mississippi River, I reached down and pulled out my clip board. Sure enough, the trip sheet indicated that our destination was KBNA; the identifier for Nashville, Tennessee.

It's tough to look cool when your passenger, who also happens to be the Governor of your state, is sitting beside you while you pretend to know where Nashville, Arkansas is. (This was 1974. We did not have GPS.) Finally, I found it on the map about thirty miles north-northeast of Texarkana. I did a scientific "WAG" (wild-ass-guess) on the heading and flew the Baron as fast as it would go to that Nashville. It wasn't fast enough. We were really late.

Jerry W. Cook

EXACTLY HOW LONG WILL IT TAKE?

Little Rock Adams Field, AR; Mid 1970s

The charter customer fit the definite "type A" personality. He was probably in his late thirties, he was rude, and he was obviously *very* important. He hardly acknowledged me when he arrived at the Beechcraft Baron that he had chartered for the flight from Little Rock to the Tallahassee Regional Airport in northern, Florida.

In fact all he said to me was, "I do not want to be late."

He sat down in the back of the Beechcraft Baron 58 in the forward facing seat and immediately focused his attention on the papers that he removed from his expensive leather-covered briefcase.

The one time that he looked up from them during the flight he asked, "How much longer?" As I gave him my answer, he checked his big gold Rolex and returned his attention to the papers.

When he exited the plane in Tallahassee, he said that he would be back to the airport on time and that he did not want to be late leaving Tallahassee for Little Rock that afternoon. After I wrote my name on it, I handed him a business card from the FBO and told him to call me if there were any changes. He looked at me like it was an insult to suggest such a thing, but he took the card and stuck it in an inside pocket of his dark blue several thousand dollar suit.

Since our scheduled departure time was quite a few hours away, the FBO provided a van ride to lunch for me and a couple of other transit pilots who also were not scheduled to depart until later that afternoon.

When we arrived back at the FBO after lunch, I checked for messages and I had none. Then I checked the weather for the flight back to Little Rock although it was still about two hours before departure. I walked out of the flight planning room and over to where a couple of other pilots were standing by the coffee pot. Just about then my passenger walked in. He saw us and made straight for me.

Before I could say anything he said in a loud voice, "I need you to fly me to Sarasota. I want to know exactly how long it will take and I don't want any bullshit about how it depends on the winds or the weather or air traffic control."

The two surprised pilots looked at him and then quickly back at me probably wondering how I would react to his outburst. I mentally calculated that Sarasota was about 250 miles from Tallahassee. I also knew that the whole state of Florida had been clear from my weather check of a few minutes ago. I quickly did the math in my head and added forty-five minutes to the probable flight time.

I then smiled at my rude passenger and said; "It'll take exactly two hours and fifteen minutes; *even if I have to circle or slow down to make it happen.*"

One of the other pilots laughed out loud and the other one snickered. My passenger's face turned red as he realized what I had done with his demand.

Finally he said, "Okay. How long do you *think* it will take us to get there?"

"*About* one hour and thirty to thirty-five minutes," I answered.

"Fine," he replied.

"How soon do you *think* we can take off?" he said.

"In *about* fifteen minutes," I responded.

He glared at me just a little before he finally said, "All right. Let's go."

I flew him to Sarasota. It took *about* one hour and thirty minutes.

Jerry W. Cook

SECOND GUESSING

Little Rock Adams Field, AR; Early 1970s

I was at Central Flying Service to fly a charter but my trip had just canceled. I was pretty bummed because money was in short supply and I had just lost that day's income.

I was talking and drinking coffee with a couple of transit pilots from Mississippi that I knew when I got paged. It was Central's charter scheduler. She said that a customer was on his way to Central from the airline terminal. His commuter airline flight to Fayetteville, Arkansas had just been canceled and he had to get there as soon as possible. She was planning to use the same Baron that I had previously pre-flighted and fueled for my canceled trip.

I was elated. Although it was a lower paying trip, it still meant some compensation for that day. I went to the flight planning room to check the weather enroute to Fayetteville and northwest Arkansas. There had been a line of storms forming earlier toward the northwest, but because I had previously been going to head eastbound on the canceled trip, I hadn't been that concerned.

However, now I had to be concerned. Unfortunately, everything that I saw indicated that the line of thunderstorms had intensified and lengthened. They were stretching all the way from Dallas into Illinois with tops in the 40 thousands. Disappointed because once again I wasn't going to make any money, I headed to the charter office to give her the bad news. The potential charter customer had just walked in and was talking rapidly to the scheduler.

I introduced myself and said, "I'm sorry sir but we can't go. The weather is too severe."

"What do you mean it's too severe? I have to go. I'm a lawyer and I have to be in Fayetteville, in court, at 10:30," he insisted.

"I'm sorry but there's a solid line of thunderstorms stretching all the way from Texas into Illinois between here and Fayetteville. In my opinion it's too dangerous to go," I said.

"*I guess you don't understand. I have to go!*" he stated firmly.

"Sir; the weather is too bad. I can't take you," I replied.

Now he was angry. "Do you mean *can't* or *won't?* Maybe I need to get myself another pilot who *will* take me," he stated emphatically and looked expectantly at the charter scheduler.

The scheduler finally spoke up, "Sir I'm sorry, but if the weather is that bad, then we can't take you."

After a few choice expletives, the young lawyer picked up his briefcase and stormed out of the building.

I looked at the charter scheduler and said, "I think I can guess why his Scheduled Skyways flight got canceled. They probably couldn't get their incoming plane down here from Fayetteville."

At about that same time I saw three well-dressed gentlemen enter the front door and walk past us and through the door to the aircraft ramp where a local company's twin Cessna sat waiting. The pilot greeted them. He had a spirited discussion with one of the men. Finally they all boarded the plane.

After I watched them taxi toward the runway for takeoff, I walked over to the flight operations desk. I asked the operations clerk if she knew where the twin Cessna was headed.

"Sure," she said; "Fayetteville."

Now began my second guessing of my decision. I walked back into the flight planning room and looked at the weather again. It had not gotten any better. In fact, it looked worse than it did before. I got another cup of coffee and sat down.

"Maybe it isn't as bad as I imagine. Maybe I should have gone," I kept thinking.

It was about forty-five minutes later when I heard a plane taxing toward the ramp. I walked over to the window and looked out. It was the twin Cessna that had headed for Fayetteville. The entry door opened and the three passengers started stumbling off the plane. Their faces were ashen and one of them was dabbing at the front of his suit pants with a handkerchief. The pilot just sat there in the cockpit not seeming to move.

When the three men got inside they all headed for the restroom. They did not look well. Finally the pilot got off the plane and began to slowly walk around it. He appeared to be looking it over very carefully.

The passengers came out of the men's room and headed for the front door leading to the parking lot. It was painfully obvious when they passed me that at least one of them had vomited all over himself. After the passengers had driven away, the pilot came in from the aircraft ramp. He got himself a cup of coffee and came over to the area where I was sitting.

"Everything okay?" I asked.

"I think so," he said.

He then added, "At least the wings are still attached to the fuselage. There for a while I wasn't so sure they were going to be."

He continued, "I tried to tell him that we shouldn't try it. He wouldn't listen and told me that they had to go."

Right then and there I decided to quit second-guessing myself whenever passengers tried to pressure me to go.

Postscript: One of the most insidious things involved when flying some passengers in corporate and charter aviation is the pressure that they sometimes apply to their pilot(s). When these passengers are driven by their desire or need to get somewhere, they have no qualms about letting the pilot(s) know that.

The pressure to try to get them to their destination becomes greater if the pilot is working directly for the passengers or perhaps competing for the relatively few dollars that are to be made in flying charters for a customer. At times some aircraft owners even threaten to fire their pilot(s) and hire someone who will take them; whenever and wherever they want to go. If the pilot doesn't want to lose the job and succumbs to the pressure to attempt the trip against his or her better judgment, then the stage is set for a potential disaster. Under such pressure the stressed pilot may rationalize that perhaps the weather isn't as bad as they first believed or that they can find a way through, around or over it.

Interestingly enough, it seems that the same passengers who are applying the "go" pressure are also the ones who expect to be flown to their destination unruffled and in complete safety. Then, when they get bounced around in the rough air while the pilot is trying to circumnavigate thunderstorms or during the winter when they end up diverting to another airport because of icing or runway closures, they complain bitterly and blame the pilot(s).

A passenger (or a company) applying pressure on a pilot to go when he is trying to make rational "go-no-go" decisions based on all of the aspects of the flight, is one of the absolute dumbest things that anyone can ever do.

Trust me on this passengers; *"You are not bulletproof."* Just keep pressuring your pilots to go and someday you may arrive at the scene of the accident just a fraction of a second after they do.

Toward The Evening Sky

WE'LL PAY CASH

Little Rock Adams Field, AR; Mid 1970s

I had not had the opportunity to fly the Learjet very much. There just weren't that many people around the Little Rock area who were chartering the little jet because of its cost. And those who did use it did not pay in cash.

It was early evening when my home phone rang. It was the lady who was working at the flight operations desk that evening at Central Flying Service. She said that she had just received a call from a man who wanted to charter our fastest plane for a flight to Laredo, Texas. She then asked me how soon I could get to the airport.

I walked into the flight operations area about forty-five minutes later. The Learjet had already been pulled out. It was parked near the exit doors to the ramp. There was a fuel truck standing by, but before I went out to talk to the line service crew about the fuel load, I needed to confirm how many passengers were going with us. When I checked with the operations clerk, she said that there were supposed to be three. She then said that when she had asked the guy for a credit card number for payment that he told her he would be paying with cash. Then, when she told him to hold for a minute so she could give him the amount, he had told her, "It doesn't matter."

Red flags suddenly went off in my head. I said, "Does this whole deal sound a little strange to you?"

She replied, "I'm glad you said that because that's what I was thinking."

I could just picture myself and my co-pilot about an hour and a half after takeoff with a gun to our heads being told that we were not going to be landing in Laredo after all.

I said, "Do you know anyone in the police or sheriff's department that you could ask what they think about this whole situation?"

"I sure do," she said; "I'll call him."

Her friend in the Sheriff's department was *very* interested and said he would "get right back to her". He called back in about five minutes and said that he was sending someone to the airport. In about twenty minutes an unmarked police car arrived and two plain clothes detectives walked in. They asked me if I was the pilot and I replied, "Yes, one of them."

My co-pilot had arrived a few minutes before them and was outside preflighting the Lear. They asked me to go get him. When we came back inside they briefed us on the situation.

They said a very high profile criminal had just made bail earlier that evening and that he was to be released shortly. They suspected that the person who requested the charter was one of two men that they thought would be picking him up at the jail. They briefed us that they would pretend to be the Lear pilots if the guys showed up. We were to stay back out of sight.

We assured them, "That will not be a problem."

Another car with two men in it pulled into the parking lot across the street. It was the detectives' backup. One of those two gentlemen replaced the lady behind the operations desk. He said that if they asked, he would tell the passengers that she had finished her shift and had already gone home. She told the detective how much she had calculated the cost of the trip to be and then we got out of there. However, we only went to a room in another part of the flight operations building. From there through a window we could see the Learjet waiting on the ramp. The two detectives who had arrived first were now standing in front of the left wing by the jet's entry door in their new role as pilots. We could not see the third detective.

It was about another half an hour when we observed three men walking quickly out of the flight operations area of the building. They hurried up to the entry door of the Learjet and began to talk to their "pilots". They did not have any luggage.

It happened very fast. The next thing that the three guys knew, they were bent over the leading edge of the wing and were being placed in handcuffs.

I sometimes wonder where my co-pilot and I would have ended up that night without that phone call to the good guys; possibly in a ditch somewhere in Mexico.

Obviously, that was one Learjet trip that I didn't mind not flying.

Toward The Evening Sky

I *AIN'T* GOIN' IN THERE EITHER

Saint Louis International Airport, MO; Mid 1970s

It was summertime and it was hot. Cumulus clouds were scattered everywhere you looked. Most of them had bases around five thousand feet and I estimated that the tops were somewhere in the "teens". In an unpressurized aircraft, that was well above us. It was also very bumpy. In a Baron it was usually about an hour and a half flight to Saint Louis from Little Rock but today, it would probably take at least one plus forty-five. That was because I had to slow the plane down to one hundred and seventy-five knots because of the rough air. Fortunately my charter passenger was a very seasoned flyer and he just rolled with the punches and tried to get some paperwork done.

The weather forecast had called for scattered thunderstorms in the Saint Louis area but, so far, there had only been haze and the smaller cumulus clouds. We crossed into Missouri and the buildups began to disappear while the visibility increased. I had the Baron's radar operating but it wasn't the best one that I'd ever seen, so I was glad that the visibility was improving. The air began to smooth somewhat; so I pushed the throttles forward on the two 285 horsepower Continentals to regain the normal Baron cruising speed. I hoped it might shorten the flight time by a few minutes.

Fifty miles south of Saint Louis, I began to see some cloud tops that appeared as if they might be at least forty or fifty thousand feet high. As we continued northward, I tried to pick up the thunderstorms on the Baron's radar. I wanted to see where the storms were situated in relation to the Saint Louis airport.

As the Kansas City ARTCC switched us over to Saint Louis Approach Control, I was finally able to determine that there was a huge thunderstorm to the east of the airport. It appeared to be located over the Mississippi River near where the Missouri empties into it. The ATIS (Automatic Terminal Information Service) indicated that there were presently no thunderstorms at the airport but did report the one that I could see. The ATIS stated that they were utilizing the ILS to Runway 30R.

Saint Louis Approach Control acknowledged my radio check-in and assigned me the RW30R ILS. They then told me to keep my speed up as long as possible because I was number one for the runway and there was an American Airlines 727 to follow me. Consequently I kept the gear and flaps up and the Baron's speed at 180.

As I intercepted the ILS localizer, I heard the American 727 check-in; "Saint Louis, American 123 with information 'Hotel'." The controller assigned him the RW30R ILS and advised him that he was number two behind a Beech Baron and to "Hold 170 knots until the outer marker." They told him I was at my maximum forward speed.

He acknowledged the instructions in a deep Texas drawl; "Roger, ILS 30R, 170 knots to the marker, American 123."

I looked off to my right at the huge thunderstorm. It was located almost due north of us now and it looked extremely wicked. It was one of those monsters that have a deep green tint to the heavy rain shaft and lightning was spiking to the ground every few seconds. I was glad that it had formed where it was instead of at the airport or on the final approach course.

Suddenly Saint Louis Approach called, "Baron 52W, there is a TWA 727 turning a six mile final in front of you for 30R and your spacing is too close." (Now who had just assigned me maximum forward speed?)

Approach then continued, "Baron 52W, turn right immediately to a heading of 360 and climb to 3000 feet."

I looked over at the huge green wall north of me over the river with its virtually constant spikes of lightning and replied, "Negative on the 360 degree heading for Baron 52W. That's right into a thunderstorm. I'm climbing to 3000."

"Baron 52W, I said I want you on a heading of 360…*now*," was the controller's immediate and determined response.

I firmly replied, "Baron 52W is *not* going to head 360 or even anywhere close to it. You can give me a heading back toward the east if you wish, but *I will not head north."*

"Baron 52W, turn immediately to a heading of 090 and climb to 4000," the controller ordered.

Before I could acknowledge his instructions he continued; "American 123, we are in the process of switching the runways to 12. Turn now to a heading of 360 and climb to 3000 feet."

The American pilot with the deep Texas drawl answered; *"I ain't goin' in there either!"*

Toward The Evening Sky

WE HAVE A "CHRISTMAS TREE" AND A "MOLE HOLE"; *WE'RE SCREWED*

Little Rock AFB, AR; Mid 1970s

The 189th Group and 154th Squadron had been in the reconnaissance business for many years and before that it had been a fighter outfit. And now, most satisfyingly, it looked like we were going to get to continue flying in the high performance fighter category for quite some time to come. We had been informed by higher headquarters that we were slated to receive RF-4C Phantoms to replace our RF-101C Voodoos. I don't recall if the planes were to be brand new or if they were coming from other reconnaissance units in the Air Force; but in any case there had been a message received which included eighteen tail numbers identifying the exact aircraft that we were to receive. Those numbers seemed to verify that the information about the new planes was correct. We were elated that we were going to be getting the newer Phantoms to replace our still capable but aging Voodoos. Our elation was not to last long.

Elsewhere, it was being reported that the Air Force was making plans to get rid of some of their KC-135 aerial tankers before they could receive a new replacement tanker. There had been several aircraft being evaluated as that replacement including the Douglas DC-10. It was eventually chosen and was designated the KC-10 Extender. I hadn't paid much attention to anything having to do with the Strategic Air Command since I had managed to avoid it back in 1959. I was busy thinking about our upcoming transition into the RF-4C and not concerned about SAC's problems.

Suddenly, seemingly in the blink of an eye, our eighteen supersonic Mach 2 RF-4 Phantoms morphed into eight big gray lumbering KC-135 Stratotankers. The needs of the Air Force apparently outweighed my need and that of the other Arkansas Air Guard Voodoo pilots to continue flying jet fighters. SAC was unloading eight of their programmed excess KC-135s onto our Air National Guard ramp. *Crap!*

When we received the disturbing news of our substitute replacement aircraft, I felt that same sinking feeling that I had experienced when my F-86 fighter-gunnery school class learned in early 1959 that we would not be going on to fly F-100s in the Tactical air Command. In that particular instance, if your fighter-gunnery school class standing was high enough, you could choose either the Air Training Command or the Strategic Air Command. If your F-86 fighter-gunnery course standing was not high enough, you did not get a choice; you took what was left. Not one pilot who had a choice selected the Strategic Air Command. That included me.

Pilots who love to fly fighters usually do not choose to fly multi-engine aircraft. That is unless they are flying them in the livery of a major airline. Even then, they usually try to get into an Air National Guard unit or an Air Force, Navy or Marine Reserve element that flies fighters. Then they can fly multis for a living and fighters for the pleasure; i.e., "Having your cake and eating it too."

We eventually were informed that what sunk our fighter future was the former mission and resultant facilities of Little Rock AFB. It had been activated as a Strategic Air Command Base in 1955 and remained as such until 1970. At various times during its tenure at Little Rock, the Strategic Air Command operated RB-47s, B-47s, KC-97s, KC-135s and B-58s. To accommodate such aircraft and missions, the airbase had been constructed with a nearly 12,000 foot long runway. A large ramp connects directly with the northeast end of the runway. This ramp was built to park bomber and tanker aircraft that were "on alert" (takeoff as soon as possible) and a facility to house the alert aircrews was constructed adjacent to the alert ramp. SAC referred to the alert ramp as the "Christmas Tree" and the crew facility as the "Hidden Hilton" or "Mole Hole". These former SAC facilities were likely what landed the KC-135s on our Air Guard ramp.

I had just thought that I had escaped SAC for good when I got out of the Air Force. *Wrong!* Welcome to the Strategic Air Command.

Postscript: While fighter pilots wanted no part of flying bombers or tankers for SAC, it is true that, during its existence, the Strategic Air Command was arguably the best organized and most influential command in the Air Force. Probably because of its critical mission of deterrence, it exhibited the most sway with Washington in terms of money and support.

Lt. General Curtis Lemay became the Commander of the Strategic Air Command in 1948 and, during his tenure, became one of the most persuasive military leaders in our country during the Cold War. He necessarily operated under the premise that any future war would be a World War involving nuclear weapons. Under his leadership, SAC grew and modernized, becoming a solid deterrent to any military aspirations against the United States that the former Soviet Union may have had.

Also, for a few years, the Strategic Air Command actually possessed its own fighters. They were tasked as bomber escorts. Then in 1957, as its bomber aircraft and weapons were upgrading, SAC's fighter aircraft were transferred to the Tactical Air Command. Finally in 1992, SAC was dissolved as a Command and its bomber assets became a part of the newly formed Air Combat Command. The Tactical Air Command also became part of the Air Combat Command. SAC and TAC had been formed as separate Commands in 1946. Now once again, strategic bombers and jet fighters were flying in the same Command. Most of SAC's KC-135s were assigned to the newly formed Air Mobility Command, also in 1992.

Toward The Evening Sky

THE STRATEGIC AIR COMMAND WAY

Little Rock AFB, AR; 1975

Our "SACumcision" had begun. We were still in the 189th Group but that's where the similarity ended. In addition to our eight dull gray Boeing tankers, we had gained a small cadre of instructors from Castle AFB, California.

Castle was home to the primary KC-135 aircrew training organization in the Air Force. Consequently, they had been tasked to provide instructors to assist in the conversion of the 189th Tactical Reconnaissance Group into the 189th Air Refueling Group. They included pilot, navigator, and boom operator instructors among other specialties.

Unlike the Voodoo pilots, the personnel who were cross-training from other specialties into the boom operator slots and those joining the unit to fill some of the positions such as the navigators were pleased with the aircraft and mission change for the 189th. Instead of one person to crew a plane, it now took four: pilot, co-pilot, navigator and boom operator. And on some flights where the plane was to operate temporarily from another base the crew chief joined the rest of the normal crew, making it five.

None of the pilots who would be transitioning into the KC-135 from the RF-101 were happy. In fact many of us were actively looking for pilot positions in other units that possessed either fighters or reconnaissance fighters. Although such vacancies were rare, we did lose at least two pilots to other Air Guard units. The rest who were committed to remaining in Little Rock for various reasons, were attempting to adjust to our new mission.

He was one of the higher ranking officers of the instructor team that had come to Little Rock AFB from Castle. As far as I know, he had been a member of the Strategic Air Command since he graduated from pilot training. It was reported that he had over five thousand hours in the KC-135 and had been an instructor pilot in the aircraft for several years. It was my first flight in the big bird and he was scheduled as my instructor. We were to take off and climb to an altitude of fifteen thousand feet for some airwork and demonstrations. That would take about an hour. Afterwards we were to return to Little Rock AFB for multiple touch-and-go landings for me and for a younger pilot who would be checking out in the KC-135's right seat as a co-pilot.

I thought at the time that I was a big brave fighter pilot; but I confess that what we did in the tanker that day did not give me any warm and fuzzy feelings. In fact, the approach to stalls and the "how to get it out of a 'Dutch-roll' demonstration" scared the Hell out of me. Especially when I looked out of the left cockpit window at the number one engine and saw it shaking from side to side so violently that it looked like it would separate from the wing at just about any second.

Simultaneously, along with the engines seemingly attempting to tear themselves from their mounts, the wing tip was flapping rapidly up and down through a huge arc. I wondered if there would be a demonstration disclosing how to fly the plane without one of the wings. I had done much wilder maneuvers in a jet fighter; but they were built for it and I was sitting in an ejection seat at the time. There was no way that any of the nine crew members on board that day could have gotten out of that plane if something important had snapped. Oh well, nothing did. Boeing obviously builds very tough airplanes.

We had miraculously survived the airwork without losing a wing or an engine and had just entered the traffic pattern at Little Rock Air Force Base. I was being instructed on the SAC way to fly the pattern in a KC-135. It was summer, it was hot, and it was windy. To add even more challenge, the KC-135's parallel-type rudder yaw damper had to be turned off prior to landing. So of course, SAC chose to leave it off while flying anywhere in the traffic pattern; no matter how many miles or minutes that was going to comprise.

Additionally, we were dragging the landing gear and we were dragging the flaps through the sky as we wallowed along in the hot and windy summer afternoon. We were really rocking and rolling in the rough air at traffic pattern altitude. I had to use much higher engine power just to drag all of the stuff that we had hanging out during our twenty-five to thirty mile long traffic patterns. We were burning a lot of extra fuel and I might add making a lot of extra noise. I could not understand the reason for such a philosophy so I asked the instructor why we were leaving the landing gear and flaps down while we flew around the almost thirty mile traffic patterns. I was not given a response.

Another ten miles went by and I asked him again, "Why are we not raising the landing gear and flaps after takeoff until we get to the base leg?" (90 degrees to the runway and just before the final approach)

He said, "We'll talk about it later. Just leave them down."

We were on the downwind for my third touch-and-go landing. I was working hard as we pulled everything but the barn door through the air. (If the KC-135 had possessed a barn door I'm sure SAC would have wanted to pull it too.) And if I remember the numbers correctly, SAC wanted you to keep the airspeed within five knots, the heading within three degrees and the altitude within forty feet. I was sweating so much in the hot cockpit that it was dripping off the end of my nose. Even my socks were sodden and my gloves were soaked all the way through. My hands and feet were moving continuously. The control yoke, the throttles and the rudders were in constant motion as I tried to keep everything within the SAC limits. And because, according to the SAC rules, the yaw damper on the rudder had to be turned off all during the traffic pattern, the tanker's tail was swinging from side to side in the turbulence and the 130 foot wings were floundering around like a cork on the ocean.

In spite of all of this, I thought that under the circumstances, I was actually doing a reasonably good job of staying within the ridiculous SAC guidelines when the instructor pilot looked over at me and said; "You seem to be having to work awfully hard to fly the plane within the parameters."

I agreed with him wholeheartedly and so I answered, "I sure am."

Then he looked at me again as he made his next comment; "I would think that a pilot with your experience wouldn't be having so much trouble keeping within the desired limits." To add to my displeasure at his remark, there were several other crewmembers in the cockpit area who heard the sarcastic statement.

I looked over at him and said, *"Okay Colonel. You show me how to do it."*

Simultaneously with my statement, I took my hands off the control yoke and throttles and my feet off the rudder pedals. I folded my arms across my chest and just looked at him.

He looked somewhat stunned as the big plane increased its Dutch-rolling and said, "What the…," as he grabbed for the flight controls. I sat and watched him for several minutes as the KC-135 continued to wallow along through the rough afternoon air. The heading, altitude and airspeed were all over the place.

He had begun to sweat profusely and was very red-faced when I finally said to him, *"Well Hell Colonel. You can't do it any better than I can."*

Then I said, *"I've got it,"* and put my hands and feet back on the controls. He didn't say anything but let go of them.

Except for reading the checklist, I don't think that he said another word to me during the remainder of the flight. As a matter of fact, I don't remember that he ever scheduled himself to fly with me again. (Perhaps he did not like having to demonstrate how to fly the KC-135 within SAC's parameters on hot and gusty days.)

I finally got my answer from another instructor about why SAC dragged the landing gear and flaps around the traffic pattern after their first touch and go landing. (I assume that the explanation was accurate.) The answer that I received; sometime in the past, the pilots on a SAC aircraft forgot to put their landing gear back down after a touch and go landing and consequently landed the bird on its belly. The powers-that-be came up with a foolproof answer; "Leave the landing gear down after the first landing when staying in the traffic pattern."

"Wow; good thinking!"

As the Standardization-Evaluation Officer of our Group I talked to the Group Commander about my objections to these ridiculous and costly procedures. Although SAC was our gaining Command, our higher headquarters (boss) was the Air National Guard Bureau in Washington. They eventually saw it our way and it was approved to stop such nonsense after our training ended and we got rid of the SAC contingent.

Not long after the SAC instructors returned to Castle, we began raising the landing gear after every takeoff and raising the flaps to zero when our airspeed permitted. SAC continued to do it their way as far as I know.

I suppose that I can't argue with SAC's premise that their crews would not forget to lower the landing gear again after touch and go landings if they just left them down. But I wonder what procedure they would have established if, instead of a touch and go, it had been the crew's first landing when they forgot to lower the landing gear? Using the same logic, I suppose SAC would have never raised the landing gear!

By the way, I never did get an answer as to why they dragged their flaps around. Perhaps that crew forgot their flaps too.

Toward The Evening Sky

SEE? WE DIDN'T FALL OUT OF THE SKY

Little Rock AFB, AR; 1975

He was probably the youngest pilot instructor from Castle. A very likable young Captain, he and the other KC-135 instructors had been assigned a very difficult job. That job was transitioning hardheaded fighter types like me into the plane. It wasn't that we had much difficulty flying the KC-135; we just didn't like flying the KC-135.

Very much like the Pan Am 707 in which I had done landings in 1967, the KC-135 flew like a truck. However, when I had made the short checkout in the similar 707 about eight years before, it had been a little bit different. That plane also had been heavy and slightly unwieldy but it had a much improved full-time series type yaw damper. That limited the vertical stabilizer from swinging back and forth quite so much. That in turn reduced the Dutch-rolling tendencies of the thirty-five degree sweptback wings. And, because we could fly the pattern and land with it engaged, it made a big difference during traffic patterns and landings.

Also, at Pan Am after takeoff, we had raised the landing gear and flaps and left them up until we were preparing to land again. Similar to the KC-135, the 707's four engines were also built by Pratt and Whitney; however they were turbofan versions with a total of nearly thirty thousand pounds more thrust than the KC-135's four J-57's. And most importantly, that plane had Pan Am painted on the sides which at the time I had foolishly believed was a good thing. (Note: In 1974 I had again been recalled from furlough by Pan American. I was assigned to Miami flying on the Boeing 707.)

The young Captain knew the airplane very well and was a good pilot. However he was SAC all the way. He was trained in and bound by their philosophy and rules. Things had gone well during the navigation and air refueling portions of our training flight. We had proceeded to a refueling track near Tucumcari, New Mexico and rendezvoused with a B-52 Stratofortress from Barksdale AFB which is near Shreveport, Louisiana. As luck would have it, the "BUFF" (nickname for a B-52 meaning, big ugly fat fellow) had a "PUP" at the controls. (PUP means pilot upgrade trainee.) So we had newbies refueling a newbie. Perfect.

We had flown up and back down the refueling track while the inexperienced B-52 pilot practiced hooking up with our inexperienced boom operator. (I have to hand it to the B-52 pilots. That thing has to be a bear to control, especially while refueling.) At times the big bomber would begin swinging from side to side. Its bow wave would try to push the tail of our tanker up as the B-52 passed through the refueling position and to the opposite side. In the cockpit we could tell how exciting it was getting under the tail of our plane by the pitch of the boom operator's voice. If it was getting higher and squeakier, we knew to get ready for a possible breakaway. If our boomer suddenly began sounding like a fourteen year old girl, we instantly became spring-loaded for a breakaway with our hand on the throttles, our thumb on the autopilot disconnect button and a pucker on the seat cushion. (The breakaway maneuver was an emergency procedure designed to hopefully get some immediate separation between our KC-135 and the receiver aircraft.)

Additionally, we could predict a possible breakaway by how much the stabilizer trim was moving as it frantically trimmed the horizontal stabilizer while trying to keep the tail of our tanker pushed down as the B-52 passed under us. Then it would rapidly trim in the opposite direction trying to keep the tail level as the big bomber swung out to the side. As I have mentioned before, there was a slim to none chance of getting out of a KC-135 in an out of control situation; such as immediately after having a midair collision with a B-52!

Finally, the Buff was finished and on his way and we could unwind a little and eat our flight lunches as we headed toward Little Rock. We arrived back in the base traffic pattern and proceeded to make our first landing. As we rolled down the runway, the instructor re-trimmed the stabilizer tor for takeoff and reset the flaps. I pushed up the throttles toward the takeoff setting. At his "Rotate" call I raised the nose and the now relatively light Stratotanker lifted off the runway. When I noted that both pilots' instruments showed a positive rate of climb indication, I said to the instructor, "Gear up."

The startled young Captain looked over at me and replied, "What did you say?"

"Gear up," I repeated.

He looked apprehensive and stated, "We don't raise the landing gear while in the traffic pattern in SAC."

I replied, "But I'm in the Air National Guard," as I reached across and moved the landing gear handle up. The young Captain just sat there and stared in disbelief at the handle as the landing gear came up. It was if he thought that the plane would fall out of the sky if we didn't go by the SAC rules and leave the gear down. When we got adequate flying speed I looked at him and called "Flaps 20." Again he just looked at me dumbfounded. I placed the flap handle in the flaps 20 slot myself. He just stared at me again, seemingly in shock. It was now time to turn to the crosswind leg and I did so. While we were in the turn the instructor pilot looked at me, then out of his side window at the ground, and then back at me.

I grinned at him and said, "Didn't fall out of the sky did we?"

I then said, "Flaps up," and raised the flap handle to the zero position myself. I pulled back the power as we reached 200 knots. Compared to the SAC way it was so much quieter and the plane handled markedly better at the higher speed. Additionally, I would wager that we were burning at least thirty percent less fuel in the traffic pattern than with the Strategic Air Command procedures.

On the downwind leg I looked over at him and said, "Okay, we'll go back to flying by your SAC rules." He quickly nodded his head affirmative. After the final landing, we parked the airplane and completed the parking checklist.

After the rest of the crew had left the cockpit I said, "Listen Captain; I know that you are bound by your Command's rules no matter how absurd they might seem to me. But I wanted to demonstrate that the plane will not fall out of the sky with the landing gear and the flaps up in the traffic pattern. It is also much quieter, easier to fly and burns a lot less fuel. You can report my actions to your boss if you wish but I will tell you this. This Guard unit is going to fly patterns the way that I just demonstrated as soon as you guys have packed your bags and are out of here."

I continued, "I could understand leaving the landing gear down for brake cooling purposes after repeated full stop landings, but we're not touching the brakes during a "touch and go" landing. Besides that, if tire and wheel cooling were the concern after a "touch and go", flying the ten miles or so with the gear down after it is re-lowered on the base leg should be plenty of time for cooling after a touch and go. Even if the idea is for cooling, that doesn't explain dragging the flaps for thirty miles."

I then said, "I would hope that someday your SAC powers-that-be will come to their senses, change their procedures and quit squandering fuel needlessly; but I bet that they won't."

Jerry W. Cook

SCREEEEEEEECH......BANG...BANG!

Little Rock AFB, AR; 1975

It was my next training flight after the gear up and flaps up demonstration. My instructor was the same young Captain. The first part of the mission was overwater training across the Gulf of Mexico so that our Navigator could practice his Celestial Navigation procedures. During that portion, he had to navigate the plane using only his sextant and celestial position charts. The instructor navigator required that we be completely out of range of all ground based navigational aids for more realism.

With the navigation portion finished we were back at the base and it was traffic pattern time. I was to make the first landing to a full stop. Afterwards, I was to park the plane on the large ramp in front of the control tower. At that point I would exit the left seat and the instructor pilot would move from the right seat to the left. The co-pilot trainee who had been riding in the back would then man the right seat and we would proceed back to the traffic pattern in order for him to practice several touch and go landings.

I don't know why he did it. Perhaps it was an attempt at payback because of what had transpired with the landing gear and flaps on our previous flight together. In any case we were on the base leg for an ILS to my full stop landing when the young instructor looked over at me and said, "Major, do you think you can land and turn off on taxiway Charlie?"

(Taxiway Charlie is less than halfway down the twelve thousand foot long runway. That would leave me less than six thousand feet of runway to land and slow down enough to turn off. A normal touchdown point is about one thousand to twelve hundred feet from the approach end of the runway. Additionally, the KC-135A had old style brakes and no thrust reversers on the engines. If I touched down at the beginning of the normal zone I would have less than five thousand feet of stopping distance remaining. That day I probably had a grand total of fifteen hours in the tanker so I didn't have a clue as to whether I could do it or not.)

"I don't know, but I will try it if you want me too," was my answer.

He was smiling oddly when he looked at me and said, "Yes sir, why don't you *try* it."

Several of the crew members were standing in the rear of the cockpit and heard the challenge. They quickly headed back to their seats to strap in. I guess they thought that the landing and rollout might prove somewhat exciting. The wind was fairly light that day and was right down the runway so the air was relatively smooth. As we flew down the final approach, I worked hard to keep the airspeed right on the bug (proper airspeed). I began the landing flare just above the overrun and managed to touchdown just short of the one thousand foot marker. I quickly lowered the nose wheel to the runway and called for the airbrakes. I got on the wheel brakes and pressed as hard as I dared. As we slowed, I steadily increased the brake pedal pressure. We turned off on taxiway Charlie. The instructor didn't say a word. I was pleasantly surprised that the plane would do it.

I parked the aircraft as had been briefed, set the parking brake and exited my seat. I was really hungry and looking forward to tackling my flight lunch. I felt the plane begin to move again and settled in for the rest of the sortie.

We had been going round and round the traffic pattern for probably another hour and the co-pilot was making some pretty nice landings. The boom operator who had been standing in the cockpit during the last twenty mile pattern came back to me with a grin on his face.

"The Captain just told the co-pilot that he was going to make the final landing and that he planned to turn off on taxiway Charlie."

"Okay thanks," I replied. I was glad it was the final landing.

Things seemed normal as we turned base leg and onto the seven mile final approach. I was sitting against the cockpit wall on the floor near the galley. We weren't supposed to sit there during landings but I liked my back against the wall during heavy braking. I could feel the pilot flare the big tanker. It seemed like it floated quite a while before it touched down. He lowered the nose gear quickly to the runway and the brakes started forcefully slowing the big plane, effectively pinning our backs against the wall.

Suddenly; "Screeeeeeeech......Bang...Bang!" Two tires on the right side of the tanker had blown out. We lurched and rumbled down the runway as chunks of rubber flew off the wheels and hit the flaps and bottom of the wing. We rolled and bumped right on past taxiway Charlie still at a fairly rapid clip. Gradually we slowed down and finally turned off the runway at taxiway Delta. It took about an hour for our maintenance team to bring out the equipment to jack up the plane and change the two tires before they could tow it back the Air Guard ramp.

I never brought up his landing to the instructor pilot and neither did he. And I still don't know why he challenged me that day. What he may not realize is; I was lucky. Less than six thousand feet was not very much stopping distance for a KC-135A with the old type brakes and no thrust reversers; especially for a PUP.

Postscript: We finished our KC-135 checkouts and then we established our own procedures which depended on the professionalism of the pilots instead of a nonsensical and wasteful remedy for an imagined problem. In the more than ten years in which our unit flew the KC-135, we never did land one with the landing gear retracted. Imagine that! And I can't even begin to guess how many thousands of gallons of fuel that we saved.

WHAT DO YOU MEAN *SHORTEN* THE RUNWAY?

Little Rock AFB, AR; 1976

To say that takeoffs in a heavily loaded KC-135A on a hot day were critical is somewhat of an understatement. We had a standing joke that after you pushed the throttles to takeoff power and released the brakes, if the plane didn't start to roll within fifteen seconds you should probably abort the takeoff. Sometimes that didn't seem to be much of an exaggeration. Although it was supposed to be a joke, I will say that on a hot day with a maximum fuel load the plane seemed like it would never gain flying speed before it ran out of runway. That wasn't so funny.

According to our takeoff performance charts, at the point where you reached "S1" (decision speed) if you were to have an engine failure, you could either continue the takeoff with the three remaining engines or you could stop on the runway that was remaining. I always thought the stopping part was the real joke. Additionally, I had some serious doubts about the aircraft's ability to take off on three engines from that point and if it did get airborne whether it would climb, especially after the water augmentation ran out.

In a heavy KC-135A on a hot day, by the time S1 speed was reached, we were so far down the runway and going so fast that stopping in the remaining runway was not something that I ever wanted to attempt. I didn't care what the performance charts indicated; in my opinion it never looked like there was nearly enough runway remaining to get stopped. Fortunately for us most of our flights were flown with tens of thousands of pounds less than maximum takeoff weight, so such takeoffs were relatively rare.

Located several thousand feet from the end of runway 24 at Little Rock AFB is a small hill. (That runway is now runway *25* due to a change in the area's magnetic variance.) The hill is not very high but it was considered to be an obstacle for planes taking off to the southwest. For most aircraft it was not even a factor because of their higher performance. That was not the case for the KC-135A. Its performance (actually its lack of performance) was such that a certain amount of clearance above the hill had to be computed in case of the loss of an engine. In actuality we usually operated at relatively light weights and the obstacle was so far from the end of the runway that it rarely posed any problem when using full takeoff power.

Our dilemma was that we did not want to have to use full takeoff power every time that we took off on runway 24. We wanted to save our engines by using what was called a "Reduced EPR Takeoff" (meaning reduced engine pressure ratio). That reduction resulted in cooler exhaust gas temperatures and lower engine turbine RPMs. Those in turn could substantially extend the periods between major engine overhauls and more importantly, perhaps reduce the chances of engine failures. Under normal circumstances, in order to use reduced EPRs, pilots would compute aircraft weight, outside air temperature, airport elevation and runway length. Based on the results the engine EPR's were then set for takeoff to ensure all safety parameters were met. However, at Little Rock AFB we were not allowed to use them at all.

Our problem originated in the performance charts because of a certain statement that had been included in them. It prohibited the use of reduced EPR takeoffs if the number of feet to the obstacle from the end of the runway was less than a specific distance. In our case the small hill from the end of runway 24 was too close by slightly less than one thousand feet.

One day I was approached by the head of our jet engine shop. He took me to their facility and showed me a couple of engines that were being overhauled. He wanted to point out to me the damage that was being caused by the constant high temperatures and rpm on full power takeoffs. He had been in contact with other guard units equipped with KC-135s that did not have obstacles prohibiting them from using reduced EPR takeoffs. Their engines were much less damaged and were operating for longer periods between overhauls. He pleaded with me to try to do something about it.

The damage that he had shown to me got my attention. I went back to my office and reread the limiting statement several times. I tried to see the logic of a set distance from the actual end of the runway being a limiting factor. I could not. To me the restrictive distance should have been from the point on the runway where the aircraft became airborne to the obstacle and that varied with every change in the parameters: aircraft weight, temperature, etc. What did the actual end of the runway have to do with it?

I called the KC-135 performance engineering section at Tinker AFB for an explanation of the statement. The gentleman that I talked to did not explain it; he just confirmed that it had been that way since the plane was certified and probably would not be changed. I then posed the question, "Are you saying that if our runway was one thousand feet shorter on the southwest end that we would then be able to make reduced EPR takeoffs?"

There was a long pause and then he replied, "Well, I hadn't thought of it that way, but yes. The southwest end would then be far enough from the obstacle to allow for reduced EPR takeoffs."

He then laughed and said, "What are you going to do; bulldoze the last thousand feet?"

"Maybe," I said. I thanked him for the information and hung up the phone.

I sat there for quite some time considering the information that I had just received. Basically it was; "If our runway was shorter by one thousand feet on the southwest end, then it would be safer to reduce our engine power for takeoff." What a ridiculous premise. I began writing.

The Group Commander listened closely and then he looked at the proposed Flight Operations Procedure that I had handed to him. He finally said, "What do you mean, shorten the runway?"

I went over the whole thing including my conversation with our engine shop Chief and with the KC-135 engineering section at Tinker.

"Colonel, it's a local procedure to overcome a restrictive and perhaps inadvertent statement in the takeoff performance manual, which accomplishes nothing but to effectively hamstring us and compel us to use full takeoff power and needlessly burn up our engines."

He still wasn't sure that he understood until I said, "Sir, put it this way; according to the statement that you just read, if I borrowed a Caterpillar D8 bulldozer and went out tonight and bulldozed away the last one thousand feet of runway 24, would we then be legal to use reduced EPRs?"

"Yes, I guess according to their statement we would; but you're not going to do that," he said.

"Sir, essentially I am, on paper," I replied.

The procedure that I had written basically stated; "For takeoff planning for Runway 24: reduced EPR takeoffs may be made if they result in a balanced field length of less than eleven thousand feet and provide adequate obstacle clearance. For these takeoffs the last one thousand feet of the southwest end of runway 24 is assumed to be nonexistent. However, in the case of an aborted takeoff, the full runway length is available for stopping.

When takeoff computations are made and a reduced EPR takeoff would result in a balanced field length of more than eleven thousand feet, or if obstacle clearance requirements cannot be met, utilize maximum power takeoffs. In this case the full twelve thousand feet of runway is available for takeoff."

The procedure was approved by the Group Commander with blessings from the Guard Bureau. I published the change to our local Ops Procedures and briefed all of the aircrews. It triggered some jokes about me stealing a bulldozer and tearing up one thousand feet of runway in order to achieve safer KC-135 takeoffs. But everyone, especially the engine shop Chief, thought it was a great idea.

Well…actually not everyone….

Eighth Air Force headquartered at Barksdale Air Force Base was our gaining Numbered Air Force in case the 189th was called to active duty. As such, they made occasional visits with a Standardization Team (referred to by us as the Hatchet Men) to check our flight standardization and compliance with flying regulations. The team was headed by a Lieutenant Colonel who was a stickler for "by the book". After their team had been there for less than a day, he made a beeline for my office. By that time I was also a Lieutenant Colonel and the head of the 189th Standardization Section.

It seems that one of his check pilots had flown with one of our aircrews who had performed an "illegal" reduced power takeoff. When he was queried about it the aircraft commander informed the check pilot that we made them on a regular basis when conditions permitted.

When the check pilot told him that he was going to fail him for violating performance standards, the aircraft commander then showed him the local takeoff procedures that I had written. The check pilot of course immediately went straight to his boss who now was charging into my office. I had expected him.

He had my Ops Procedure in his hand. "What is this?" he stated rather emphatically as he lifted and wagged the folder in his hand.

Admittedly being somewhat of a smartass, I replied, "I should think that its title would be self-explanatory."

"That's not what I mean," he said.

Of course I knew what he meant but I continued, "Perhaps you'd better sit down and tell me what you do mean."

He sat down opposite me; "You cannot make reduced EPR takeoffs from Runway 24 at Little Rock Air Force Base." He sounded like a frustrated headmaster counseling an unruly child.

"Why would you say that?" I answered.

"You can't because the end of that runway is too close to your obstacle," he said.

I smiled as I replied, "Sure we can. We 'shortened' the southwest end of the runway by one thousand feet. Now the obstacle is far enough away from the end."

"You didn't shorten the runway," he said.

"Effectively, we did," I replied. "It's right there in that procedure in your hand."

He looked at me and with a very authoritative air repeated, "You can't do that."

I was still smiling as I said, "Okay Colonel, you love 'the book' so much; you show me in writing where it says that I can't do what I did and we'll stop doing it."

Of course he couldn't. It wasn't there. We kept right on making reduced EPR takeoffs, even during the inspection team visit.

We not only passed that Stand/Eval inspection but over the years we saved a tremendous amount of wear and tear on our engines.

There was one other Air National Guard KC-135 base with a similar obstacle problem. They heard about our procedure, contacted me as to how I did it, and then they "shortened" their runway too.

Postscript: The KC-135A was an effective but under-powered aircraft especially during takeoffs. Its maximum takeoff weight was listed as 297,000 pounds while its four jet engines only produced a total of 40,000 pounds of dry thrust or 52,000 pounds with water injected into them. Even with water augmentation the power to weight ratio was only 1 pound of thrust to each 5.7 pounds of aircraft weight at maximum takeoff weight. To add further complications to takeoff computations, the 670 gallons of water only lasted about 2 ½ minutes and then the ratio went to 1 to 7.4.

As a comparison, the Boeing 707-320B had a power to weight ratio of about 1 to 4.7 at its maximum takeoff weight of 336,000 pounds and it did not require water injection to achieve it. Its four engines produced 72,000 pounds of total thrust. They were a derivative of the same engines as on the KC-135 and had first become available in 1959. It is very unfortunate that the Air Force did not retrofit these engines to the KC-135A at that time. That would have given the plane a thrust to weight ratio of 1 to 4.1 at maximum takeoff weight with greatly improved operational capabilities and much safer flight operations. (The Air National Guard finally did exactly that in the 1980s.)

Of course that would have taken away all of the excitement of making a maximum weight takeoff on a hot day in a "water-wagon" (a KC-135 using water to increase thrust).

(Just for comparison purposes, the F-4 Phantom's thrust to weight ratio at maximum takeoff weight was 1 to 1.7. Ask me again why I like fighters.)

Toward The Evening Sky

ROCHESTER?

Preface: In an earlier postscript, I mentioned that I had been recalled to Pan Am in 1973 and had given up my GS-13 instructor pilot position in the Air Guard. Then I had been furloughed again while still in Boeing 727 ground school at Miami. Subsequently in early 1974, Pan Am evidently decided the 1973 furlough was a mistake and in mid-1974 recalled me. Like the fool that I evidently was, I returned to the "World's Most Experienced Airline". (Perhaps they meant the most experienced at furloughing pilots.) Back I went to Miami; this time on the Boeing 707.

Once again the wise men in charge of Pan Am evidently decided *that* recall was a mistake. It lasted less than two years until March 1976 when I got furloughed again. "Fool me once…etc." At least I had sense enough to stay in the Air National Guard.

As an Air Guard part timer, I was trying hard to pay the bills by flying the KC-135 as much as possible and by volunteering for alert duty. We were required to keep one of our KC-135s on standby and ready to fly 24/7 in response to a launch message from Strategic Air Command Headquarters. It was part of our commitment to SAC as our gaining Command. As a result, we kept a crew on alert twenty-four hours a day, seven days a week.

Little Rock Adams Field, AR; 1978-1979

It was early in 1978 when I received a call from a friend at Little Rock National airport. He had heard that a company in another town had just ordered a new Learjet and was looking for a Lear qualified pilot. He knew that I had a Learjet type rating and that I had flown the plane on charters for Central Flying Service. He was not Lear qualified, so he had kindly decided to phone me. The owner of the company was the contact individual; so I called him. After asking me a few questions, he said that he was interested in talking further and set up an appointment for me to meet with him.

The company was operating a conventional twin-engine plane and was replacing it with the soon to be delivered new Learjet. The deal was for me to checkout in their present aircraft and to fly it until the Lear was delivered in a few months. It was a full time job and I would be the Chief Pilot. The owner of the Company had been flying the conventional twin himself. He had no jet time but he wanted to fly as a co-pilot on the Lear when it came and to eventually obtain his Lear type rating so he could fly it as a Captain. Part of my duties would be to help him get his type rating. Since I had been instructing in jets off and on for nineteen years I did not see that as a big problem. Also I was to find and hire a part time co-pilot to fly with me when the owner was not aboard. The pay was pretty good. It would help solve my cash-flow problems. He offered me the job and I took it.

I checked out in the company's conventional twin-engine plane and began flying it mostly around the state. Several of the regular destinations were small airports with runways about three thousand feet long. I quickly learned that three thousand feet seemed to be about how much runway this particular aircraft needed to get airborne on a hot summer day. The way that it loved the ground reminded me of the KC-135 and its ground-loving tendencies.

In the meantime, my new co-pilot Bill Kyzer (who was also a part-time Air Guard pilot) and I headed off to school on the Learjet at Wichita, Kansas. We had an enjoyable time checking out in the little fighter-like corporate jet simulator. Bill had also flown supersonic Voodoos in the Air Guard before the KC-135 conversion but he was still impressed with the performance of the Learjet. Although it wasn't a jet fighter, some of its characteristics weren't all that much different. We finished the familiarization course and went back to Little Rock to await the completion of the company's new Lear.

Wow! When it was finished and we flew it the first time, that little machine was impressive. It was a real hotrod. It was designated by its builder as the 24E and it had the highest performance of any Learjet built. There were corporate jets that were faster in cruise but none of them could out climb it. It would climb to forty-one thousand feet in twelve minutes flat. That is an average climb rate of nearly three thousand, five hundred feet per minute. That was a higher average climb rate to forty-one thousand than some of the Air Force's earlier jet fighters.

In fact the little Learjet would climb so quickly that it was equipped with a special rate of climb indicator. Normally the maximum climb rate indication on a standard instrument was six thousand feet per minute. The 24E's IDC electronic climb rate indicator's maximum reading was ten thousand feet per minute; and even that wasn't enough. On most days it would stay pegged at ten thousand feet per minute through an altitude of at least twenty thousand feet.

The jet's major shortcoming was that it had very "short legs" (not much range). The plane took off quicker and climbed faster simply because it was lighter. And it was lighter primarily because it did not have a fuselage fuel tank and therefore carried less fuel than the Lear 24. My perception was that Lear built it without the fuselage tank to better compete with another company's small jet that was being manufactured. That jet was selling like hotcakes partly because it had very good performance for short runways. However, it was relatively slow for a jet aircraft. In fact, pilots of other type jets (including me) liked to joke that it had protective screens installed on the back of the engines to prevent bird strikes from the rear. It wasn't quite that slow.

The Lear 24E also had good short field performance but...it was equipped with General Electric CJ-610 turbojet engines that were very similar to and developed with the J-85 engine that powered the supersonic Air Force T-38 jet trainer. The major difference in the engines was that the T-38 version had afterburners. A major similarity was that both versions burned a lot of fuel. So much in fact that anytime we were going very far away from Arkansas, such as the east coast or very far to the west, we were usually approaching a minimum fuel situation upon arrival at our destination.

One of the typical destinations for the owner of the company was New York. The flight time from Little Rock was around two and one-half hours depending on air traffic control handling. If I recall correctly, the 24E had enough fuel for about three hours and twenty minutes. Consequently when we arrived in the New York area, we could ill afford any delays. We were usually approaching the minimum required fuel remaining which was thirty to forty-five minutes depending on the weather. We had to land; and soon. Sometimes things got very tense, especially if the weather was causing approach delays. My answer to the problem was that we could stop for fuel on the way. His answer was to buy himself a new plane with longer range.

This time he bought the longest range Lear, the 36A. Instead of running low on fuel in three hours as we had been, the 36A had about seven hours of fuel endurance. We went from flying the Lear with the least range to the Lear with most. It wasn't nearly as much fun to fly as the 24E, but it was a lot easier on the nerves after you had been airborne for three hours. However there can be upsides and downsides to such long range.

We had not possessed the 36A for very long. It was a couple of days before the New Year and the weather in Arkansas had been awful; cold and dreary. The phone rang at home and when I answered it was my boss. He sounded terrible.

After he identified himself and coughed a couple of times, he said, "Jerry, can our new Lear 36 go from here non-stop to Acapulco?"

I thought just for a moment before I answered, "Yes sir it can. But we don't have Mexican insurance so we'd have to stop in Laredo and buy some on the way."

"Do you want to go to Acapulco? You sound terrible," I asked.

"I feel terrible. That's why I want to go. I think I've got the flu and I want to go down there and sweat it out in the hot sun on the beach," he answered. (That was certainly a remedy I had never been rich enough to try out but "Hey", maybe it would work.)

"When are you thinking about going?" I inquired.

"Tomorrow morning about ten," he said.

I answered, "I'll have everything ready." (One of the realities of flying for an owner pilot is that you usually get to do everything except fly when he's in the plane.)

"Hope you get to feeling better," I concluded.

He didn't sound any better the next morning at the airport and he didn't look that good so I asked him, "Are you sure that you feel well enough to go?"

"Yeah, let's go," he coughed.

"Man," I thought; "I hope I don't catch that."

I had called ahead and the fixed base operator at the old Laredo AFB, now the Laredo International Airport, Texas, had our Mexican aircraft insurance papers ready when we arrived. After about thirty minutes on the ground we were on our way. Less than two hours later, we were landing in Acapulco. It was beautiful; seventy-eight degrees with a light ocean breeze. Perfect. The kamikaze cab ride to the hotel; not so perfect, but we survived it.

The boss still looked and sounded terrible, but he said that as soon as he changed clothes he was going to the beach to "sweat it out". His wife just looked at me, rolled her eyes, and shook her head slightly.

The hotel was right on the beach and it was a wonderful place. When we checked into our rooms we were booked to stay for several days. The next morning after breakfast I walked down the beach and was almost back to the hotel. People were having a great time parasailing, waterskiing, swimming, playing volleyball, all kinds of activities. The weather again was picture-postcard-perfect.

Back in Arkansas there was still freezing drizzle and fog but here it was idyllic until; "Hey Jerry; over here," was the call coming from beneath the thatched-roof bar by the swimming pool. I looked in the direction of the voice and it was the boss. He was sitting at the bar with his wife. He was motioning for me to come over to where they sat. As I walked closer I could already see the glow. His face and arms were shining bright red with a terrible looking sun burn. And he still sounded terrible. His wife was just quietly sitting beside him. She was wearing a wide brimmed straw hat and sipping a mimosa.

"Good morning," I said as I walked up closer to them.

"I don't like it here. Can this new Lear make it to Rochester, New York nonstop from Acapulco?" he said in reply to my greeting.

His wife, very surprised, stared at him and said, "Rochester? Why would you want to go to Rochester?

He looked at her and very seriously replied, "Because they have a good place to eat in Rochester." She looked anxiously back at me.

Somewhat recovered from his incomprehensible answer I crossed my fingers and replied, "Well yes it could fly there nonstop, but not anytime soon. They had a blizzard up there yesterday with snow drifts about twenty feet high." (I *may* have exaggerated just a little.)

Then I quickly said, "I'll see you later," and disappeared. I became hard to find for the next two days.

Toward The Evening Sky

ME? YES YOU

Little Rock AFB, AR; 1979

Very early in my Air Guard career I'd been assigned to the 189th Standardization/Evaluation Section; consequently I only got to fly for a short time in the 154th Squadron where most of the pilots were assigned. At the time we were operating RF-101 Voodoos and Lieutenant Colonel "Buck" Wassell was its Commander. I would have really liked to have been a squadron pilot under his leadership. He was a part-timer and in his "real life" was a successful Little Rock architect. I didn't know him outside of work all that well but he was an impressive individual and an excellent pilot. I had flown as his check pilot on occasion and had participated in quite a few flights with him as a flight leader. He had an outgoing personality and was always a gentleman. All of his squadron pilots liked him and so did I. He was always one of us, but at the same time he held our respect as a leader.

Lieutenant Colonel Wassell had been transferred from his Squadron Command to take over the 189th Group when health problems caused the retirement of his predecessor. He was promoted to full Colonel and had led the Group with distinction for several years. And now, Colonel Wassell was to continue his climb in the Air National Guard. He was to become the Commander, Arkansas Air National Guard and as such would be promoted to Brigadier General.

The 189th Group Commander position was going to be vacant. Vying for the position and the probable promotion to full Colonel that came with it had begun. Some Lieutenant Colonels were making calls and talking to anyone that they thought might have some influence with the Adjutant General. It was he who would make the selection.

Although I had been promoted to Lt. Colonel, my date of rank was so junior to the others that I had not thought that there was any possible chance that I would even be considered for the position. In fact I was rather enjoying watching the rivalry between two of the "contestants".

Evidently one of those two senior Lieutenant Colonels did not think that I was in contention either because he rather sarcastically told me one day that, if I wanted to be the Group Commander, I'd better call the Adjutant General and let him know. (I had been told earlier that he had already called the AG's office himself.)

I replied, "Anyone who calls the AG to tell him that they want the position reminds me of the 'Arnold Horshack' character on the 'Welcome Back, Kotter' TV show. When Mr. Kotter asks a question, Horshack always raises his hand and shouts; *'Oh...oh...me...me...please!'*"

Then I finished, "If the AG wants me to be the Group Commander, he'll call me."

The now somewhat red-faced senior Lt. Colonel laughed and said, "Yeah sure; fat chance of that happening," and walked away.

It was a few days later when Major General Jones, the Adjutant General, called. He wanted me to come to Camp Robinson and talk to him about something. I said, "Yes sir," and hung up the phone. The first thing I wondered was whether the red-faced Lt. Colonel that I insulted had called the AG and told him what I had said. If so, I just might be in for a dressing down from a two-star General. My next thought was, "Oh man, me and my big mouth."

I reported to the Adjutant General in my best military manner. I tried but could not decide from his expression if I was in trouble. He returned my salute and then ordered, "Sit down Colonel." I sat.

He then looked at me and said, "I'm going to get right to the point. How would you like to be the next 189th Group Commander?"

I know that I must have looked at him with an expression of disbelief and I said, "Me?"

He finally smiled as he said, "Yes, you."

He continued, "A couple of the individuals who are also qualified for the position contacted me to express their interest. In your case you did not call, but Colonel Wassell did. He said that he had not talked to you about it, but if you would accept the job it was you that he wanted to replace him. Although the other individuals who are qualified are several years senior to you, after looking over your military record, I agree with Colonel Wassell. Now I repeat, how would you like to be the Commander of the 189th?"

"General, I think that I would like that very much," I answered.

"Then the 189th is yours. Congratulations," he replied.

ORI

Little Rock AFB, AR; Early 1980

It had been a few months since I had taken over the 189th Group and things were going well, or so I thought. Colonel Wassell was now a Brigadier General and I had been promoted to full Colonel. The General called me from his office downtown one day and said, "Colonel Cook, we need to talk." His tone sounded serious. He instructed me to meet with him at the next Guard drill weekend.

I reported to his office in the Arkansas Air National Guard State Headquarters building with some level of concern. He grinned and shook my hand after returning my salute and then said, "Have a seat." He then sat down behind his big mahogany desk.

As I sat down I stated, "Okay General, you certainly got my attention with your call. Please tell me what's going on."

He began, "Colonel Cook, I told the Adjutant General last year that one of the reasons that I wanted you to replace me is because you have exhibited an ability to solve problems."

The General continued; "Of course we're all well aware that the 189th has a Strategic Air Command Operational Readiness Inspection (ORI) in just a few months and I know that you have already begun preparing the Group for it." (An ORI was conducted by Strategic Air Command Headquarters. It was a large team of inspectors who were specialists for each section within a unit. It was a full-blown examination which scrutinized everything within a SAC gained organization to determine its war fighting capability, i.e. combat readiness. It lasted for several days and checked every detail in the unit down to and including even haircuts and mustaches.)

The General then stated, "I have recently received some disturbing information that there is a section in your organization where the people assigned to it are so unhappy with their senior leadership that they are talking of intentionally failing the ORI to teach them a lesson. He leveled his gaze at me and said, "Have you heard anything of this?"

I replied, "No sir; I have not."

He said, "I didn't think so," and then he continued; "Of course this kind of 'wrong-headed' thinking would also take the whole of the 189th and you down with them. I want you to find out if this is accurate information and if it is, fix it."

"What is the section?" I asked as I tried to hide my anger. When he told me the identity of the section, I was not all that surprised mainly because of the personality of its Commander (The same Lt. Colonel who had told me that I needed to call the Adjutant General). But I knew that I must not make any assumptions at this point about fault. The General was right. The vital role of that individual's unit was such that if it failed the inspection, it would bring down the entire 189th with it.

"I'll find out if it's true and take care of it General, and I have a request to make," I said.

"What is it?" he answered. "Sir, I have been waiting for an opportunity to talk to you about this and this may not be the right time; but I request that after this ORI is successfully passed, I be considered for the State Operations Officer position," I said. I continued, "And I fully realize that if the ORI is not successful, that my career in the Air Guard will likely be over."

The General looked at me and sternly said, "You're not fooling me Cook. You just want to get away from the Strategic Air Command and fly F-4s again." (Our other flying unit in the state was the 188th Tactical Fighter Group in Fort Smith, Arkansas. They had begun flying F-4C Phantoms in 1979.)

"I said, "Yes sir, you are correct sir." (As the State Headquarters Staff Air Operations Officer, I could be allowed to fly any type of aircraft that the state possessed.)

General Wassell finally smiled and said, "Well, I would not have expected anything different from you. Okay Colonel; you fix the 189th and do well on this upcoming ORI and I think I can make that happen."

He stood up and stuck out his hand, "Good luck 'Jer'." (The General had begun calling me "Jer" several months before whenever we were speaking informally. In turn, I called him "General", although his nickname was actually "Buck").

I began by pretending to make a casual visit to the section that General Wassell had briefed me about. I walked around and talked to everyone while asking some general questions. I hoped that the answers would inform me if there really was a problem. And if so, perhaps there would be some clues as to what the problem was. At first, the personnel seemed nervous at my presence in their work areas, but after a brief time spent talking and joking with them, they relaxed somewhat. It helped somewhat that I had known most of them since I had come into the unit as a Captain some ten years before. I began to detect some slight hints in their answers. I identified a couple of people that I wanted to speak with further. Of everyone that I talked to, they were the ones who seemed surer of themselves and the most comfortable around me. I took them aside separately and asked them to come to my office later that day, but at different times. I also asked them to keep the fact that they had been invited there to themselves.

Although completely separate from each other, the two individuals told a very similar story. It seemed that the unit Commander and a Senior NCO (non-commissioned officer) were having constant disagreements about organizational policy and procedures. Their difficulties with each other had not been kept within the confines of their office and consequently the unit's morale was being affected in a very negative way. The members of the unit had started taking sides and that was causing further problems in their areas.

After talking to the two individuals, I insisted on their silence pertaining to our meetings. After several days of further investigation, I spent a lot of time considering the situation and about the best way to fix it. The truth of the matter was that, if I had to choose which individual was more vital to the unit, it would not have been its Commander. However, I did not want to try finding a replacement for either of them. It likely would not have been a feasible solution with the ORI only a few months away.

I was finally confident that I had determined the source of the problem. I required the two individuals to report to my office during the next Guard Drill weekend. They were to report to me at the same time. I will not go into details of the private meeting, but suffice it to say that it ended with me making to them a promise that they could not refuse.

When it came we not only passed the ORI, but did not have a single finding below Satisfactory. That was an almost unheard of result.

The troubled unit did an outstanding job.

General "Buck" was very happy. So was I.

Postscript #1: The 189th did so well on the ORI that we decided to have a big Group picnic on the Saturday afternoon during the next Guard Drill weekend to celebrate the outcome. Everyone was having a great time playing volleyball, pitching horseshoes and playing tug-of-war. It was after duty hours, so we were all in civvies and the atmosphere was like a huge happy family reunion.

I was standing in line to get a couple of hotdogs when a young airman walked up to me with a big grin. "We kicked their asses didn't we Colonel," he happily exclaimed.

I laughed and replied, "Yes son, we certainly did."

As he cheerfully went on his way I thought, "And there were two more asses kicked that you don't know about."

Postscript #2: On a Saturday morning drill several months after our successful Operational Readiness Inspection, I went to see General Wassell in his office at Air Guard State Headquarters. He was sitting behind his desk as I knocked on the door jam. He looked up from some papers in front of him and said, "Come in Colonel Cook. What brings you over here this morning?"

After he returned my salute he motioned for me to sit down. "General I was wondering whether you had thought any more about the conversation that we had a few months before the ORI," I said.

"Yes I have," he answered; "And I have speculated on when you might come to collect."

"Well sir, I was wondering when that assignment change might be possible," I replied.

General Wassell folded his hands together and said, "Colonel, you just led the 189th through the best ORI that they've ever had. No finding below Satisfactory was unheard of before then. Why would you want to leave now? Things are going great."

I looked at him and replied, "Sir that is precisely why I want to leave now."

He looked at me and said, "So you're a believer in quitting while you're ahead, huh?"

"Well sir; I can sure think of worse ways of leaving," I said.

He laughed and agreed, "You have a point."

Then he continued, "Jer, I would love to let you transfer to the State Operations job right now, but unfortunately I don't have anyone that I feel is ready to take over the 189th. I need you to stay as its Commander for a while longer. I'll let you go as soon as I feel that I can. I know that you want to get back to flying F-4s as soon as possible."

"Yes sir. I understand sir," I replied.

"Anything else?" the General asked.

"No sir," I said as I stood and saluted."

"Sorry Jer," General Wassell said as he returned my salute.

So; I was to be the 189th Air Refueling Group Commander for a while longer. As I walked back toward my office, I was wondering just how much longer I would be dealing with the Strategic Air Command and their doctrines. I was soon to find out.

Toward The Evening Sky

YOU'RE JUST THE MAN WE NEED

Offutt AFB, Nebraska; 1980s

Not long after my meeting with General Wassell about my future, I was notified that the Strategic Air Command was planning a world-wide exercise. It would simulate the Command's reaction to and its capabilities in the case of the Cold War becoming hot. They wanted the Air Guard and Air Force Reserve KC-135 units to participate.

I became somewhat enthusiastic about having the 189th take part because the exercise was to include short notice rapid generation of our tankers, launching them with combat fuel loads and then actually flying very lengthy distances and refueling our war-plan designated receivers. It promised to be a very realistic scenario and, because of that, I felt it would benefit our unit. Information about the upcoming exercise was restricted to add realism for unit members and, at that time, only I and my senior staff were aware of it.

Air National Guard units plan and publish to their members the once-a-month drill weekend schedule. The planning is done up to a year in advance. This arrangement is a necessity because the vast majority of unit members are part-timers. This allows them to arrange time off with their civilian bosses and to make plans for family activities. Unfortunately the big SAC exercise was scheduled during a time period which did not coincide with our planned drill weekend for that particular month. After meeting with my staff, I decided that the benefits of participation warranted changing our drill weekend to correspond with the exercise. Fortunately the lead time was far enough in advance to allow the members to change their schedules with a minimum of difficulty.

A couple of months prior to the exercise, I was required to attend a Strategic Air Command Commanders' Conference. It included all SAC Wing Commanders along with the Commanders from the other KC-135 Air Guard and Air Reserve units. These conferences were designed to apprise Commanders of recent intelligence affecting SAC operations and, in this case, update the latest information on the approaching worldwide exercise. On the evening of arrival there was a mixer at the Offutt AFB Officers' Club and conferees were expected to attend. These things weren't my cup of tea mostly because I didn't drink and they were basically cocktail parties. However, they were designed to get to know the other Wing and Group Commanders in SAC and some of the senior staff at Headquarters: so I attended and carried around my ginger ale for a while.

I was talking to a couple of other Colonels when I noticed a Brigadier General looking in our direction. He was obviously asking a question to a Colonel talking with him because the officer looked in our direction and then turned back and nodded to the General. The Brigadier started walking toward our little group. As he came to a halt beside me, he said "Hello" to one Colonel who obviously already knew him and then introduced himself and shook hands with me and the third Colonel.

He then looked back at me, "Aren't you Colonel Cook, the Commander of the 189th Air Refueling Group at Little Rock?"

I replied, "Yes sir General, I am."

He continued, "That's what I thought. Congratulations on your recent ORI. Well Done."

I replied "Thank you sir. We were very happy with the results."

"I don't blame you. I've never seen one with no score below Satisfactory," he said and raised his glass.

He then said, "Aren't you a furloughed airline pilot?" I was a little surprised that he knew that and I wondered why he had asked the question.

I answered, "Yes sir, I am."

He then said enthusiastically, "You're just the man we need."

I was a little uneasy as I replied, "Need for what General?"

"Well Colonel, as you already know SAC is losing a lot of our pilots to the airlines. We need you to travel around to all of the SAC bases and tell our young pilots about all of the pitfalls of getting out and going to the airlines like you did," he finished with a smile.

"General, it sounds like you've assumed that I'm sorry that I got out of the Air Force," I replied.

He looked surprised and said, "Well, aren't you?"

"Well actually sir, I'm not. But I certainly agree that there is a big problem of pilot retention in all of the Air Force including the Strategic Air Command," I answered. A small group of curious Wing Commanders and staff officers began to gather around us.

I continued, "In my opinion, the airlines are not the root cause of the Air Force's pilot retention problem."

The Brigadier General looked surprised and said, "So Colonel Cook, what do you see as the problem?"

"General, it has been my observation that like me, most pilots don't give a flip about any job other than flying airplanes. That is the reason most of them joined the Air Force in the first place. Also they don't particularly care about rank or how they're referred to besides as a pilot. What they want, and what I think the Air Force should want, is for them to be the best pilot that they are capable of being. In contrast; a successful career in the Air Force demands so-called continuing education, most of which contributes nothing to piloting skills. On the contrary, the time spent away from the cockpit is counter-productive when considering pilot proficiency and knowledge. Also, many times they are then stuck behind a desk in a non-flying job. I believe that to be a waste of a very expensive-to-train pilot. It is as if the United

States Air Force expects all of us to someday be the Air Force Chief of Staff. If instead, pilots were left to develop their piloting skills, they would be a much better fighting force in case of a conflict. Moreover there would certainly be fewer accidents during war and peacetime. Additionally, vast amounts of training money would be saved because of the resulting lower turnover in our cockpits. In my view we are training pilots for the airlines because the Air Force effectively drives them away by expecting them to be a student of just about everything but aviation." By now the crowd of listeners had grown considerably.

"That's a very interesting theory Colonel, but how would you propose to fix the problem as you see it?" the General challenged.

"There is a way sir, but the Air Force would never do it," I replied.

"Let's hear it anyway," the General said.

I responded, "Very well sir. First, don't use the rank system for our pilots. They could be just Pilot, Senior Pilot, or Command Pilot. Second, don't require the study of any subject that doesn't have to do with their primary duty of flying an airplane. Third, don't assign them to additional duties that have nothing to do with their piloting skills. Fourth, hold them to even higher standards than now. After that, if they can't hack it, fire them. Let those pilots go to the airlines."

The General interrupted with, "So do you really think that those changes would keep our pilots in the Air Force?"

I replied, "Those...coupled with one other thing sir. Pay them based on an average airline scale. The Air Force wastes a lot more money than that would cost in training new pilots to replace them."

The General responded, "That all seems pretty far-fetched Colonel; that pilots would stay in simply because they don't have to accomplish the additional things that Air Force officers have to do to be promoted."

I took a deep breath before I replied; "No offense intended sir, but most pilots that I know, including me, would rather fly airplanes than be promoted to General with a desk job." After my statement there was a lot of coughing and whispering and shaking of heads among the full Colonels listening.

The Brigadier General leveled his gaze at me before he finally said, "No offense taken Colonel, but I don't believe that the Air Force would ever change to such a system."

I replied, "As I said before General, I don't think so either."

He smiled and nodded as he raised his glass toward me. I nodded in return and he left the group. For a few more minutes several of the officers standing around me asked some further questions about my pilot retention theory. One of them remarked that it sounded to him like something that might work. I laughed and told him to keep up his professional education and then, when he got to be the Air Force Chief of Staff, perhaps he could change it.

The next morning the base theater was packed with Colonels and Generals. We were there for the briefings that I mentioned earlier. After a welcome by General Ellis, CINCSAC (Commander-in-Chief Strategic Air Command), the individual briefing officers began their presentations. The briefings were very detailed and well done. The capabilities of the Command were indeed impressive and hopefully, never to be tested.

After the general briefings the attendees broke out into smaller groups for further information concerning only their areas, i.e. bombers, tankers or missiles. After these sessions the Air National Guard and Air Force Reserve Tanker Unit Commanders were invited into a conference room to receive information that applied only to us.

In just a few minutes a SAC Colonel entered. Just as I did, the other Commanders knew him and the usual pleasantries were exchanged. He was the SAC liaison officer to the Air Guard and Reserve units. I expected that the information we were to receive was concerning the worldwide exercise in which we had been asked to participate. I was correct but the information was a little different than what I had anticipated. He began by telling us that the dates of the exercise had been changed from what we had initially been told. It would now encompass a completely different weekend from the one to which I had just changed. The second bombshell he dropped was that none of our units would actually be flying, but that our people would be accomplishing all of the other tasks required just as if we were going to fly.

I cleared my throat and said, "Colonel that is unacceptable."

He looked surprised and replied, "Why would you say that?"

"I say that because this is a completely different scenario than the one that was presented to me when I signed on to this exercise. I have already changed my unit's drill weekend once in order to participate. And that was when we were going to be actually flying and not just playing games to fill some squares for the Strategic Air Command."

I continued, "My unit already knows how to fuel, maintain and generate aircraft to alert status. We already know how to operate and produce the support required to create our war-fighting forces. We just did all that during our ORI a couple of months ago. I will not change my drill schedule again for something that I now consider to be of little value to my unit."

The liaison Colonel looked at me and said, "Colonel Cook; your breaking of your agreement to participate in this exercise is going to attract four-star attention at SAC Headquarters."

I replied, "Really? Well my agreement to participate was based on some very important facts that have now been changed. I'd say that I'm not the one breaking the agreement."

There was some grumbling from some of the Commanders around the table but I don't think any of them opted out of full unit participation. They certainly didn't while they were sitting there at the table. It appeared that they all were going to change their plans again and participate. The SAC Colonel was looking concerned. I knew that he wasn't the one who had changed the rules.

"Look Colonel," I said. "I am not going to reward my people for a job well done in our ORI just a couple of months ago by changing the drill date again and then making them come out and essentially do it all again but not launch and fly. But I'll tell you what I will do. I will bring the members of my Battle Staff and my Intelligence Section out during your exercise and we will do a BSX (Battle Staff Exercise). To the personnel in the SAC Command Post the message traffic will look exactly as if we are generating the force. We will send responses to your messages just as if we were participating."

I continued, "There will be absolutely no change on SAC's end since you're not letting us fly in the exercise anyway. In fact, if you didn't inform your Command Post Staff, they would never know the difference. My people will pretend up to the point of launching our planes just like your people are going to pretend that we are actually flying."

The liaison officer finally responded after he thought over my proposal, "I'll have to run this by our senior operations staff. If they don't approve they'll probably want to notify the Guard Bureau about you pulling out of the exercise."

"You tell them that I said to do what they think they need to do," I replied. The meeting adjourned. A few days after I got back to Little Rock, I received a message from SAC that a Battle Staff Exercise would be acceptable.

After the SAC exercise had come and gone, I wondered if they had told anyone working in the SAC Command Post. If they didn't, those folks never knew the difference.

My people were spared some needless aggravation, except for my Battle Staff team. There was a little grumbling from them so I reminded them that, "Rank has its privileges" and "Taking one for the team" is sometimes one of them.

Jerry W. Cook

COUPLED APPROACH

Little Rock AFB, AR; early 1980s

We had been operating the KC-135 for several years and I was still the commander of the 189th Air Refueling Group. Additionally, I was designated as an instructor pilot in the KC-135. On this particular day I was "riding shotgun" in a seat behind the two pilots. Manning the left Aircraft Commander position was an experienced lieutenant colonel who I'd been flying with since our RF-101 days. In the right seat was a young lieutenant who was new to our unit and to the KC-135. He was in the co-pilot checkout phase for the big tanker which was the reason that I was aboard that day.

We had already accomplished most of our planned mission including the air refueling of a B-52. We had returned to the airbase traffic pattern where we would complete several visual and instrument approaches and landings with the newbie co-pilot flying the aircraft. The young pilot was visibly and understandably nervous with a lieutenant colonel in his left seat and a full colonel looking over his shoulder. However, in spite of this added pressure, he was doing a very admirable job of flying and landing the unfamiliar aircraft.

After several approaches and touch and go landings we were flying on the traffic pattern downwind leg. I checked the list of required training items and announced to the two pilots that this would be an ILS approach and to make the landing to a full stop. They both acknowledged my instructions and the co-pilot was visibly relieved. He flexed his shoulders slightly and tried to find a more comfortable position in his seat. The aircraft commander called the control tower and relayed our intentions.

The young co-pilot rolled out on a ten mile final and was established on the ILS course. He was still hand-flying the plane. Suddenly the aircraft commander looked over at him and said, "Lieutenant, have you ever made a coupled approach?" (Normally this refers to using the autopilot to fly the ILS.)

The young co-pilot answered, "No sir, not yet."

The aircraft commander said, "Want to try one?"

The co-pilot said, "Yes sir, I guess so." With that the left seat pilot reached over and softly placed his right hand on top of the young lieutenant's left hand where it grasped the four throttles and smiled sweetly at him.

I've never seen a hand move as fast as the co-pilot's did as he jerked it off the throttles. He was very relieved when the "left-seater" started laughing.

Postscript #1: The jokester aircraft commander was the same guy who "spooked" the Braniff captain with the big sinister gray glove in an earlier story.

Postscript #2: "He who laughs last...." The young lieutenant co-pilot eventually became the Commander of the Arkansas Air National Guard with the rank of Brigadier General. We still laugh about his first "coupled approach" every time we see each other.

Jerry W. Cook

COLONEL; DON'T YOU THINK THAT WE SHOULD GO AROUND THAT STORM?

Tucumcari to Little Rock AFB, AR; 1980s

We had just completed another "Tucumcari Turnaround" as we had begun calling the recurring flights to the refueling track near Tucumcari, New Mexico. We were flying so many of these same missions in our KC-135s that we almost didn't need a map. We knew how long it should take and how much fuel we would need and that our receiver was usually a B-52 out of Barksdale AFB. It had been a late evening air refueling and now it was a beautiful clear night as we headed home. Our navigator that evening was a very experienced Lt. Colonel. He was an excellent officer and was additionally the ranking officer and Chief of a very important section of our Air Refueling Group. He possessed a serious demeanor and seemed a little edgy at times.

Not many minutes prior, we had passed over Amarillo, Texas. We were cruising along on autopilot and enjoying the beautiful night. The navigator was busy at his desk, which sat facing the right side of the cockpit a couple of feet behind the co-pilot. He was stowing his maps and various other paraphernalia in his big case. Located above the plotting area at his duty station was a radar scope. It provided an easy way for the navigator to see the radar return by just leaning forward and placing his face up against the shroud. The shroud was designed so that it kept out any cockpit lights from interfering with the view of the scope. It usually was padded with a soft sheepskin material.

"Colonel Cook, I'm painting a very large thunderstorm at our twelve o'clock position about one hundred and fifty miles," said the navigator. I looked out of the windscreen for telltale signs of lightning in the distant dark sky. At the same time, I recalled our weather briefing before the flight. It had forecast no convective activity of any kind anywhere along our route. I saw no signs of thunderstorm activity, just clear skies with lots of stars. I looked over at the co-pilot who had been peering out of his forward windscreen also. He looked back at me and shrugged as he shook his head to indicate that he too had seen nothing there. I turned and looked at the navigator. He had his face buried in the scope shroud peering intently at his radar return. I glanced down at the repeater radar scope near the co-pilot's left knee. Sure enough, there was a huge radar return on the scope dead ahead of us. Now it was about one hundred and forty-five miles. I looked out of my windscreen again.

All I could see out in front of us were the distant lights of Oklahoma City. They were glowing up into the night sky. I looked down at my DME (distance measuring equipment) which was tuned to the VORTAC station near Oklahoma City. It read one hundred and thirty five miles. The co-pilot looked over at me and grinned as we simultaneously identified the "thunderstorm". (The tilt of the antenna on a weather radar unit is usually adjustable. If it is tilted just slightly too low, it will reflect objects on the ground; such as the buildings in a city for instance.) I turned in my seat slightly so I could better observe the navigator. Some navigators in our unit were just as interested in what was visible outside of the plane as were the pilots; however, others it seemed, not so much.

"How far out is the thunderstorm now, 'Nav'?" I asked.

"About one hundred and thirty miles Colonel," was the answer. I looked at my DME…Check.

"Okay," I said and occasionally glanced at him out of the corner of my eye. The lights of Oklahoma City were getting about eight miles closer with each minute as we continued straight ahead. The navigator had not moved a muscle from his watch position.

"Colonel, don't you think that we should tell Fort Worth Center that we need to make a turn soon for weather avoidance?" came the navigator's call over the interphone. We were now at about one hundred miles.

I looked down at the radar return and it was huge. (At that time, Oklahoma City was one of the largest cities in the world when measured in square miles.)

"No, let's continue a while longer so we can get a better *visual look* at this storm," I said as I dropped the hint. The co-pilot was about to burst a blood vessel trying to suppress his mirth.

"I don't know Colonel. That thing is awfully big," the navigator stated emphatically. After that concerned sounding statement, the co-pilot was really struggling to maintain his composure.

"Let's get closer so we can *see* it better," I answered while emphasizing the *"see"*. We continued straight ahead. The navigator still had not removed his face from his radar shroud. We now were approaching seventy miles from Oklahoma City and its lights were shining up into the night sky.

Just as I turned to look at him again, the navigator said, "Colonel, if we go much farther we won't be able to miss the storm by twenty miles like we're supposed to do."

I answered him with; "I tell you what Nav. It doesn't look that bad to me and I haven't flown through a thunderstorm in a long time. I'm just going to keep this heading and fly right through it." My co-pilot was about to stroke out by now. His eyes were bulging out and his face was a bright red.

I was watching the navigator. He finally stopped peering into the radar shroud but he still didn't look toward the front of the cockpit. Instead, he hurriedly began stowing items that were left on his table and then tightening his safety belt and shoulder harness. We were so close to Oklahoma City now that the city's lights were glowing onto the overhead panels of our cockpit. As we passed over the area of his concern, our navigator still had not bothered to look out of the plane. His face was back buried in his radar shroud.

As we passed over the far eastern edge of the city and the sky began to darken again, I announced, "Well, that wasn't so bad. I've sure seen a lot worse." At that the co-pilot finally lost his self-control.

I said, "Nav, your radar beam was tilted too low. Your thunderstorm was actually Oklahoma City." The navigator just looked at me, unstrapped, got out of his seat and went to the back of the plane. I supposed that he was upset; hopefully mostly with himself.

But I figured that he would never make that same mistake again. I was more than a little surprised that he made it that night.

LAUNCH

Little Rock Adams Field, AR; 1980

I was at Hiegel Aviation at the Little Rock airport where we kept the company's Learjet. The Hiegel fixed base operations was where I spent my weekdays when I wasn't at the Air Force Base flying KC-135s or in my office at the 189th Air Refueling Group Headquarters. I was talking to some other corporate pilots who had an office at the FBO.

Because we had to keep a KC-135 on alert 24/7 there was always an operations specialist manning a small 189th Command Center. He or she was equipped with instant communications with the airbase's Wing Command Post and the Strategic Air Command's Command Post at Offutt AFB, Nebraska. And of course, our Command Center was also telephone or radio linked directly to our alert aircrew at all times. It was early afternoon when I received a telephone page. When I picked up the phone, it was our Command Center specialist, "Sir, we have a situation and I need a command decision."

"What's going on, Sergeant?" I quickly asked.

"I just got an emergency phone call about an airborne F-4 in our area. The pilot has a main landing gear that won't come down and he will be running low on fuel before very much longer. He hopes that with more time he can phone patch to the engineers at the McDonnell factory and maybe get the gear down. If he can't get a tanker in time, he and his backseater may have to eject."

"Launch the alert bird for the F-4; then call SAC and tell them we are going down from alert. Instruct maintenance to get another plane to the alert pad and ready to assume alert status as quickly as possible. Call out another crew to preflight and fill in for the alert crew until they get back. If you can't find pilots soon enough, let me know and I'll come out."

"Yes sir. Sir, we have another problem," my ops specialist said.

"What problem?" I asked.

"The Wing Command Post has just advised me that the runway has been closed by order of the Wing Commander for a C-130 Operational Readiness Exercise."

"You call them back and inform them that we are launching our alert tanker for an emergency and they need to open the runway right now."

"Colonel, one more question. What do I tell SAC if they ask why we're taking our bird down from alert?"

"Tell them that we have a problem with a landing gear. You don't need to mention that it's not *our* landing gear." I said.

"Yes sir. Thank you. I'll call you with an update," the ops specialist finished as he hung up.

My ops sergeant called back about forty minutes later. "Colonel, the alert bird is in formation with the F-4. They've already refueled once and they're working the landing gear problem with the factory engineers at Saint Louis. As we speak, maintenance is towing the replacement alert bird to the pad and a crew should be here before they get it parked and cocked (ready to go). We should be back up on alert in about forty-five minutes."

"Excellent work; did SAC give you any static?" I asked.

"No sir. I just told them that there was a landing gear problem and we were replacing the aircraft on alert. They just said, 'Roger; call when you're back up.' I said okay," the sergeant replied.

"Thanks Sergeant. You did great. Everyone did," I said.

"That's what you expect from us isn't it sir?"

I could tell that he was grinning when he said it.

I replied, "Yes it is and you guys never fail me. Thank you."

The sergeant replied, "Yes sir, thank you."

The F-4 pilots were eventually able to get their landing gear down and landed safely. Our alert bird recovered to Little Rock.

Because of their professionalism and expertise, the Arkansas Air National Guard team probably saved a valuable fighter aircraft and possibly two lives.

"Another day, another dollar."...In this case *several million* dollars.

Toward The Evening Sky

WHAT TIME DO YOU HAVE?

Little Rock AFB, AR; Winter 1980

He was one of the nicest people that I had ever met. He was a gray-haired Lieutenant Colonel and was older than our average crew member. He was highly experienced; just quietly went about his job and performed his duties very well. He was one of our KC-135 navigators. He lived in an Arkansas town located between Little Rock and Memphis, which required him to drive quite a few miles to fly a training sortie or to attend a drill weekend. Rather than having to get up very early, so as to be there by 07:30 for drill on Saturday morning, he preferred to go to the Air Force Base on Friday evening. There he would check into the Visiting Officers' Quarters which were located right next to the Officers' Club. He would go to the O Club dining room and have a nice quiet meal, relax for a while in the reading lounge, and then walk back to his room in the VOQ. Back at the VOQ, he would request a wake-up call for Saturday morning and then go to bed early. The next morning after his wake-up call he would go through his usual morning routine and then leave the VOQ in plenty of time to have some breakfast at the 24 hour Flight Line Snack Bar located in the Base Flight Operations Building. He was very well organized and always planned ahead. He evidently was very time conscious also because; he wore three watches.

It was the Friday evening before the scheduled drill weekend and the Lt. Colonel had just checked into the VOQ. He walked next door to the O Club and ordered his favorite meal. A couple of hours later he was back in his room preparing to retire early. It had been a busy week at his civilian job and he was tired and sleepy. He picked up the phone to the front desk and requested his usual wake-up call. Afterwards, he turned out the light and fell right into a sound sleep.

The phone on the little bedside table rang. He finally awakened enough to answer it but the caller had already hung up. It was in the middle of winter so it was still dark outside when he had finished shaving and showering. He slipped into his flight suit, put on his flight boots, his three watches and his winter jacket and left for the Flight Line Snack Bar and a hot breakfast. He was the only one there besides the cook as he ate his bacon and eggs and sipped his coffee. He figured that some other Air Guard members would start coming in soon like they usually did.

He had already finished his food and was on his third cup of coffee and still no one else from the Air Guard had come into the snack bar. They usually had by the time he finished his second cup. Finally, he pulled up the sleeve of his flight suit and looked at his three watches. They indicated that it was 03:35, 03:32, and 03:28.

He then looked at the cook and said; "Excuse me. What time do you have?"

Toward The Evening Sky

NEAR MISS

Pease AFB, NH; Late Fall 1981

The 189th Air Refueling Group had been tasked to join another KC-135 unit in a fighter drag for a squadron of F-15s that was deploying to Europe. (Tankers rendezvous and fly formation with the fighters for a set distance while refueling them one or more times.) The sixteen fighters were staging from their Air Force Base located several hundred miles to the south in Virginia and were to join up with our four KC-135s well offshore over the Atlantic just prior to the first scheduled air refueling. After topping off the fighters' fuel tanks, we were to return to Pease AFB for recovery and debriefing; then return to Little Rock the following day.

The 189th ARG was the only Air National Guard unit participating in the mission. The rest of the crews and planes were regular Air Force. The lead tanker was to be flown by a Lieutenant Colonel and he had been tentatively appointed as the Mission Commander. As such, his crew would be conducting the flight planning and the briefings. After our arrival at Pease, I had been asked if I wished to lead the mission but I declined the offer. I didn't want the extra hassle. I had come for the flying time and to accomplish my air refueling requirements.

We had landed the day before in rain and it had not stopped raining since. It evidently was typical weather for this time of year in the northeast with low visibilities and thick clouds with very high tops. Fortunately, the temperature on the ground was above freezing and forecast to stay there for the duration of the mission. We gathered in the large Wing briefing room and were welcomed to the base by the Wing Commander, a full Colonel. When he had concluded his short remarks, the Flight Leader/Mission Commander took over the briefing. He reviewed the flight lineup and the start, taxi and takeoff procedures. We were to be the number three aircraft. The senior Wing Weather Officer briefed the entire route weather including the planned air refueling tracks out over the Atlantic. The only potential weather problems were the low visibility and rain during our takeoffs, recoveries and landings. Additionally, our climb to altitude was going to be in heavy clouds until just before our level off altitude of flight level 330. Because of this, the flight leader had the lead navigator review the procedures for flying radar trail formation during the climb and initial level off.

Each aircraft would use its radar to close on the aircraft in front of it until established at one mile in trail. It would maintain that mile spacing until the entire flight was clear of the clouds and at cruise altitude before closing up the formation to more normal spacing. There were no questions; so supposedly everyone understood.

It was still raining heavily as we started engines and went through our Before Taxi Checklist. Then we waited for the lead aircraft to call us on the ground control frequency. Precisely on schedule the leader called for our flight to check in. Everyone did so and all aircraft were reported as ready, including our one spare. I waited as the numbers one and two aircraft passed in from of me on the taxiway; and then I pulled in close behind number two. Number four turned onto the taxiway behind us and our four heavy gray tankers lumbered slowly toward the active runway. The water on the taxiways was running off as rapidly as it could; but the engines were kicking up large clouds of it and blowing them over the plane behind. Sometimes it would hit the windscreen and obscure parts of the tanker in front of us in spite of the windshield wipers. Occasionally we could see a mini-tornado of water being sucked up into the intake of an engine on the tanker in front of us. It appeared to be raining even harder as we approached the runway.

I wondered how much effective water depth was on the runway and how severely it would affect our takeoff roll. The Mission Commander in the lead aircraft was also thinking the same thing as he asked the Supervisor of Flying to make a quick trip down the runway to estimate the depth of the water near the centerline of the runway and where it flowed nearer the edges of the concrete. The SOF made the pass down the length of the runway with his pickup truck and called back his estimates. Hopefully they were correct.

While the lead tanker was computing the takeoff penalties, we were doing the same. Our computations showed that we had enough runway length for the conditions, but just barely. The Mission Commander came to the same conclusion. He transmitted the numbers to the Tanker Wing Commander who was in the SOF truck. After a short time considering the factors, the Wing Commander cleared the mission for a "Go".

The number one KC-135 was holding just short of the runway with the other three aircraft close behind him. He changed our flight's radios to the Pease control tower and after checking us in on that frequency called, "Holding short with four." We were just slightly behind schedule because of the last minute takeoff computations. The tower answered with a weather update and cleared the entire flight for takeoff and to maintain MARSA (Military Assumes Responsibility for Separation of Aircraft). The first tanker started moving almost immediately toward the runway as we began completing the checklist. His added engine power blew water over number two and past us. As he straightened out on the runway centerline, the pilot added power and began his takeoff roll. Number two moved into position while counting down the interval before his takeoff roll was to begin. Our checklist was complete as we entered the runway as number two began his takeoff. He completely disappeared ahead of the water kicked up by his engines at full takeoff power.

I lined up on the centerline and waited for our navigator to finish counting down our takeoff interval. As he began his ten second count-down, I began gradually adding power. When he announced "Go" I released the brakes and the tanker slowly began to pick up speed on the flooded runway. The heavy KC-135 seemed to be really struggling as it dragged its landing gear through the water. I wondered if it would be able to accelerate enough to lift the wheels clear of the wet runway. Finally the co-pilot called "S-1". Now it was too late to abort the takeoff if anything went wrong. Through the rain I saw the end of the runway lights approaching rapidly as I waited for his "Rotate" call. It seemed to take forever.

"Rotate!" he called urgently and I hauled back on the yoke. I stopped the nose at the preplanned nose-up angle and the two hundred and ninety five thousand pounds of aluminum and jet fuel at last broke free from the water on the Pease runway. I had begun to have my doubts and I wasn't the only one who did. We were much closer to the end of the runway than the performance charts had indicated that we would be. Oh well, we were finally airborne, the wheels were up and we were accelerating as quickly as possible to the flaps up speed.

We had not seen the number two aircraft again after he had begun his takeoff roll and likely would not until we were on top of the clouds in fifty minutes or so. Our navigator was adjusting the radar intensity and beam angle searching to pick him out of the ground clutter. We were rolled out on the first course and accelerating to climb speed.

"Okay. I've got him; two and one half miles dead ahead," said the Navigator.

"Have you got lead also? We want to make sure we're looking at the right guy," I said.

"Yes sir, I've got lead about two and one half miles in front of two," the Nav replied.

"Okay, call it," I said. He called the rest of the flight with the information that we had radar contact with numbers one and two aircraft and that we were presently in a two and one half mile trail with number two. It was a few more minutes and several miles later when number four tanker called and announced that he was in a three mile radar trail with number three (which was us). He did not give any more information but to say that he was slowly closing (getting closer).

As we were climbing through about twenty-five thousand feet, our climb rate was falling off rapidly. We had moved to about one and one-half miles behind our number two tanker as he was approaching his one mile trail position on our lead tanker.

It was approximately five minutes later and we were just settling into our one mile trail position behind number two. Two had called his position as being one mile behind lead and that checked with our radar. The number four tanker had not given any recent information but suddenly radioed that he was moving into a one mile trail position behind number three. At about that same time we heard a loud roar in the cockpit. The sound came from directly above us. The co-pilot and I looked up.

The co-pilot shouted, "I've got him! He's right on top of us!"

I punched the autopilot off and pushed the nose down. Everything in the plane that wasn't tied down floated toward the ceiling. I don't know how but our vertical stabilizer didn't hit him. The co-pilot said that "four" was so close that he thought that it would. I descended five hundred feet in a slight left turn and as I did, I called the number four tanker.

I told him. "Four; turn immediately ten degrees to your right; slow down twenty knots and get back where you belong in the number four position." I then proceeded to inform him that his navigator was evidently looking at the number two tanker and misidentifying it as our aircraft. I then told him that they had just come less than fifty feet from having a midair collision with us and to not get any closer than two miles again unless they were looking at all three tankers ahead of them on their radar.

His only response was a very sheepish, "Yes sir."

The rest of the mission went as planned. We rendezvoused with the flight of F-15s several hundred miles out to sea and the refuelings went like "clockwork". The weatherman was right. It was still raining when we got back to Pease but the approach and landing were no problem; especially since we were about one hundred and sixty thousand pounds lighter than when we took off.

When he was asked during the mission de-briefing the young aircraft commander of the number four tanker stated that they had not seen us before my radio call.

I replied, "What about on radar? Had your navigator identified all of the other three tankers to you before that?"

His sheepish reply once again was, "No sir."

I continued, "Was not your crew at the same briefing on radar in-trail procedures as the rest of us?"

There came an even weaker, "Yes sir."

I then asked, "Do I need to say any more?"

"No sir," was his quick reply.

"Then you and your crew take the valuable lesson that hopefully you learned today and apply it in the future. It is truly a miracle that we are not all dead," I finished.

"Yes sir. We will sir. Thank you sir," the young pilot said.

"Don't thank me son; thank God that we're all still alive," I suggested.

Toward The Evening Sky

BECAUSE *I'M* AN 0-6

Hickam AFB, HI; Winter 1981

The first segment of the most popular assignment that was tasked from time to time for our unit's KC-135s by the Air National Guard Bureau was a non-stop flight from Little Rock AFB to Hickam AFB, Hawaii. From there, the next part of the task was to make several flights while staging out of Hickam Air Force Base to provide a tanker for the Hawaii Air National Guard's F-4 fighters. To maintain combat ready status, fighter pilots were required to fly a certain number of air refueling sorties on a recurring basis. Our tanker's flights were closely coordinated with their schedule in order to refuel as many fighters as possible during each sortie.

These particular trips were much sought after for several reasons. They provided many opportunities for training our crews and to accomplish our recurring requirements. Of course there was the extended over water flying which provided much more realistic training for the Navigators than our regular Gulf of Mexico over water navigation training flights that took off from, and landed back at Little Rock Air Force Base. Consequently we sometimes took an augmented crew so as to share the realistic training. And of course the fact that the flights were staging out of Hawaii for several days was not a factor in the appeal of these flights; especially in the winter months. I usually made it a practice to not take advantage of my rank but what the heck; I needed to accomplish my flight requirements too. In any case, I *somehow* ended up as the Aircraft Commander/Instructor Pilot on this particular one.

It was a wonderful trip from the very beginning. For one of the few times in my years of flying, we enjoyed a tailwind while flying westbound. And this one lasted most of the way from Arkansas to Hawaii. (For non-pilot readers this is an extremely rare occurrence because prevailing winds at higher altitudes are predominately from the West to East.) The flight went off without a hitch and we landed in Hawaii in record time. We arrived early enough for a nice dinner after checking in at the Visitor's Quarters on the Air Force Base.

The next day, my crew and I reported to the briefing room at the Air National Guard Base for the flight briefings with the fighter pilots. It was an enjoyable experience. One of my pilot training classmates was a full Colonel and F-4 pilot in the unit. The Phantom pilots were easy-going and friendly and my crew enjoyed their time at the fighter unit (especially the free donuts) but with the joint briefing over, we headed for our big gray heavy KC-135 tanker.

The Boeing was almost full of fuel because of the multiple fighters to which we were scheduled to pass gas that day. I was glad that the runway was over twelve thousand feet long. I remembered watching the KC-135 tankers struggle into the air from this same runway sixteen years ago when I was flying an F-4C headed to Vietnam. At that time I never envisioned myself doing the same thing.

It was hot and once again we seemed to roll forever before the co-pilot called, "Rotate". I did and the "KC" finally lifted off the runway. As soon as we had enough speed so we wouldn't stall and fall out of the sky, I started the close-in right turn to avoid Waikiki Beach and the city. Now we were in the race to get the flaps up before the water boost to the engines ran out. (When the water quit, the KC-135 immediately lost about twelve thousand pounds of badly needed thrust.) If the flaps were not yet all the way up by then, the Stratotanker was a real hand-full. (Recall that the six hundred and seventy gallons of water only lasted for two and one-half minutes.)

We won the race with the water and our flaps were up. I rolled out on course and held the plane level for the few minutes it would take us to accelerate to our climb speed of two hundred and eighty. Of course by now we had two F-4 Phantoms already flying on each wing; Smartasses! Clearly I remembered doing the same thing sixteen years before; sitting on my tanker's wing with my throttles pulled way back while the big gray beast struggled to accelerate to climb speed. Somehow it had seemed different then.

We finally reached climb speed and started up toward the refueling altitude. The Phantoms loosened their formation a little and a couple of the fighter pilots unhooked their oxygen masks to relax. My boom operator brought me a cup of coffee. I held it up to my cockpit window as if to offer some to the F-4 pilot on my left. Although he knew that I was a full Colonel, he still gave me the universal one-fingered salute. (Can you believe that? Of course you can.)

After quite a few more minutes we leveled off and proceeded toward the designated refueling area several hundred miles to the west and north of Oahu. The first flight cycled through and each pilot practiced several hookups and disconnects. A lot of these guys were also airline pilots in their day jobs and they were good sticks. The second flight of Phantoms checked in with us as we bid "adieu" to the first. We refueled four flights that day with the rest of the refuelings going as smoothly as the first.

The next two days were pretty much the same except we had fewer receivers and were able to takeoff with less fuel. Therefore we were much lighter than the first day and our takeoffs were not nearly as exciting. All of the remaining F-4 pilots completed their refueling requirements and it was mission accomplished. Now pretty much all that remained was a nice final evening in Hawaii sharing a good meal with my crew and then the flight back to Little Rock tomorrow.

Toward The Evening Sky

The phone rang in my room just as I got out of the shower. I presumed it was someone from my crew calling to finalize the plans for dinner. I lifted the receiver and just said, "Hello."

A very brusque sounding voice answered me with, "Are you the pilot of the KC-135 going to Little Rock AFB tomorrow morning?"

"Yes I am," I answered while wondering what this was all about.

The voice continued, *"I am Colonel A_____ and I want to go with you."* Again he sounded very stern and authoritative.

"Well Colonel, I believe that we have some seats available. You will need to check-in with the Aerial Port Squadron at the flight line to confirm that there *is* a seat available and then take your bags to them for manifesting tomorrow morning," I politely replied although I was getting a little tired of his abrupt manner.

"What are you going to be doing?" he said in a very demanding tone.

"When?" I replied.

"Now, and tomorrow morning of course," he said.

I suddenly realized where he was heading with this conversation. He was obviously expecting me or someone from my crew to take care of listing him for the flight and tote his luggage for him.

I was struggling with my temper as I answered, "Well right now I'm getting ready to go to dinner and tomorrow morning I'm going to be preparing for the flight. *Why do you ask?"*

His pompous reply came flying back; *"Because I'm an O-6!"* (Full Colonel)

At that I "lost it" and answered him rather forcefully; "Well so am I you egotistical *s___*, and if you want to ride with me tomorrow then *do what I told you!"* There was a long silence and then he slammed down the phone.

I don't know how he got back to the mainland, but he didn't show up for my flight. I had been disappointed in the arrogant O-6 and his attempted bullying; but glad that I was the one he tried to bully.

Jerry W. Cook

FALCON 10

Flight Safety Training, Moonachie, NJ; January 1982

Although I was the Commander of the 189th Air Refueling Group, I was a part timer. Foolishly enough, I was still hoping to be recalled from my third furlough back to Pan Am so I could resume my big time airline career. In the interim I needed a more stable income than occasional active duty days earned while pulling alert. The alert duties were spread among all of the flight crews in the 189th and therefore came too infrequently to provide any semblance of a steady income.

A close businessman friend of mine with whom I had partnered in a Beechcraft Bonanza a few years before had purchased a fixed base operation at the Little Rock airport. He was adding some Falcon 10 corporate aircraft to his charter fleet. He contacted me and asked if I would like to join his business as the Director of Flight Operations. He was aware of my Air Guard commitments and he assured me that they would not be a problem. I readily accepted his offer and since I had never flown a Falcon 10 aircraft I went to the Flight Safety International Falcon training facility near the Teterboro airport in New Jersey. There I would spend about two weeks training in the little French-built jet and then receive a flight check in the simulator. The check ride would qualify me for a type rating in the aircraft. With that rating I would then become qualified to fly as a captain on the plane.

One of the things that stand out in my mind about those two weeks was the bitter cold. Consequently this old southern boy did not spend much time outside. Another thing that was impressive was the aircraft itself. Dassault Aviation, the French manufacturer of the plane, had built jet fighters for years. Probably the most well-known is the Mirage. You may remember from an earlier story that it was a Mirage taking pictures that flashed across the Beirut airport that day in in 1968. Most of the Dassault aircraft are beautiful machines. In my eyes the Falcon 10 may have been an exception because it seems a little short for its girth. However, beneath its aluminum exterior it is gorgeous. It is exceptionally well-built and it shares some similar major system features with its jet fighter brethren. It has dual, three thousand pound per square inch hydraulic systems for the flight controls, landing gear and various other components. This is a very complex system for a small jet. I was told that its aileron actuators are the same as on some of the company's fighters. Its swept wing design with its leading edge devices allowed the aircraft to be both very fast and very slow. It had fast speeds in climb, cruise and descent; then slow speeds for landing; a great combination. The airframe structure was built like a tank; not literally of course, but in comparison to some other manufacturers it seemed like it. In fact, the airframe had no "life-limited" parts; very unusual. Again this probably stemmed from Dassault's long history of building sturdy jet fighters.

The training at Flight Safety was thorough and somewhat intense because of its relatively short length. The first days were spent in the classroom studying the various systems and aircraft performance. The last part of the training was some cockpit mockup sessions and then several simulator training periods leading up to the final ride. This last "flight" was usually with a Flight Safety Instructor who was also a designated flight examiner for the Federal Aviation Administration. Of course the examiner could not be one of the simulator instructors who had trained you.

The training course had gone well and I had developed a friendship with another class member named Don. He had also been an F-4 pilot in the Air Force so we had a lot in common. He had been hired to fly for a company out of Omaha, Nebraska that had recently purchased a Falcon 10. We had teamed up when it was time to choose our sim partner. The drill for the simulator rides was for one pilot to fly the left seat for the first two hours with the partner as the co-pilot. Then the roles were reversed for the second two hours. There was usually about a fifteen minute break between the two sessions. I don't remember how many training sessions there were in the course but pilots would normally alternate in which seat they started each session. The simulator training went well and if the actual jet flew anything like the simulator, it was going to be fun to fly. It has been my experience that simulators are usually harder to fly than the airplane they are designed to simulate. Neither Don nor I were having any difficulties "flying" the simulator and we rapidly progressed to the final day. It was checkride time.

When we reported to the briefing room there were two gentlemen sitting there talking. One of them stood up and introduced himself as our examiner for this check ride. He wore the usual Flight Safety attire. He then introduced the other person. I had already spotted his name tag with the FAA symbol on it. He was there to observe our examiner as he administered our type checks. Great…it immediately brought back memories of the two sorry bastards who had ganged up on me back at Pan Am in San Francisco some fifteen years before. "Oh well," I thought. "They can't possibly be as bad as those guys." Don and I tossed a coin to see who would be checked first. The toss determined that it would be him. I felt like I had lost the toss because I would have preferred to "fly" first and get it over with.

We finally finished the oral part of our check ride which involved answering a multitude of questions about the Falcon 10 with some on procedures and Federal Aviation Regulations. It had seemed to me that our examiner had gone far past the time that our simulator period was supposed to begin. When we finally got into the simulator, it was already well into the first two hour time slot. Consequently during most of Don's check the examiner was constantly pushing us to hurry. That certainly did not contribute to the realism of the flight and it definitely did not give us time as a crew to properly evaluate the situations that he was constantly throwing our way.

In spite of this my sim partner was doing great. He had finished everything except for his last approach which was a raw data ILS (without the use of the flight director's computer, a more difficult task). Our flight examiner was also acting as the approach controller and was giving us radar vectors around the ILS pattern at Teterboro. We were on the downwind leg and Don called for the approach flaps. They would not lower. I quickly pulled out the checklist and Don told me to ask our "controller" for an extended downwind while we addressed the flap problem.

Our controller/examiner said, "No. We don't have time. Just assume that your flaps have failed and you can't get them back. Turn left now to 280 degrees for your base leg."

Don opened his speed brakes and called, "Gear down." I repeated his order and lowered the landing gear handle.

He continued, "Ask him for another mile or so on the downwind leg while we slow down."

"No, go ahead and start your turn now," said the examiner before I had a chance to ask.

Don started his left turn. He already had his throttles in idle and the Falcon was still fast. The examiner then gave us a left turn to 235 degrees and cleared us for the ILS. Just as Don rolled out on a 235 heading the ILS course indicator began to move quickly.

I called, "Course alive."

Don "Rogered" and started his turn to intercept. We were still fast and the needle was moving rapidly toward the center. Don was turning with as much bank as was legal. We overshot the final approach course so he continued the turn to head back toward the course intercept. He still had the speed brakes out and the throttles in idle. We were slowing very gradually. Don overshot slightly to the left of the needle but immediately corrected back to the course line.

He did a good raw data ILS from that point although we were still fast as we passed over the final approach fix. At about five hundred feet he lowered the speed brakes and adjusted the throttles to hold the proper speed for a no flap approach and landing. I had been making the required instrument callouts and was now looking for the runway. I spotted the runway approach lights dead ahead and called them out. I then saw the runway and called it in sight.

Don announced, "Runway in sight," and then switched from instruments to visual for the landing. He touched down right on the centerline and rolled to the end of the runway.

The examiner at that point put the simulator on "freeze" and said, "Let's take a break and have a quick debrief."

Don and I looked at each other and he shook his head. I grinned at him and said, "Nice job."

I grabbed a cup of coffee and sat down with the other three men. The instructor was debriefing Don and had covered everything quickly down to the final ILS. I was pretty relaxed because I felt that Don had done a good job of getting the plane down after being given a very difficult situation.

"Don, I'm going to have to fail you because of that last ILS," the examiner stated. Don looked stunned but didn't say a word.

I almost spilled my coffee as I exclaimed, "What? What about that last ILS?"

The flight examiner glared at me across the table and said, "Well, he overshot the final approach course twice and was fast during almost the whole approach."

I couldn't believe my ears and said, "*Right; and just whose fault was that?*"

The examiner looked startled as I continued; "Don asked twice to extend our downwind after you failed his flaps. You refused and then you turned us in a tighter pattern than even a normal ILS should be."

I continued, "In the real world we would not have asked but instead *told* you that we were continuing straight ahead until we had our new situation stabilized and then we would have insisted on and flown an extended final approach. *You* are the one who screwed things up by placing us in a time crunch in the first place. If anyone failed his check ride, it was you."

I looked straight at the FAA Examiner and said, "Isn't that right?"

Without even looking up from his coffee cup he quietly replied, "Sounds about right to me."

Our flushed flight examiner finally stammered out something to the effect that, "I hadn't thought of it that way," and "Maybe you're right." He then immediately proceeded to un-fail Don.

Now; I had to go and take my check ride with this guy. Fortunately it went well. After I had been debriefed and the other two had left, Don shook my hand and said, "I guess I would have just sat there and not said anything while he busted me."

I replied, "That's because you weren't with me at Pan Am in San Francisco."

He looked a little confused and said, "What does that mean?"

I laughed and answered, "Never mind; you would have had to be there to believe it."

The next time I went to Flight Safety Teterboro, I didn't see our flight examiner on their instructor picture board so I asked about him.

They just said, "He's not with us anymore." I guess he did fail *his* check ride.

Jerry W. Cook

THAT DIDN'T HAPPEN

Omaha to Little Rock, AR; 1983

Johnny, one of our pilots and I had been on a day trip from Little Rock to Omaha, Nebraska in a Falcon 10. We were heading back toward Pine Bluff, Arkansas to drop off some passengers before flying back to Little Rock. We had just passed central Missouri southbound and were cruising at flight level 330. We had been switched from the Kansas City Air Route Traffic Control Center to Memphis ARTCC just a few minutes before. It always seemed like we were almost home when switching to the Memphis Center because it included Little Rock and most of Arkansas in its area.

Johnny had flown the plane to Omaha so I was flying in the left seat on the return flight. We were about one hundred and fifty miles out of Little Rock and sixty miles or so from beginning our descent into Pine Bluff, our destination. The Master Caution Light suddenly illuminated followed immediately by an amber generator failure light on the warning panel. Johnny called out the failure and confirmed that the generator switch had tripped. I asked for the abnormal checklist and reached up to "load shed" the electrical system. This brought our total amperage load below the maximum that one generator could support.

Johnny read the checklist and we followed the steps. The generator was not re-settable. No problem; we turned off some more unnecessary electrical equipment and continued our flight. About two minutes later the Master Caution Light came on again accompanied by the other generator fail light. It reminded me of a simulator training session. Johnny got the checklist again and he read the procedure aloud as we followed its directions. We could not get a generator to reset. We were now batteries only and we continued electrical "load-shedding" down to bare essentials. The batteries were supposed to last about thirty minutes in this condition. We were close enough now to Little Rock so that should have been just enough time. I asked Johnny to inform Memphis Center of our situation and ask for a descent into Little Rock instead of Pine Bluff. Johnny pushed the microphone button for our remaining radio and it would not transmit. He tried again to no avail.

The Memphis controller heard the microphone clicking and called us; "Falcon 837F, if you are trying to call Memphis, click your 'mic' twice," Johnny clicked twice.

"If you are requesting descent, please click twice," the controller said. Johnny did so.

"Are you having any other problems besides your radio?" Memphis asked. Johnny clicked twice.

"Do you wish to change your destination to Little Rock?" the controller asked. (This guy was sharp.) Johnny immediately clicked twice.

"Roger Falcon 837F; you are now cleared direct to Little Rock Adams Field. Descent is at your discretion. I will tell them you're headed their way. Fire and rescue will be standing by."

I had already pushed the power up to maximum cruise speed to get to Little Rock as soon as possible. Now I lowered the nose and accelerated to remain just below the maximum airspeed in descent. Memphis Center called and asked us to click the mic twice if we had received our clearance. Johnny tried to click again but the radio was completely dead. The voltages on both batteries had dropped drastically so I asked Johnny to turn them off with the hope of regaining enough electrical power to lower our landing gear normally without having to free-fall it. I couldn't believe how soon the batteries had lost charge. It must have been less than fifteen minutes with just minimal electrical equipment on.

It started getting warmer in the plane. Our air conditioning controls and gasper fans were now inoperative and, as we descended to warmer altitudes, the temperature in the cabin was climbing. I quickly briefed the passengers about our electrical situation, our change of destination and why the cabin was warm. I reassured them that they were not in danger (I didn't think that they were at the time.) but said that we couldn't do much about the temperature.

As we descended, Johnny re-read the Complete Electrical Failure procedure with me and we reviewed what equipment would be operational for landing. We reset the airspeed reminder indices for a no-flap landing (faster than normal) in accordance with the checklist's instructions. I leveled off at two thousand feet and Johnny turned on the battery switches in an attempt to lower the landing gear with the normal gear handle; nothing. The batteries were completely dead. I slowed to 190 knots and we lowered the landing gear using the emergency free-fall procedure. The control yoke was very heavy because I had trimmed the stabilizer for our high speed in the descent (nose down trim). Since the normal and the emergency trim were both electric, they were both inoperative. As we slowed toward our newly computed no-flap final approach speed, I instructed Johnny to operate the throttles for me because the nose was so heavy that I decided to use both hands to hold it up.

Then I told him, "Don't let the airspeed drop below bug plus ten." Fortunately the weather was clear as a bell as I lined up for a long straight-in final to runway 22. We had noted from smoke on the ground during descent that the wind was from the southwest.

Johnny was keeping the airspeed ten knots faster than the computed approach speed called for by the emergency procedure. We could see that the runway was clear and that the emergency equipment was standing by for our landing. Just as we approached about 500 feet above the ground the airspeed began to bleed off. The nose started down and I pulled the yoke further back to stop it. The yoke hit its backstop with a thunk. The nose of the Falcon stopped dropping but it was too low.

I called; *"Airspeed!"* and Johnny pushed the throttles up to regain the few knots we had lost. The nose was pushed further down by the added engine thrust. The Falcon was now pointing toward the far bank of the Arkansas River. The runway overrun began several hundred yards beyond that. Things weren't looking very good for us. The airspeed was increasing and as it did the Falcon's nose finally began to rise. I kept the yoke pulled to its backstop. As we got our airspeed back up to bug plus 15 the nose raised still more until the descent stopped. Gradually we began a slight climb as we flew over the river. I held the yoke near the backstop until we had climbed back to about two hundred feet.

"Hold bug plus 25, small corrections," I instructed Johnny.

I eased off the aft yoke position slightly and then descended slowly until we were over the runway threshold. I eased off a little more of the back pressure and we descended toward the concrete. At ten feet I pulled back the yoke and it hit the backstop just as we touched down. It was a firm landing but I was just proud to be there. Johnny looked at me as we rolled toward the far end of the runway.

Sweat was pouring off his forehead as he said; "No sweat in a Falcon jet; right?"

The passengers were still complaining about the heat as we taxied behind the "follow me" truck to the ramp. We got another Falcon 10 ready and took off for Pine Bluff about forty-five minutes later. That plane's cabin was cooler and they were all happy again.

When we landed back at Little Rock, Johnny and I began trying to figure out why we had almost landed in the Arkansas River after accomplishing the emergency checklist. We reviewed it again and determined that we had followed it to the letter. Of course it was obvious that what had almost killed us was that our airspeed was too slow; "But why?" We had followed the checklist's instructions for setting the airspeed bug precisely. But had we? The correct answer suddenly hit me and then I got angry. I was angry at myself for not thinking of it; but even angrier at Flight Safety. What the Flight Safety Emergency Checklist had failed to even mention was that with a Complete Electrical Failure, possibly your biggest issue is your jammed stabilizer.

There was an entirely different procedure for that emergency. That procedure included a special method for determining approach and landing speeds. If we had used that method, we would have been flying our final approach and landing at higher and safer speeds than the "Complete Electrical Failure" checklist numbers.

Checklists are intended to assist pilots in operating their aircraft safely, especially in Abnormal and Emergency conditions. One could say that either I or Johnny should have thought about the Jammed Stabilizer checklist during the "heat of battle". (I'm certain that the ones responsible for the checklist would say exactly that.) But…why should we have had to? With a complete electrical failure a jammed stabilizer is one of the most important aspects of it. So why wasn't it included in the complete electrical failure procedure or at the least referred to?

A few months later Johnny went to Falcon 10 Recurrent at Flight Safety Teterboro. While he was there he related our incident in the classroom. Then he asked them why they thought we almost crashed. Not one of the Falcon 10 pilots in the class, or the instructor for that matter, thought about the jammed stabilizer. (And that was while they were sitting in an air-conditioned classroom; not in a 120 degree cockpit trying to deal with an emergency situation.) Until then it had always been stated in Falcon 10 electrical system classes that there had never been a complete electrical failure in a Falcon 10. They couldn't make that statement anymore.

A couple of months later I went to Teterboro for my recurrent training. The ground school instructor had heard about our complete electrical failure and he had me relate it to the class of Falcon 10 pilots. After I had done so, I asked the other pilots if they knew why we were too slow and almost crashed the aircraft in the Arkansas River. Not one of them came up with the jammed stabilizer; again including that instructor. He obviously hadn't heard that part. That was thirty years ago in 1983. I wonder if they've changed the checklist *yet*.

Postscript #1: After I related my complete electrical failure incident to the class, the instructor told us to take a ten minute break. When we returned to the classroom, the instructor was talking to a man wearing Flight Safety instructor attire. As I started to walk past them, the instructor stopped me and introduced me to the individual. Then he asked me to relate my electrical failure incident to the man. I did so as he listened intently.

After I finished he looked at me, shook his head negatively and said, "That didn't happen." I looked at my surprised instructor and then back at the man.

Then I leaned forward and seriously invaded his personal space. I replied, "I don't know who in the Hell you are, but I do know that you are not big enough to stand there and call me a liar." The guy didn't say a word but he quickly left the room. My instructor's face was now bright red and he started to apologize.

I stopped him and said, "You didn't do anything to apologize for; but who is that guy?"

He answered, "He's an instructor in the maintenance ground school. I had no idea he was going to do anything like that."

"Well, you might want to tell him to avoid me while I'm here," I stated.

The instructor nodded vigorously and said, "Yes sir, I will. But I doubt that it will be necessary."

Postscript #2: In 1986 I retired from the Air National Guard, changed civilian jobs and began flying a Falcon 10 out of Monterey, California. Instead of Flight Safety Teterboro, I attended the Falcon 10 recurrent course at Simuflite near the Dallas Fort Worth airport. Because of a late schedule change, I did not have a Sim partner for one session so my instructor also served as my co-pilot. Harry was a very good instructor, a great guy and a very experienced pilot.

When we had finished all of the training for that session he said, "We've still got a few minutes before our sim time is up. Is there anything else you want to do before we pull the plug?"

I replied, "Yes sir there is. I want you to fly and I'm going to give you a situation."

"Oh, okay," he smiled broadly as he said it. I turned the controls over to him and had him climb to ten thousand feet and accelerate to 350 knots. He did so and, when he had the stabilizer trimmed, I reached up and turned off both batteries and both generators.

"You have just suffered a complete electrical failure and nothing is resettable," I said as I finished turning them off.

I continued, "The Dallas weather is clear and sixty with calm winds. You are cleared to land on any runway at Love Field."

He replied "Okay," and pulled the throttles back while calling for the Complete Electrical Failure checklist. I turned to the procedure and read it as we accomplished all of the items. He proceeded toward Love Field. We could see it in the distance nearly straight ahead. As he slowed the aircraft so we could lower the landing gear manually, he had to hold the yoke further and further aft. While he was yawing the plane back and forth to lock the main landing gear down, he was working hard to hold the nose up. Although the simulator air conditioner was working just fine, he was sweating. Once the landing gear was down, he reduced the throttles to achieve the computed approach speed in accordance with the complete electrical failure checklist. The yoke moved further and further back. I asked him if he wanted me to operate the throttles for him so he could use both hands on the control yoke.

He said, "No thanks, I'll do it." He had lined up nicely for Love Field's Runway 13L. I watched him further reduce the engines' power to slow toward the computed speed. His left arm that was holding back the control yoke was quivering with the effort. We were about five hundred feet above the ground. As our speed approached the indices that we had set, the nose started to drop. I heard the control yoke hit its aft limit. The instructor immediately pushed the throttles forward and that pushed the nose down still further. The simulator was still accelerating when it crashed into the simulated ground. It lurched violently on its hydraulic legs and all sorts of terrible noises ensued for a few moments; then; quiet. The simulator slowly settled down into its resting position.

The astonished instructor looked at me and said, "What in the heck just happened?"

I replied, "I'll show you in the briefing room. Let's get out of this thing."

"Amen," he said.

As we sat down in the briefing room he said, "Okay tell me. What just happened?"

I didn't say anything but handed him the Jammed Stabilizer checklist with its approach and landing speed computation procedure.

As the revelation struck he just shook his head slowly and said, "I never thought of that." He was visibly upset with himself.

I replied, "If it makes you feel any better; no one else has either." Two days later I was back at my apartment in Monterey when I received a phone call from the Simuflite instructor.

He said, "Jerry, we've made a change to our Emergency Checklist and I'm Fed-Exing it to you today. It adds a Complete Electrical Failure checklist bold face note that instructs the pilots to utilize the Jammed Stabilizer Procedure to set the approach and landing speeds."

I thanked him and he said, "No sir, thank you."

I hung up the phone and thought, "Three years with no improvement to an inadequate checklist versus two days and a change." It was a very interesting difference in attitudes.

Jerry W. Cook

JUST TO MAKE SURE

Little Rock Adams Field, AR; 1983

To retain their authorization to fly charters, pilots are required to take a FAR Part 135 Check Ride every six months. Part 135 is the section of the Federal Aviation Regulations pertaining to Charter Operations. It was time for my six month flight check in the Falcon 10.

Just a few weeks prior, the FAA had instituted a new procedure in the Falcon 10 for checking the flaps. It required lowering the flaps one increment at a time until they were in the full down position. Then, you were to place the flap handle in the full up position. The idea was to see if the leading edge slats and trailing edge flaps retracted in the proper sequence. Only after all of this "monkey motion" were the flaps to then be placed in the takeoff position. The new rule evidently was in response to a Falcon 10 incident that occurred after takeoff when the leading edge slats came up prior to the flaps fully retracting. If that happened, the nose of the aircraft would pitch down; not a good thing.

When I had received the new flap procedure, I immediately thought it was ridiculous. In my opinion it not only did not prove a thing but it increased the chances of such a failure and of forgetting to set the flaps in the proper position for takeoff.

First: Just because the flap system worked properly during the new flap check procedure, this didn't prove that it would work properly after takeoff. It only proved that it worked that time.

Second: Cycling the flaps an extra time did exactly that; it added another cycle on the flap system and that increased the chances that it would fail sooner.

Third: Adding all of the motions of moving the flap handle so many times could cause the unintentional exclusion of the most important one…to the takeoff setting.

I know that the third one is true because, after trying the new procedure for a few flights, I had observed the final flap setting was missed twice by my co-pilots. On one of them I also missed the omission and it was caught by the takeoff configuration warning horn. I cautioned my pilots about using the procedure. I told them that, if the flaps worked properly on the prior flight, that proved just as much as the new procedure and it didn't wear the damn flaps out.

My co-pilot and I finished the oral exam which always preceded the check flight. The examiner had even asked me to relate the new flap check procedure to him. I did so and managed to keep my low opinion of the rule to myself, for the time being. Our Falcon 10 sat outside the FAA facility and, as the three of us walked toward it, I kept thinking about the absurd new procedure. The examiner watched and listened closely as we went through our checklists and started the engines. We received our IFR clearance and taxi instructions. As we taxied and arrived at the item "Flaps" on the checklist, I said to the check pilot, "Although I think it's absurd, we're going to do the new flap check procedure because you are sitting there watching."

He was surprised to say the least and replied, "Does that mean you're not going to do it when I'm not watching?"

I looked at him and repeated, "We're going to do the new flap check procedure because you are sitting there watching." He said nothing in return but wrote something on his notepad. My co-pilot was looking uneasy as I instructed him to check the flaps.

After he had done so I said, "As an added briefing item, after takeoff and when we are safely airborne with the landing gear up, I am going to have you lower the landing gear again to the down and locked position. Then I'll call for you to raise them again."

The surprised FAA flight examiner took the bait. He said, "Why are you going to do that?"

I looked back at him and said, "Just to make sure that they will work properly later when we get ready to land."

"That won't prove they will work later," he said sarcastically.

I answered back to him with the same sarcasm; "Exactly; just like the FAA's new procedure for the flaps and slats."

He glared at me for a moment before he finally said, "Okay, you've made your point." Then he wrote again on his notepad.

I looked back at the co-pilot and said, "Okay, cancel the gear recycling after takeoff."

Amazingly enough I passed my check ride. A few months later, the FAA canceled the ridiculous procedure.

Postscript: While on the subject of charter flights; for some reason that eludes me, the FAA's flight rules are stricter when a pilot is flying a passenger who is paying for the trip as a charter than if the pilot is flying a passenger who owns the plane. For instance, the same exact trip in the same exact plane with the same exact pilot when flying as a charter requires a longer runway. Additionally, that pilot requires more flight checks and more rest than if he or she were flying the plane's owner. In fact, suppose the owner sells the plane to a charter company and his pilot now works for them. The former owner then charters his former plane with his former pilot. According to the FAA, the pilot now requires a longer runway, more flight checks and more rest; same pilot, same passenger, same airplane.

"Some things I see and understand; other things I just see."

Jerry W. Cook

OH S___!

Eglin AFB, FL; Late 1983

Major General "Starbuck" Wassell (his nickname was also promoted from just Buck when he got his first star) looked much younger than his age. He was trim, slim and his hair was still dark at fifty. He ran several miles every week and he looked about thirty-five. And like me, he loved flying fighters. As the Commander of the Arkansas Air National Guard, he could fly whatever aircraft the state possessed and consequently had checked out in the F-4. However, because he was a general officer and it was a two-seated fighter, Air Force regulations required him to fly with an instructor with him in the plane.

The general had gone to Eglin AFB, Florida in an F-4 for a meeting of some sort. The next morning the other pilot had already gone out to the fighter to preflight it. General Wassell was inside Base Operations and had checked the weather in Fort Smith for their return flight. He finished filing his flight plan and was preparing to leave the building for the aircraft. He had been carrying his G suit draped over his shoulder. Just before he got to the door leading out to the aircraft parking ramp he stopped, took his G suit off his shoulder and was putting it on. He zipped it up at the waist first and then bent over to zip the legs.

A young lieutenant who was walking across the room nearby evidently thought that he knew the other "young" pilot bent over facing the other way. He walked up behind him and snapped his fingers across the bent pilot's butt and cheerfully said, "Good morning." General Wassell straightened up and turned around to face the young man.

When the lieutenant saw the two stars on each shoulder he hit a stiff brace, snapped a very shaky salute and said, "*Oh S___!*" (Probably the most common exclamation in aviation)

General Wassell smiled at the young man, returned his salute and said, "Good morning lieutenant." The red-faced officer dropped his salute and stood at his stiff position of attention.

The general then said, "You're dismissed. Have a nice day."

Stammering, "Yes sir, thank you sir," the young pilot spun on his heels and took off down the hall as fast as he could walk.

General Wassell told me that it was so funny that he couldn't get angry. He said he had almost laughed when he saw the lieutenant's face and heard his exclamation, but managed to wait until he was outside and walking to the plane. I guess that was one of the problems of looking so young. Unfortunately I have never had that problem.

PHANTOMS AGAIN

Little Rock AFB, AR; December 1983

It was early during Saturday morning drill period when my secretary came into my office. "Colonel Cook, General Wassell wants to see you in his office right away," she said.

"Did he say what it was about?" I asked.

"No sir he didn't," she replied. I hadn't thought that he would, but figured it was worth a try. Anytime a General wants to see you right away, it is not necessarily a good thing. Because I was scheduled to fly later that day, I was already in my flight suit but decided not to change because of the "right away" instructions. I headed for the General's office. As I entered the headquarters building, I nodded to the Senior Master Sergeant whose desk was right outside the General's office door.

I said in a low voice, "Do you know why he wants to see me?"

The Sergeant replied, "Sorry sir, I can't say, but he said to send you right in as soon as you arrived."

I knocked on the open door and the General said, "Come in Colonel," when he saw me. I entered and saluted. He returned my salute but did not ask me to sit or to relax from my position of attention.

I thought, "Oh crap. Who at SAC did I piss off now?"

Finally he spoke, "You going to enjoy wearing a G suit over that flight suit again?"

I tried not to smile as I said, "Sir?"

He said "Relax and sit down Jer," and handed me a piece of paper. It was from Air National Guard Headquarters and was an order. It was authorizing me to fly F-4 Phantoms at the 188th Tactical Fighter Group in Fort Smith, Arkansas. Additionally, I was authorized to continue flying the KC-135 with the 189th. I was to be dual qualified. I couldn't believe my good fortune.

The General grinned and said, "You are to be the Operations Officer for the state and as such, you will be authorized to fly both aircraft. Think you want to do that?

"Absolutely General, but I didn't expect that they would approve me to fly both types," I said.

He replied, "It is a little unusual but I told them that I wanted you to do so for a while. With a new Commander being assigned for the 189th, I thought it would be good for you to keep flying with them for the transition. After a few months you can drop the tanker."

"Yes sir. Thank you sir," was all I could think of to say.

"You're welcome Jer. You deserve to have a little fun after successfully taking the 189th through two SAC ORIs," he replied with a smile;

"Now get out of here. I've got work to do." I stopped in front of the Senior Master Sergeant's desk and frowned down at him.

He grinned as he said, "Sorry sir. I knew, but he told me not to tell you."

I added, "And he seriously outranks me too, right?"

"Yes sir, there's that too. Congratulations Colonel. Do you want me to show you your new office?" he said as he stood up and stuck out his hand. I was one happy camper.

Postscript #1: Not many months before this great news for me, the 189th had indeed gone through another Strategic Air Command Operational Readiness Inspection. I had not planned or wanted to still be the Commander through another of these rather stressful extended assessments by a SAC Inspector General team. However, once again the 189th proved to SAC that we could perform our wartime mission with no problem. And this time our overall score on the inspection was even higher than the prior one. The 189th was a wonderful and extremely capable organization and I was proud to be their Commander. I have many fond memories of the four years that I served in that position.

Postscript #2: Credit is due. In an Air National Guard Unit there is a cadre of full-timers who keep the organization running smoothly when the part-timers, like me, are not there (which is most of the time). Some might think that this arrangement would not work very well, but it was a fact that Air Guard units stacked up quite well against regular Air Force units when in competition against them. It is also a fact that in my day in the Air Guard, we accomplished it on a lot less money than the regular units. I was told that the figure was something like two thirds to three fourths as much. Consequently the Air Force basically got the same bang but for fewer bucks. These kinds of performances could never be achieved without the above mentioned full-timers. There were many of them that I owe my gratitude for my successful tour of duty as the 189th Commander.

However there was a particular individual who was responsible for all of the part-timers and the continued operation of the unit between drill periods. During the majority of the time he was my liaison not only to them, but to the Air National Guard Bureau. His in-depth knowledge of how things functioned up and down both the Military Chain of Command and the Air Guard Civil Service organization was vital to me as a part-time Commander.

He was also the first individual whom I had talked to in the Arkansas Air National Guard back in November of 1969. He was Colonel Bob Byrd. Thank you Bob. Well done.

Toward The Evening Sky

CRUISIN' ON 40

Interstate I-40; Arkansas: January 11, 1984

I was excited. I could remember feeling the same way some twenty-one years prior while I was a Captain in the United States Air Force. It was when I had received my assignment to fly F-4s. This morning I had gotten up at my home in North Little Rock at three-thirty a.m. so as to be on I-40 by four-thirty. I was well past the halfway point to Fort Smith and my shark-gray Camaro Z-28 was on cruise control. My portable CB radio was tuned to the truckers' channel as I listened to them for any "Smokey" information. Because of my present cruise speed, that knowledge might prove useful.

I was approaching Clarksville, Arkansas about five forty-five a.m. and I had just passed an eighteen wheeler when my CB came alive; "Little gray 'Z' west-bound with the hammer down at mile marker sixty-three; what kinda license plate is that you're sportin' this fine mornin', 10-4?"

I picked up my mic and said, "Arkansas Air National Guard."

"Oh okay. Where you goin' in such a hurry this mornin'? You pretty much flyin' low, 10-4?" he said.

"Well actually, I'm heading over to Fort Smith; to *fly*," I answered.

He laughed at that and said, "You getting a little practice on the way huh?"

I said, "Well, fortunately I haven't gotten this thing airborne yet."

"10-4; well, what you goin' there to fly today?" he continued.

"F-4," I replied.

"F-4; that one of them fast 'smokers' I see sometimes when I pass north of Fort Smith on 40?" he said.

"Probably so, the Air Guard's got them at Fort Smith Municipal Airport," I answered.

"10-4; how fast is one of them things?" he asked.

"Pretty fast, it set a world speed record a few years ago at sixteen hundred miles an hour, plus a few."

There was a long silence then he said, "Now say that again; how fast?"

I replied, "You heard it right friend; one thousand and six hundred miles per hour."

"Holy Toledo; well then I guess that little gray "Z" don't give you much trouble at eighty-five or so then," he laughed.

"Not too much," I said.

"10-4; well all righty then. Fly safe little buddy, if you can do that in one of them things. I ain't had any Smokey reports between here and Oklahoma so keep her rollin'. I got your back door," he finished.

Then he quickly added, "By the way, what's your rank? I was in Uncle Sam's Army for twenty-four; retired as an E-7." (Master Sergeant)

"O-6," I answered. "Holy Toledo Colonel; in that case fly safe *Sir*," he laughed.

I signed off with, "Thanks again Sergeant; and 10-4."

Toward The Evening Sky

PHANTASTIC PHANTOM

Fort Smith Municipal Airport, AR; January 11, 1984

I settled into an F-4 cockpit for the first time since Homestead AFB, Florida in July, 1967. Then I had been the instructor. Today and for the next week or so, I was to be the student. As I looked around the cockpit I was surprised at how much I recalled after seventeen years. I could shut my eyes and correctly move my hands to switches, handles and knobs. I remembered equipment locations almost like it was just yesterday. There had been some new equipment installed since I had flown them, such as a radar missile warning system and a new switch on the fuel panel, but everything else was very familiar. These planes had hardly changed since I flew my last C model in Vietnam in 1966. In fact, a couple of these Phantoms I suspected that I might have flown in Vietnam. Their tail numbers seemed very familiar. I felt right at home in the big fighter sitting there on the ground. I hoped I would feel the same when I got into the air.

Another difference in the plane since I had flown it last was a modification in the boundary layer control air. The F-4 initially had a system installed which blew hot air from the engines over the wing and trailing edge flaps. This air blowing over the wing provided more lift and allowed the Phantom to slow to about 132 knots for normal landings. On takeoff, its effect was to enable the plane to get airborne at slower speeds and therefore use shorter runways. This system had been partially deactivated which meant higher takeoff and landing speeds. The final approach speed was now around 165 knots. I think that the cost of maintaining the system as the planes got older became prohibitive and was at least one reason for the change.

As we lined up on the runway, I felt the old familiar surge of adrenalin into my body. I released the brakes and lit the afterburners. The transverse Gs pushed me back into my seat as the big Phantom accelerated rapidly down the runway. 165 knots; I pulled the stick back and the fighter was airborne and gaining airspeed at a fast clip. I raised the gear handle and the landing gear retracted into position. I could feel the nose gear thunk into place as it locked below my feet. After fumbling a bit because of its unusual position on the vertical area outboard and behind the throttles, I raised the flap handle. I rotated the nose up still further to slow the rate of acceleration and quickly glanced down at the flap indicators. The leading and trailing edge flaps both indicated zero. I pulled the throttles out of the afterburner range at three hundred knots (345 mph). We were already over the end of the runway and I pulled the throttles back still further to stay at three hundred. Although we were carrying two under-wing external fuel tanks they were empty; consequently the Phantom was really moving. It had been quite a while since I'd accelerated this fast.

I called the control tower and requested a right turn out of traffic. They approved the turn and I racked the Phantom into a sixty degree bank and pushed the power up to military (full power without afterburners). The fighter surged forward. I raised the nose to about thirty degrees and rolled out on a westerly heading. As we climbed through ten thousand feet, we were about two miles south of the control tower when they handed us off to the departure control. I thought about the KC-135 for a moment; if I had been flying it, we would be just getting the flaps up about now. My next thought was, "Two completely different worlds of aircraft performance; and I get to fly them both."

We would be coordinating with Fort Smith Departure/Approach control during the initial part of this Transition #1 mission and staying within thirty miles of Fort Smith and below 18,000 feet. We were only cleared to 15,000 feet and it was already time to level off. I advised Approach/Departure Control that we would be performing some airwork under visual flight rules between 10,000 and 17,000 feet and in an area about halfway between McAlester, Oklahoma and Fort Smith. I then requested to remain with them for traffic advisories. They approved my request and then assigned me a code to squawk on my IFF (identification friend or foe).

The mission was basically a re-familiarization with the Phantom's handling characteristics and then back to the "Fort" for some touch and go landings. My instructor said "Okay Colonel, do a few turns and then when you think you're ready, take them up to max performance (turn as hard as possible)." Heck, I was already ready. I rapidly rolled the F-4 into a ninety degree left bank and pulled back until the angle of attack indicator was at 19.2 units (maximum rate turn). The wingtips were vibrating and the big fighter was shuddering and shaking just like I remembered. I had already added full military power because the speed would bleed off rapidly in a hard turn. I had started the pull at 450 knots and we were down to 400 already. I selected minimum, then second stage afterburner. At 180 degrees of turn, I rudder-rolled the Phantom into a right ninety degree bank and kept the control stick pulled back to hold the maximum AOA (angle of attack).

I was now in full afterburner and the speed was still bleeding off. I kept the bank angle at near 90 degrees and the altitude at fifteen thousand feet with rudder inputs. I knew that any aileron input during high G turns in a Phantom II would result in adverse yaw. That yaw tried to pull the fighter's nose toward the down aileron. Consequently, when flying the Phantom during hard maneuvering, the rule was; "The more the G; the less the aileron." It took quite a bit of rudder/aileron skill to max-perform the Phantom correctly. I was in Hog Heaven. (Appropriately enough, the Fort Smith fighter unit was known as the Flying Razorbacks.) Here I was, forty-six years old, grunting to stay conscious against the G forces, sweating like a stevedore from the effort, and I was having a blast. As I had hoped my feel for this big fighter was coming back rapidly. I could hardly believe that I was back in this great machine that had pulled me through some very tight spots in Vietnam eighteen years before. After a few more minutes, we went right into some simulated combat maneuvers such as pitch-backs, nose low slice-turns, Yo-yos, Immelman turns, etc. Afterwards, I did some slow flight with the landing gear and flaps down to simulate the handling during a landing pattern.

I informed Approach Control that we were ready to head back to the airport. I pointed the big fighter's nose back toward the ribbon of the Arkansas River that I could see to the northeast and pulled the throttles back for our descent. I soon had Fort Smith and the airport in sight and at about fifteen miles out, Approach switched us over to the control tower. Inbound, the instructor pointed out several reference points on the ground that the local F-4 drivers used for their visual traffic patterns. I entered the traffic pattern at the prescribed 300 knots and 2000 feet and executed several touch and go landings. With the exception of the higher approach and landing speeds, the Phantom felt just like it had seventeen years ago; Phantastic.

Jerry W. Cook

YOU CAN'T DO THA.......

Fort Smith Municipal Airport, AR; February 10, 1984

"I saw the Colonel standing there in operations when I came in this morning. I thought; 'So he's the old guy I heard about who's flying with us now.' Then I saw some gray hair and thought, 'Wow, he does look old.' No offense Colonel. Then I looked up at the scheduling board and saw that I was flying a '1-V-1' (1 fighter vs. 1 fighter) against him this morning and my next thought was; 'This should be a piece of cake.'" The young source of this testimonial paused. He was an early thirty-something Captain/F-4 pilot and had been my flight leader and air combat opponent earlier that morning.

I was still in the check-out phase but my instructor had decided to cut it short of the normal ten sorties. He had stated after the second transition flight that we were wasting time with more transition sorties and were going to go right into some air to air combat missions. After those and a couple of air to ground flights, he would turn me loose. So here we were sitting around a table in a briefing room and the young Captain was reviewing our just completed two-ship flight, my first air to air combat training sortie.

He continued, "Well, along about the third time the Colonel 'shot my ass down' I decided that I had made a serious error in judgment."

He then said, "Colonel you should be debriefing this flight. I didn't know an F-4 could do some of the things that you made it do today."

He then said, "Sir, for instance, on that last high side pass, what did you do to keep from overshooting? I thought I broke into you at just the right moment. I lost track of you when you went behind us and when I reversed I expected you to be way out to my right in an overshoot. You weren't there. I asked my back-seater if he had you in sight and he said, 'Yep.' I said, 'Then where is he?' He said, 'Right on our ass.'"

The Captain then looked at my instructor, "Major, maybe you can tell me; how did you all keep from overshooting on that last pass and then end up right on our tail? Did I break too soon?"

My instructor replied, "No Captain, I thought you broke into us at the perfect moment. Then when the Colonel started his countering maneuver, I said to him, 'You can't do tha....' But he had already done it by the time I got my vision back. I'm not sure exactly how, but we ended up slightly low at your six o'clock and gun-tracking."

The flight leader looked back at me and said, "Sir, would you please tell me how you did it?"

I said, "Captain, all I can tell you is that when you broke into me, I immediately snatched the nose up and started a maximum angle of attack, high G rolling scissors to our right. Our initial semi-vertical path and the maximum AOA roll maintained our turn radius at a minimum and kept us from overshooting. That combination finally put us into position behind and below you. I used maximum afterburners to maintain energy. By the way Captain, I thought your defensive break was at just the right moment too." The Captain looked quizzically at my instructor. The Major shrugged and said, "Don't ask me. I was blacked out during most of it."

That was a very enjoyable flight and this is the way I remember it.

However, I also remember that there is a saying; *"The older I get; the better I was!"*

Jerry W. Cook

TWO "WORLDS"......SAME DAY

Little Rock AFB, AR to Fort Smith Municipal Airport, AR; 1984

I was flying both the KC-135 and the F-4. Talk about differences in airplanes. In addition to these two vastly different types of aircraft, I was also flying Falcon 10s and an occasional King Air for the Little Rock Air Center. At least I was down to just four types from the thirteen different kinds of planes that I had been flying ten years before...dumb!

I had served as an instructor in the KC-135 for several years but I dropped that status because I was not flying it very much. I had now become an instructor in the F-4. Although it took more of my time and effort, I didn't mind, just so I got to fly the F-4. I was driving to Fort Smith once or twice a month to fly the big "smoker" and I loved it. An added bonus was that my parents lived a few miles west of Fort Smith and it gave me numerous opportunities to visit them.

The KC-135's main purpose for being was as an airborne tanker. It could pass gas to any fighter or bomber that used the boom refueling method. That of course included the F-4. (Additionally a hose and drogue could be attached to the end of the refueling boom to accommodate numerous aircraft of the Air Force, Navy and Marines that utilized the probe and drogue method of air refueling.)

One morning I checked the upcoming flight schedule and there was a KC-135 mission that captured my imagination. It first went to Fort Smith. Once there, it would take on some passengers and then depart for a refueling mission with F-4s from the 188th TFG at Fort Smith. The passengers boarding the KC-135 were wives of the F-4 pilots. It was labeled a "wives' orientation flight" and was to show the fair ladies a part of what their husbands did for a living. I decided that I would fly the KC-135 to Fort Smith and after landing, I would turn the left seat over to another aircraft commander. I would get off the tanker, go to the 188th flight ops, attend the briefing with the other fighter pilots and then fly an F-4; refueling from the KC-135 that I had just flown there. Why not? I needed an air refueling mission for my requirements just like the other guys.

What a rewarding day that was. I felt extremely privileged to be in the position that I was in. I had a great time flying both airplanes. I have a picture from the refueling part of that mission and it includes both of the planes that I flew that day. I think it was probably an unusual experience that few pilots ever get to have.

It was also an unusual experience to glance up at the boomer's window and see all of those curious feminine faces staring down at you as you tried to hook up to the boom. Talk about pressure.

Toward The Evening Sky

DIAMOND IN THE ROUGH

Little Rock Adams Field, AR; 1984?

My civilian boss, the owner of Little Rock Air Center (formerly Hiegel Aviation), had added several jets in the past year to his managed and charter fleet. We were operating three Falcon 10s and I believe that we had a Citation for a while also. One day he told me that a sales representative was bringing a new Mitsubishi Diamond Jet to demonstrate to us. I had recently read the specs on this relatively new jet design and admittedly, I was not that impressed with its performance numbers; but I was curious to see how it flew. It was equipped with the same type of Pratt and Whitney jet engines as were certain models of the Cessna Citation.

The jet arrived and, while my boss was talking to the sales representative and the demo pilot, I walked out to the little jet and climbed aboard. I glanced back toward the passenger area. It was small but that wasn't my main area of interest. I had thought the Learjet had a small cockpit but this one looked even tighter for a pilot my size. First I located the landing gear handle and made sure that it was in the down position. (You'd be surprised what hidden "Easter eggs" have been found after others have been in the cockpit before you.) Then I tried to figure out a way to get my six foot, one hundred and ninety-five pounds into the left seat. Before attempting it, I had checked to see if there was an up/down adjustment. I can't remember exactly what I found, but I do remember that the seat was as low and as far back as I could get it. Eventually, I twisted around enough to get into the seat but, when my feet were positioned on the rudder pedals, the tops of my thighs were jammed up into the bottom of the control yoke. I leaned forward intending to move the rudder pedals to their most forward position. The space was so small that I finally felt around with my hands for the pedal adjustments. They were already full forward. I placed my feet flat on the floor and I could only move the yoke an inch or two in each direction. With my feet up on the rudder pedals I couldn't move the yoke at all; very impressive. It was as if the manufacturers had finished the plane's design when someone noticed and said, "Oh crap. We forgot to put in a place for the pilots!" It was obvious that I wouldn't be piloting this plane.

By the time I finally got out of the cockpit (that wasn't easy either), the demonstration pilot had walked out and joined me. He asked me how I liked the plane so far. I was brutally honest and said, "Not very much." Then I told him about my difficulties in the small cockpit.

He said, "Oh; you probably didn't have the seat and pedals adjusted right." He got into the plane and bent over to adjust them for me. He finally confirmed that they were already at their maximum.

"Are you sure you can't move the controls?" he said; "I don't have any trouble at all." He was probably about five feet eight and one hundred and fifty pounds. About that time, the owner of the Little Rock Air Center came walking out with the salesman for the demonstration flight. I told him that I wouldn't be flying the plane.

He asked me why and I said, "The cockpit isn't big enough." He looked at me and smiled as if I were joking.

I said, "No seriously. I can't move the flight controls when I'm in the seat." I then told him and the demo pilot that I'd just ride along and watch from the rear-facing passenger seat behind the cockpit. The boss had been going to fly during most of the demo flight anyway so it did not present any problem. And it was assuring that he was the best businessman/pilot with whom I had flown.

Another gentleman who was going along on the flight also was a businessman/pilot who owned and flew his own Beech Baron. I assumed that he may have had some potential interest in the plane also. My boss climbed into the left seat as the demo pilot closed and locked the door. He instructed me on how to open it in case of an emergency and then slid into the co-pilot seat and talked the boss through the engine starts. The taxi to the runway and the takeoff were uneventful and we proceeded about thirty miles to the southeast of the airport for some airwork. The boss did some turns including some steep turns and just generally felt out the little jet. To prepare for the return to the traffic pattern, he slowed the plane down to lower the landing gear and flaps for some slow flight and simulated landing patterns.

I was turned sideways in my seat looking into the cockpit during all of these procedures. When the speed was slow enough, my boss called, "Gear down." The demonstration pilot reached up and lowered the gear handle. I could feel the wheels unlock. Two of them moved smartly into their down and locked position. One of them; did not. The two pilots were sitting there discussing their next move. I turned and looked at the businessman/pilot who was sitting directly behind me in a forward facing seat. I grinned at him and then chuckled as the humor of the situation struck me.

"What's so funny?" he said. He was not yet aware of our problem.

I replied, "Well, here we are on a sales demonstration flight and one of the landing gear won't come down."

His eyes got big and he said, *"What? And you think that's funny?!"*

"Well yeah…I kinda do," I said.

He looked rather stricken as he replied, *"You fighter pilots are all crazy. This is not funny."*

In the meantime the two pilots got out the emergency checklist and reviewed their options. In a short time they had all three landing gear down and locked. Of course they left them down and flew straight back to Little

Rock and landed. For *some* reason, I don't think the boss bought that airplane. I don't believe that the other passenger was interested anymore either.

And…I still think it was funny.

Jerry W. Cook

FAYETTE-NAM

Fayetteville Drake Field, AR; 1980s (Before Approach Radar)

Fayetteville, Arkansas is located in the northwest part of the state, not far from the western edge of the Ozark Mountains. It is one of the most scenic locales in the state and among other things is the home of the University of Arkansas' main campus. In comparison with mountain ranges like the Rockies or the Sierras, the Ozarks by contrast are relatively small. In fact, the highest point in Arkansas is not in the Ozarks but further south at Mount Magazine, which is located in the Arkansas River valley. Magazine is just over two thousand, seven hundred feet in elevation. These mountains do not seem at all big when compared with peaks in the above mentioned ranges that are at least ten thousand feet higher. However in terms of aviation, one mountain can be as deadly as another. An airplane cannot move them.

"Fayette-nam" was the nickname used by me and many other Arkansas pilots for the area surrounding and including Fayetteville Drake Field; the main Fayetteville area airport at the time. Approach radar has since been installed; but for many years, radar coverage at the lower altitudes during descents and approaches was non-existent. The nickname did not apply when the weather was good but during Instrument Flight Conditions it was a different story. In those days there were two primary ways to get into Drake Field when an instrument approach was required. A VOR (Visual Omni Range) from the Drake VOR or a LOC (Localizer) approach to Runway 16 were the two IFR procedures. The required weather ceiling for beginning the approaches was eight hundred feet above the airport for the VOR and six hundred above it for the LOC approach. The weather observations were provided by a FAA Flight Service Station located on the airfield.

During a home football game for the University of Arkansas Razorbacks, the number of aircraft converging on Fayetteville from all directions was amazing and of course, we all arrived at about the same time. What a complete circus it was during bad weather. Aircraft would stack up in holding patterns at the navigational fix depending on which instrument approach was being utilized. Then the waiting began. Planes would be cleared one at a time to begin the approach which took several minutes. Especially if it was a light conventional aircraft, some of the pilots would not be heard from for what seemed a very long time. Eventually, pilots in the holding pattern and Memphis Center would begin to wonder where the planes were, hoping that the pilots had not turned the wrong way or missed a level-off altitude and descended into a mountain. The next aircraft in holding could not be cleared to begin its approach until the aircraft in front had canceled its IFR clearance.

As the delays developed the waiting pilots would have to begin checking fuel remaining, the weather at their alternate airport and the present time against the game's start time. Occasionally, the pilots would then begin catching grief from passengers who were complaining about being late for the game. (It was not unusual for the complainers to be the same passengers who had been late when arriving at the airport for the flight. It was a curious but common phenomenon and not beneficial to the already very busy pilot.)

In those days before radar and improved instrument approaches, Fayetteville could be a crap shoot. Strangely, often the reported weather was very close to the published minimums for the VOR approach and even the experienced pilots who were more proficient on instruments were sometimes challenged to establish visual contact with the airport in time to make a safe descent to the runway. For whatever reason, there were times when making instrument approaches into Drake Field when I encountered weather lower than what was being reported. And on many occasions, arriving aircraft were encouraged to accept the VOR approach from the Drake VOR because that was the approach being used by the small commuter airline that was based at Drake Field and…"They were getting in okay." On at least two occasions after receiving this information, I missed the VOR approach because I was still in the clouds at the minimum descent altitude.

On one of those occasions (a night football game charter flight) as I executed the missed approach procedure, I heard one of my passengers exclaim, "Where is that stupid S.O.B. going?" (He meant me.)

Then he said loudly, "I saw the airport lights straight down below us." He was correct. The airport lights had been right below us and with about two hundred feet of clouds also right below us. There was no way that we could have gotten down to the runway and landed safely from that approach. I requested and received the LOC 16 (localizer) approach which had weather minimums two hundred feet lower than the VOR. On that approach at the minimum altitude, we were skimming the base of the clouds and finally saw the runway soon enough to land safely. As he got off the Falcon 10, I heard the vocal and profane passenger still cursing me for the delay (however not to my face).

Twenty minutes later, I wished that he had still been at the airport with me while my co-pilot and I watched in amazement as one of the commuter airliners dove out of the clouds in the rain. He landed hard about halfway down the runway, jammed on the brakes, skidded off the right side of the runway into the muddy infield between the runway and the parallel taxiway and finally came slewing to a stop. (I was told later that the pilot had been executing the Drake VOR approach.)

I guess *that* "stupid S.O.B." saw the airport right below him and thought that he could still land from that position…*Wrong!* As we watched the wet and visibly upset but very lucky passengers exit the airplane in the muddy infield and begin walking toward the terminal building in the rain, I wondered if perhaps my obnoxious passenger would have preferred flying with that pilot. I certainly wished that he had been!

Toward The Evening Sky

JUST TWENTY MINUTES LATER…

Fayetteville Drake Field, AR; April 4, 1984

My information at the time indicated that the business meeting was likely considered important and it was in or near Fayetteville, Arkansas. At 10:12 a.m. Central time, the pilot's weather briefing at Little Rock indicated that the Fayetteville Drake Field weather was an estimated six hundred feet overcast with four miles visibility in light drizzle and fog. Those conditions were at or above those required for the LOC 16 approach. The forecast was for improving conditions. Upon arrival in the area at 11:23 a.m., the pilot of Cessna 310 N8156M was advised that two aircraft had just executed missed approaches after their landing attempts. At 11:39 a.m., the pilot of the Cessna 310 was cleared for the Localizer Runway 16 approach. At 11:41 a.m., he called leaving the Elmie Intersection/Initial Approach Fix. It was located on the LOC course 6.9 miles north/northwest of the Hogge Intersection/Outer Marker and about 9.8 miles from the runway. At 11:45 a.m., the pilot was cleared to land and reminded to call at the Outer Marker.

He responded, "Waiting for it." Thirty seconds later, the control tower asked the pilot of N8156M to report his position…. One of my favorite and most respected people in the world along with the son of an individual who had literally changed the direction of my flying career had become victims of "Fayette-nam".

I was sitting in a barber chair getting a haircut when the phone rang. Harold my barber answered it, then handed it to me and said, "It's for you." It was an operations specialist from the Air National Guard.

He sounded upset as he said, "Colonel Cook, I've got some very bad news; General Wassell has just been killed in a plane crash."

As I tried to wrap my mind around his message, I said in disbelief, "What? Are you sure?"

"Yes sir. I'm sure," the Sergeant replied.

"What kind of airplane?" I asked. (The General was flying F-4s on occasion with the 188th Tactical Fighter Group at Fort Smith, but he also owned his own aircraft, a Cessna 310.)

"He was flying his own plane," the Sergeant replied; "And he was not alone. His passenger was killed also."

"Who was it?" I said.

"It was Colonel "Doc" Savage's son," he replied. "Doc" Savage's son was an architect with General Wassell's firm in Little Rock. I couldn't imagine the sorrow that was being felt by the families of the two men; but I was certainly aware of mine.

According to the National Transportation Safety Board accident summary, the twin engine Cessna 310 was on the extended centerline of the localizer course, but about seven miles south-southeast of the airport when it impacted below the crest of the small mountain at about 11:45 a.m. At 11:55 a.m., the FAA weather observer at the airport made his regular hourly observation. He reported the weather to be 500 feet overcast with 3 miles visibility in drizzle and fog. 500 feet overcast was lower than the weather minimums for the Localizer 16 approach.

If they had only been about twenty minutes later they would have received the updated weather report. General Wassell would not have initiated the approach. Just twenty minutes later....

Toward The Evening Sky

WHAT'S WRONG WITH THAT GUY?

Little Rock Adams Field, AR; 1984?

The owner of Little Rock Air Center built a beautiful and very striking building to serve as its headquarters and passenger terminal. On the second floor it housed administrative offices and charter pilots' areas. The ground floor included plush waiting areas for the passengers and transient pilots. It included a snack bar, flight planning area, conference room and a reading area. It was state of the art in every way. A grand opening event was being planned to show off the plush facility to the city and, in addition to free food and drinks, the owner wanted to have an aviation related event for the attendees.

The individual that the boss had hired as LRAC's general manager was involved in the planning. A local stunt pilot who owned a Stearman biplane was contracted to perform an aerobatic routine for the expected crowd. Several dignitaries including the Arkansas Governor had committed to attend. And it was thought that, since our charter section operated three Falcon 10s in our fleet, a short flight demonstration highlighting some of its performance capabilities might be beneficial. The GM talked to our Chief Pilot about flying the demonstration. He declined but suggested that, if I would fly it, he would fly as my co-pilot. I agreed and we began planning what we would do to highlight the Falcon 10's assets. A technician installed a G meter in the plane so I wouldn't exceed the little jet's design limits during my steep turns and the pull-up after the high speed pass.

Some of the planes' assets were speed and its short runway capabilities along with superb fighter-like handling. Since all flight demonstrations in the U.S. are controlled by the FAA, we were required to meet with them to discuss our plans and obtain their approval. The Stearman pilot was also there and he outlined his airshow plan for the Feds and us. We coordinated our flight demonstration with his and with some minor adjustments that the FAA required (my maximum speed and minimum altitude), it was approved. It was decided that, as the Stearman made his last low pass northbound over runway 18/36, he would be at 90 knots and 100 feet and emitting smoke. The crowd's attention would be focused on him as he approached from the south. Just as he flew in front of the crowd outside of the new FBO building, we were to unexpectedly arrive from the north and appear to pass directly under him. Our airspeed had been restricted by the FAA; therefore I was not supposed to demonstrate the Falcon's impressive high speed capability.

The day of the grand opening arrived and we carefully re-briefed with the Stearman pilot to assure that we all fully understood the other's role. After we had passed *underneath* the Stearman, he would turn off the smoke, break off to his left and exit the area out of sight behind the buildings to the west. At the same time, I would pull the Falcon up steeply into a modified left downwind and fly a very low speed approach about ten feet above the runway while proceeding southbound. When we arrived in front of the crowd, I was to add full power and pull into a climbing left 90 degree turn and then into a right descending 270 degree turn and land on the same runway northbound. As we rolled toward the north end of the runway, we would be out of sight of the crowd behind a hangar. There, I would stop quickly and pick up Bill Clinton, the Arkansas Governor, and my boss out of the view of the spectators and then quickly taxi back into sight. A huge ribbon was to be stretched across the ramp immediately in front of the new FBO building and the waiting crowd. I would turn the plane and taxi toward the ribbon until the nose touched it and it separated. At that point the Falcon's door would open and the Governor would step off the plane and walk up to the waiting podium.

His carefully worded remarks such as; "Wow! That was quite a ride," would leave the crowd believing that he had been aboard during the flight demonstration. More than likely, some people still think that he was aboard. They probably never considered that a politician would mislead them.

The airshow and Falcon 10 demonstration went off as planned except for one thing; well actually several small things. Just as the Stearman roared up the runway trailing smoke, I was descending over the Arkansas River from the north. I cleared the remaining trees at the north edge of the airport and pushed the nose down to level off at my planned height of fifty feet above the grass infield and just to the east of the runway. Our timing was nearly perfect, but just then the Stearman's loud radial engine startled a flock of small birds and the Falcon's windscreen filled with them. Surely he was mistaken because I don't remember saying it; but my co-pilot later told me that I uttered that famous aviation phrase, "Oh S___!" as I flew the plane level just above the grass.

We passed under most of the flock. My main concern was whether any birds had gone through the engines so I pulled the nose up even steeper than planned in case one or both of them flamed out. That would give us more time for a possible engine restart or enough altitude for a dead-stick landing if we needed it. Because of our speed on the low pass, we were able to pull up to a high downwind position of several thousand feet. The engines both looked fine and my co-pilot and I quickly agreed that we would continue the flight demonstration. The crowd never knew. Later, after the Governor's remarks were over and the guests were leaving, one of my good friends who had been watching the airshow and Falcon demonstration flight came up to me smiling.

She said that one attendee, an older lady, had exclaimed to her just after we had flashed by *under* the Stearman; "What is wrong with that guy trying to land? Doesn't he know there's an airshow going on?" It was not exactly the impression that we meant to leave.

After landing, we discovered that we had hit two of the spooked birds. One had slightly dented an area just behind the radome and the other had impacted on the center frame of the windscreen.

Postscript: One of the Little Rock Air Center's employees told me later that a local FAA operations inspector had been standing next to her as we flashed by on our first pass.

She said he had remarked as he slowly shook his head, "200 knots maximum huh; *yeah…right.*" I have *no idea* what he meant by that.

Jerry W. Cook

ASPEN ROULETTE

Aspen/Pitkin County Airport, CO; 1984

Aspen, Colorado is a beautiful place any time of the year but especially during the winter. Situated at the base of Aspen Mountain in the Rockies, it lies at nearly eight thousand feet of elevation just a few miles southeast of the Aspen airport. Situated on the western side of the highway between the airport and the town, one can view the base of Buttermilk mountain. It is often dotted with novice skiers testing their ski legs on the gentle grades of the Bunny Slope. Especially during ski season, many members of the so-called rich and famous set can be seen just about anywhere in the town and at one time or another most of them pass through the airport.

My boss at Little Rock Air Center was the owner of several other businesses in addition to the Air Center; but during ski season he and his family usually spent as much time as possible at their condominium in Aspen. They were gracious hosts and often had several friends of the family there as guests. He had planned a party in Aspen and had committed to providing transportation from Little Rock to Aspen for some of his guests in one of his Falcon 10 jets. Because of the total number of passengers compared to the size of a Falcon 10, it was going to require three trips to Aspen to convey them all. He was an accomplished Falcon pilot himself; but he wanted to stay in Aspen to get things ready for his party guests. I was one of the pilots on the day of the party and the other was named Joe. We flew the jet into Aspen on the first flight and if memory serves, we took three couples that trip. The flight was uneventful and their transportation was waiting for them when we arrived. We loaded them and their gear into the vehicle and then hustled to get the plane fueled and ready for the next leg.

The weather was clear and crisp and the scenery was gorgeous as we departed Aspen on the return flight to Little Rock. Since we had no passengers on that flight portion to make uncomfortable with a high deck angle, I "steep-climbed" the Falcon northwest up the valley at an airspeed of just 180 knots. The departure had us heading the wrong direction anyway and that kind of quick climb would let us reach 14,000 feet in a shorter distance. We knew that the sooner that Denver Center could identify us above the mountains on radar, the sooner they would clear us to proceed southeast on course. Because of the wintertime tailwinds, it was less than two hours back to the Rock. We wanted to get back as fast as possible because there would be passengers waiting there for their trip to Aspen. Then after dropping those folks off, we would turn around and head back to Little Rock and more passengers for our final flight to Aspen that day.

We taxied up to the Little Rock Air Center where our passengers and a jet fuel truck awaited us. All of our flight plans for the day had already been filed; so all I needed was a weather update. While I went inside to obtain it, the other pilot supervised the fueling. Three SUVs full of luggage pulled up to the plane as I went back outside to help. It was a good thing that we had modified our Falcon 10s with extra baggage compartments because as usual, it looked like our passengers were bringing everything that was in their closets. Finally after some creative loading, unloading, and reloading, we finally got everything aboard the little plane. The load wasn't too heavy. It is usually the volume of luggage that the passengers bring that give corporate and charter pilots headaches. With our excited passengers finally on board, we started engines and taxied quickly for takeoff. I briefed the other pilot that the weather was just like we had experienced on our other flights that day; beautiful all the way and still without a cloud in the sky. We lifted off and pointed the nose of the Falcon back toward Colorado.

That flight went as planned as well as the next leg back to Little Rock. One more trip to Aspen and we could quit for the day. This time we only had two passengers, so the baggage loading was a piece of cake. It was a young couple and they were sitting on the bench seat at the rear of the cabin holding hands and talking.

It was Joe's turn to fly again; so I crawled into the right seat for this flight. I was glad that this was our last trip into Aspen that day because as beautiful as it was, we were getting a little tired and we were also looking forward to a nice big Colorado steak.

In those days, Aspen was served by an airline called Aspen Airways. It flew Convair 580 turboprops into the airport several times a day. Its pilots obviously were very familiar with the area surrounding Aspen and, when the weather was good, they just used visual points on the ground to pass their location to the Aspen control tower. Transit pilots, such as us, were not necessarily familiar with these local reporting points. In just over two hours we were descending thirty miles to the southeast of Aspen Mountain and could see the town partially cloaked in the mountain's shadow. We canceled our instrument flight plan and Denver Center turned us over to the Aspen tower. As expected, when we checked in, the tower instructed us to enter a high left downwind for runway 15. We descended southeast of the downwind toward 11,000 feet and the tower called us "in sight". They then informed us that we were "number one in traffic and were cleared to land on runway 15." I acknowledged the landing clearance and Joe called for approach flaps and the landing gear down. Since the downwind must be flown at 11,000 feet to stay above the rocks and trees and because the airport elevation is less than 8,000 feet, a base turn is required that is nearly twice as steep as normal.

We were descending at about 1400 feet per minute and almost to the halfway point in the base turn when this radio call came; "Aspen tower, Aspen Airways 1234 over ____ Pass inbound."

The tower immediately answered with, "Aspen 1234 you are cleared to land number one. Falcon N837F you are now number two to land. Follow the Aspen Convair."

"Do you see him?" Joe asked. There was a hint of alarm in his voice.

"No," I said as we looked for the airliner. We had no idea of this guy's position from us or his altitude.

"Tower, where is the Convair from the Falcon?" I urgently questioned. Joe had rolled out some of our bank and slowed our rate of descent somewhat as we anxiously searched the sky for the Convair.

Suddenly there came a very patronizing tone encompassing an utterly stupid radio call; *"Don't sweat it Falcon!* Aspen Airways has you in sight at our 10 o'clock."

That didn't help us at all and the tower still had not said diddlysquat! This guy could be almost any direction from us. Suddenly out of my peripheral vision, I caught a sun flash just above our right canopy rail. It was from the Aspen Airways Convair.

I grabbed the control yoke and shoved the nose down as I shouted, *"I've got it!"* Our female passenger screamed. We could hear the Convair's propellers thrashing the air as we dived under the airliner. I don't know how we missed his left wing. Now I began to recover the Falcon from its rapid plunge toward the valley floor. I added full power and began lifting the nose as I raised the flaps one notch. Up to this point I hadn't had time to say anything to Joe except, "I've got it."

I called, "Gear up." In just a few seconds we were level and in a left turn back toward the airport. We had overshot the final approach course but we were above the rising terrain to the northwest of the airport which of course had been my primary concern during our dive recovery. We could see the Aspen Airways Convair about to touch down.

I said, "Joe, you've got the plane."

He said "Okay, I've got it," and took the controls back.

Just then the control tower finally called us; "Falcon 837F, go around and re-enter a left traffic pattern. Call midfield downwind." Joe added power and began to climb back to 11,000 feet.

I was really fuming; but all I said back to the guy was, "Roger." It was several minutes before we had progressed around the pattern and landed. Then it took several more minutes to unload the passengers, explain what had happened, and get them on their way. As you can imagine, they were almost kissing the ground and it looked like the young woman had been crying. I didn't blame her. I was still shaking from my anger at the utter stupidity of the so-called Airline Captain; and as soon as I could, I commandeered an FBO lineman and his vehicle. I had him drive me to the small terminal ramp southeast of us where the Convair was parked. Probably fortunately for me and the airline Captain, they had already closed the door and were starting the left engine by the time I got there. I didn't know what I was going to do to the guy if I had gotten there earlier; but I was so furious that I was definitely going to do something.

When I arrived back at the FBO, I obtained the telephone number of the control tower and called it. I asked the guy who answered if he was the controller who was responsible for almost causing a midair collision between a Falcon 10 and an Aspen Airways Convair.

He snidely remarked, "It didn't look that close to me." I could hardly believe my ears.

"Then you're as big an idiot as that so-called Captain in the Convair." I replied. He hung up on me.

To this day, my blood pressure still goes up thinking about that incident. I remember that when I looked in the direction of that sun flash (it was from the propellers) that not only did I see the Convair; but I got a glimpse of the face of the Captain looking at us as I shoved the nose of the Falcon down to avoid ramming him. *What in the Hell was he thinking?!*

The imbecile in the Convair and the incompetent Aspen tower operator had just provided two of the worst examples of aviation professionalism that I ever saw in my fifty-four years of flying. Interesting enough, just a few months later there was an article in the June 1984 FLYING magazine titled "Mountain Passage" by Nigel Moll. In it he referred to the inherent dangers of flying into Aspen. The writer used the term "Aspen Roulette" while discussing the increasing traffic caused by pilots stretching the definition of VFR.

In our case it had absolutely nothing to do with the weather but instead; a total lack of competence in an airline captain and a tower controller that caused our "Aspen Roulette".

Jerry W. Cook

NOT FUNNY

Little Rock Airport, AR; 1984

I walked around the nose of the Falcon 10 to where my co-pilot was standing by the door. I had seen the very expensive sedan enter the ramp and it had stopped behind me in front of the plane. We had been getting the bird ready for a late morning flight to San Diego, California. The passengers were first time charter customers and we wanted everything to be just right. I said something to the co-pilot, but his attention was on something else. He was looking past my shoulder and didn't even seem to hear me. I turned around to see where he was looking.

She had bent over in our direction and appeared to be retrieving something from a leather bag on the ground. Her silky white blouse was unbuttoned half way down to where it was tucked into the waist of her leather slacks. Her kneeling position had placed her left breast in full view. I looked back at my co-pilot. He had not moved his eyes from their *target*. She straightened up and walked toward us with her right hand extended.

"Hi, I'm _____," she said. Her smile was shall we say, *knowing*. She knew full well what she had just accomplished and she was enjoying our reactions, especially the co-pilot's. I introduced myself and when he didn't say anything, I introduced the co-pilot to her. He finally blinked and stuck out his hand. She was spectacular; 5'10", slim, blond, blue-eyed, a beautiful smile. She was definitely a "10". Her husband came walking toward us from behind the sedan. He was also wearing leather pants. I had never seen a guy wearing leather pants except maybe Fess Parker playing Davy Crocket on T.V.

I thought, "This is definitely an interesting pair."

He walked up to me and smiled as he said, "Are you guys our pilots today?

I shook his hand and said, "Yes, I'm Jerry and this is _____."

He smiled and, as he shook the other pilot's hand, said, "Good, let's go to California. This will be fun."

After we loaded the bags and line service had driven his car away, the other pilot and I boarded the Falcon. I glanced back at our passengers. They were sitting on the bench seat in the rear of the cabin and were snuggled close together. _____ shot me a big smile and then laid her head on her husband's shoulder. They looked like they were *in love*. About two hours later we were over New Mexico when the husband came up toward the cockpit and sat on the side-facing seat near the door.

"How much longer?" he asked.

"We should be on the ground in one hour and forty five minutes," I replied.

After a couple of questions like; "How high are we, how fast are we going, etc.," he suddenly said; "How do you like my wife?"

I thought it was a rather strange question from a husband and I said, "What do you mean?"

He answered, "She was an airline stewardess. I met her on a flight to New York. Isn't she gorgeous?"

I looked back at him as I said, "Yes; she is a very pretty woman Mr. _____."

"Please, call me _____," he said.

"Okay, anything else?" I replied.

"Nope, that's it," he said as he grinned and went back to his seat.

The other pilot and I looked at each other. The plane was too small to discuss the strange exchange without being overheard, so we said nothing. We landed at San Diego International Airport and exited the aircraft. After carrying their bags to their rental car, I gave our passengers our hotel information. It was Thursday afternoon and we were to leave Sunday for Little Rock. I was shaking hands with him when _____ suddenly stepped over, hugged me, and planted a kiss on my cheek as she said, "Jerry, thanks for a lovely flight."

Surprised by her actions, I looked at her; then back at her husband and said, "You're welcome. See you Sunday."

He was smiling rather oddly as he replied, "Yeah, see you Sunday."

I remember thinking, "This is strange."

Then I thought, "She is trouble."

We put the protective covers on the Falcon and disconnected the batteries. Then we grabbed our bags and walked into the FBO. The lady behind the desk called the hotel van to pick us up. I was looking forward to a couple of days in San Diego in some of the best weather in the world. We were staying in a nice hotel on Shelter Island on the north end of San Diego Bay and just a couple of miles southwest of the airport. I had stayed there before and knew that there were a couple of good seafood restaurants within walking distance of our hotel and I loved seafood. The hotel van pulled up to the FBO and we headed for a couple of enjoyable days in beautiful San Diego; all expenses paid. Nice.

It was early Saturday afternoon and the food, accommodations and weather had been as good as I had remembered. I hadn't given our passengers another thought since they had left the FBO in their rental car. The room phone rang and I answered, thinking it was the other pilot wanting to make some dinner plans.

It wasn't...instead it was my male passenger; "Jerry, I want to know what you have going on with _____."

I was floored. "What are you talking about?" I said.

He continued, "About all she's talked about since we got here is you and how she's looking forward to seeing you tomorrow."

"Well I don't know what that's all about but I've seen her exactly once; and you were there. So there's not a damn thing going on," I stated emphatically.

He then said, "I want you to know that I carry a nine millimeter pistol."

I hesitated for a moment in disbelief and then in anger I slowly replied; "Are you threatening me?"

He suddenly laughed and said, "I'm just kidding Jerry. I called to confirm our takeoff time tomorrow." Then he added, "But _____ really does like you." This was getting more bizarre.

I thought the situation over for a moment and then I said; "Let me tell you something _____; and I am *not* kidding. If you ever threaten me again, I guarantee that you will regret it."

He quickly replied, "But I don't really have a gun with me."

I said, "Tomorrow at the airport I am going to make sure of that."

He started to laugh again but I cut him off; *"I said I'm not kidding."* I hung up.

When our passengers arrived at the San Diego airport, things went as I had planned. _____ and I had a little private time out of sight and earshot of the others. Then as we flew back to Little Rock our passengers stayed in the back of the plane. However, when we got off the Falcon in Little Rock, _____ stepped toward me and tried to plant another kiss on me.

I put out my hand and quietly said, "Please, stay away from me." She looked surprised. I don't know if she knew about my conversation with her husband the day before. I also don't know whatever happened to _____. However, I do know what happened to her husband. Eight years later, he died under unusual circumstances in a New York hotel room.

I HAD LOST MY MIND

Fort Smith Municipal Airport, AR; 1984

The approval finally came through from Washington. My boss at Little Rock Air Center was a very enthusiastic and active supporter of the United States Military, including the Air Force and the Air National Guard. To my knowledge he had never been in the military, but he was a talented civilian trained and licensed pilot. He actively flew several different kinds of aircraft including the Falcon 10. The approval was from the Air National Guard Headquarters and it was his authorization to fly in my back seat on an F-4 simulated combat mission. I was eager to show him the F-4 and some of its capabilities and he was excited to be able to experience what it was like to fly in a high performance jet fighter in formation, low level and during ground attack maneuvers.

The day of the flight, we arrived in Fort Smith early enough for him to be fitted with a flight suit and G suit. Then he was thoroughly briefed on the Martin-Baker ejection seat by an egress technician. We went out to the F-4 early and he got a detailed check-out on the rear cockpit. We were scheduled to fly as the number four plane in a flight of four Phantoms; call-signs "Hog 11 through 14". After performing a formation takeoff on Hog 13's wing, we would join the first two aircraft and head north into Missouri. There we would turn back toward our low level route's starting point in the hills of northern Arkansas. The flight would make a high speed descent to join the route and. on a signal from the lead plane, we would slide out into combat spread formation. This formation was designed to provide mutual support, visual coverage and "six o'clock" protection for all four Phantoms. You could not see anything low and directly behind you in an F-4.

We would fly the low level route at an altitude between one hundred and five hundred feet above the ground. This extreme low altitude would provide terrain masking so that we could not be seen by ground based radars. Our indicated airspeed was to be four hundred and twenty knots (480 mph); eight miles per minute. Upon arrival at the end of the route in west-central Arkansas, we would be adjacent to the gunnery range southeast of Fort Smith. Just prior to reaching a planned initial point, the flight leader would signal us into extended trail formation. Over the entry point we would each perform a steep "pop-up" maneuver from off the deck to about eight thousand feet. We would visually acquire the target during the pull-up followed by our first bombing pass. Next we were to stay on the gunnery range for fifteen to twenty minutes to accomplish several more bombing and strafing passes.

The flight had gone exactly as briefed. We had just left the Ozarks behind and were streaking across I-40 southbound toward the Boston

Mountains in the near distance. Unknown to my backseater, who seemed to be enjoying his high speed and low altitude ride, we were soon going to have a "visitor". Our flight of Phantoms had just swept low across the Arkansas River when suddenly; *"Hog 11 flight; bogie two o'clock high moving to three. Break Right!!"* Four Phantoms immediately went from near straight and level one G flight into a seven G plus ninety degree banked hard turn toward the "threat". I spotted our "attacker" rolling in toward us from about three thousand feet. We snatched the noses of our F-4s directly at him and flashed by him in the opposite direction with a closure speed of over one thousand miles per hour. Our flight leader dived back down into the cover of the Boston Mountains and then broke hard left to rejoin our low level route. We followed and were quickly back down in the weeds. By the time our "bogie" had turned his jet around we were out of sight.

During the hard break toward the "attacker", our four Phantoms had gone from one G to about seven Gs in something less than a second. The pilot who is flying has time to tighten his stomach muscles and do the "M-1 maneuver" to stay conscious but the backseater may not; especially if he is on his first ride. Over the interphone during the break, I heard my boss grunting and straining to stay conscious. As swiftly as it had started, the violent fighter break was over and the G forces back to near normal as we dove for the cover of the trees. I could see my backseater's head in my rearview mirrors again and I asked if he was okay. I saw him shake his head in the mirror as he assured me that he was.

Upon the leader's signal I slid into trail formation about a mile behind Hog 13. Ahead of him I could see the black exhaust smoke trailing behind Hog 11 and Hog 12. Hog 11 roared over the initial point and pulled the nose of his Phantom almost straight up toward eight thousand feet. Sheets of vapor ripped off the top of his wings as he yanked the big Phantom up off the deck. Less than ten seconds later Hog 12 followed and then 13. It was our turn.

I hauled the stick back and then stopped the nose's pitch angle at about eighty degrees. I looked to my right and could see Hog 11 pulling off his first bombing pass. Hog 12 was in his forty-five degree dive toward the target. I rolled our Phantom inverted and pulled the nose down hard to the horizon to stop our climb at eight thousand feet. Hog 13 had dropped his bomb and was pulling vapor trails from the wingtips as he pulled his Phantom's nose away from the ground. I again rolled nearly inverted to begin our first bombing run. I noted the smoke drifting across the ground from Hog 13's bomb to help me judge where to place my bomb sight pipper (center dot). As we arrived at forty-five degrees of inverted dive, I flipped the Phantom right-side up and quickly made adjustments for the wind as we roared "down the chute" toward the target. Because of the extremely short time available, my adjustments required very aggressive corrections of both pitch and bank. In fact, they sometimes had to be so aggressive that I had forewarned my backseater about them. If I remember it correctly, I told him that he might think that I had lost my mind, but not to grab the controls because I had not. To add to the realism, the target area had simulated SAM (surface to air missile) and anti-aircraft gun sites. Their presence required that we perform furious "jinking" maneuvers (extremely hard turning back and forth) to spoil any possible weapons tracking as we pulled off our bombing and strafing passes. For anyone to just stay conscious while riding the bucking back seat of a Phantom on the gunnery range was an accomplishment in itself.

"Last pass," Hog 11 announced as he rolled in for his final strafing run. Following 13's last pass I pulled off our final strafe and "safetied" the gun switches. Then I quickly joined back into formation on Hog 13's right wing. As we headed back for landing, I let my boss try his hand at Phantom formation flying for a couple of minutes. I think he found that tight formation in an F-4 was not quite as easy as it might appear at first glance. As we approached the initial entry point, Hog 11 signaled for us to move into a right echelon for our fighter break and landing. I took the controls back and a couple of minutes later our simulated combat mission was over.

I have a picture taken after my boss and I had climbed out of our Phantom. We're standing by the big fighter shaking hands and grinning; however we both look completely wiped out. Lots of Gs have a way of doing that to you.

After the flight debriefing was finished, the boss told me he thought it was a good thing that I had briefed him about the extremely aggressive gunnery range patterns because he probably would have thought; "I had lost my mind."

Jerry W. Cook

YOU ATE MY DINNER

Petit Jean Park Airport, AR; September 1984

The efforts to try to defeat Bill Clinton for Governor of Arkansas were in full swing. There was to be a fundraising dinner to support a challenge by a Republican named "Woody" Freeman, a Jonesboro, Arkansas businessman. Winthrop Paul Rockefeller, the son of past Arkansas Governor Winthrop Rockefeller, was one of the sponsors and had arranged for former Secretary of State Henry Kissinger to be the featured speaker at the five hundred dollar a plate dinner. One of my boss's contributions to the effort was to provide air transportation for Dr. Kissinger to the event on Petite Jean Mountain, Arkansas and then on to La Guardia Airport in New York after his presentation. The day of the dinner, my co-pilot and I flew a Falcon 10 from Little Rock to pick up Dr. Kissinger and his security guard. If memory serves, the pickup point was Salt Lake City. After that, our itinerary called for us to bring them to the Petite Jean Park airport.

As the airport is rather isolated, we would wait in the small FBO building at the airport during the dinner. From there it was on to New York for the passenger drop-off and then back to Little Rock with an arrival early the next morning. It was going to be a very long day for me and my co-pilot. Things went as planned and we were on schedule landing at Petite Jean. A large entourage was waiting for Kissinger and off they all went to enjoy their delicious five hundred dollar per plate dinners. Because the airport was far from any place to eat, it appeared that we were out of luck for food except for some crackers and peanuts from the plane. The other pilot and I had not eaten since the flight lunches during our flight to Salt Lake City. It was looking like a very long and hungry night ahead of us.

Gary, the manager of the airport, who was also the Chief Pilot for Mr. Rockefeller, had a much better idea. He called the Rockefeller kitchen and had the cook prepare two dinners identical to the ones at the fundraiser and send them to the airport for me and the other pilot. The Chef had informed him that it was no problem because they had plenty of food. In a few minutes a car pulled up and an employee of Mr. Rockefeller delivered the two dinners complete with all the trimmings. He walked in and said, "The Chef said that these are for the pilots."

We ate them and agreed that they were the best five hundred dollar meals that we'd ever eaten. About an hour after we finished eating, we saw the vehicles containing our passengers entering the airport gate and heading toward our plane. The car with Dr. Kissinger, his body guard and accompanied by Mr. Rockefeller stopped by the Falcon's entry door where I was standing. Kissinger got out of his car, then walked up to me and stuck out his hand. It rather surprised me because he had not been overly friendly at Salt Lake City or during the flight to Arkansas.

I took his hand as he said, "I understand that you fly F-4 Phantoms."

I said, "Yes sir; in the Arkansas Air National Guard."

"Also in Vietnam?" he replied.

"Yes sir, that is correct," I said.

He continued, "The F-4 is a great airplane; much better than the F-15." I wasn't sure where the good Doctor had gotten his information, but I was surprised at his statement to say the least. I decided to keep my mouth shut and to not offer a correction to his highly inaccurate observation about the F-4 versus the F-15. He let go of my hand and got on board the Falcon. The co-pilot was already in his seat and had turned on the interior lights for Kissinger and his security guard. I was sitting down in the pilot's seat when the security guy came forward and said, "Dr. Kissinger asked if there is anything to eat on board,"

I replied, "Yes, there are snacks in the galley area."

He said "Okay," and went back to his seat. We were starting the engines by now, so I did not hear what he said to Kissinger. I remember thinking that Dr. Kissinger must not have eaten as much as I did because I sure wasn't thinking about anything else to eat. The sun had set some time ago and it had been dark for several hours as we leveled off and headed for Nashville. We were past Memphis when the Security guy came up again and asked what time we would get to New York. I told him our estimated time of arrival and that the airport manager at Petite Jean would make sure that our ETA was relayed to Kissinger's wife in New York, per his instructions. As he went back to his seat, I turned around and could see Kissinger rifling through the snack basket.

I turned to the co-pilot and said, "I can't believe he's still hungry."

The other pilot looked at me with a pained expression and said, "Man, I wish I was just hungry; I'm sick as a horse."

I said, "What do you mean; what's the matter?"

He was holding his stomach and rocking back and forth. "I think I've got food poisoning. My stomach's cramping like crazy."

"Do we need to land in Nashville?" I asked.

"No. I'm going to try to make it," he said. I got some antacid tablets from my flight kit and handed them to him. He grabbed them and chewed several.

"I'll make all the radio calls and navigate. You just stay still and let me know if we need to land," I told him. He just looked at me with a pained expression and nodded. All the way to New York I kept wondering if whatever the co-pilot had was going to hit me too since we ate the same thing (not smart). But I was lucky and felt fine the entire time. We landed at La Guardia right at the time that I had told Security and quickly taxied to the old

Marine Air Terminal parking ramp. My co-pilot was still miserable. I told him to open the door and head for the terminal building as soon as he could and I would take care of everything. He gratefully accepted and hit the ramp almost running as the engines were spinning to a halt. As I left the cockpit, I overheard Kissinger querying his security guard about why his wife wasn't there to meet them. He then made some gruff sounding remark about "estimating time" and "Arkansans" that I couldn't quite decipher but that I seriously doubted was a compliment. I went around behind the left wing to retrieve the luggage. We had been on the ground about fifteen minutes when Mrs. Kissinger finally pulled up in her Chrysler and got out.

I heard her say as she greeted her husband, "I'm sorry I'm late. I was watching a tennis match at the U.S. Open and I lost track of the time." The security guard and I loaded the luggage into the trunk of Mrs. Kissinger's car. I straightened up as Dr. Kissinger walked up to get in. He didn't shake my hand this time.

Instead he stopped, glared at me and then in his low guttural voice said, "You ate my dinner." Then he got in the car and they drove off. I didn't know what in the Hell he was talking about.

Back in Little Rock the next day, I found out what he was talking about. The Petite Jean airport manager called to tell me that Kissinger had decided not to eat at the dinner. He then said that he overheard one of Kissinger's escorts, a Little Rock lawyer, tell Doctor Kissinger that the pilots ate the dinners that the lawyer had arranged to send to the airport for Kissinger and his security guy. Evidently the guy did this after someone had told him that the pilots had eaten meals at the airport. (I guarantee that my co-pilot that night wishes that Kissinger had eaten the one that he did.) Before he called me, the Petite Jean Airport Manager had checked with the kitchen and found that the lawyer had not arranged for any meals to be delivered for Kissinger.

He had said, "Jerry, I thought you should know in case you hear about it."

I told him that I had already heard about it; from Kissinger. I could hardly believe it. It turned out that the guy who lied to Kissinger about me and my co-pilot eating his dinner was a lawyer. Can you imagine my disappointment when I found out that day that lawyers lie? (Perhaps he was the same guy who told Kissinger that the F-4 was better than the F-15.)

By the way, my co-pilot changed his mind about the dinner. He said it was by far the *worst* five hundred dollar meal he ever ate.

Toward The Evening Sky

WHAT'S THE MATTER; DON'T YOU LIKE ME?

Little Rock Adams Field, AR; 1985

It was going to be a long afternoon and a late night for Johnny, the other pilot and me; but it was going to be a profitable Falcon 10 charter for the Little Rock Air Center. We were to fly to Memphis, Tennessee empty and then pick up five passengers at the Memphis Aero Fixed Base Operator. From there we were to fly them to Fort Lauderdale and drop them off before returning to Little Rock. One week later a Little Rock Air Center Falcon was to return for them and take them back to Memphis.

We were a few minutes early when we taxied onto the ramp at Memphis Aero. There were a man and a woman standing and watching as we parked and got out of the Falcon. Johnny started around the plane for his post flight inspection and to open the baggage door. I told the lineman that we would not need any fuel and would be departing as soon as our passengers arrived. He said that he thought that the couple watching us might be some of my passengers. I walked over to them and asked if they were waiting for a charter flight to Ft. Lauderdale. They excitedly said that they were and that another couple was waiting inside. I asked if one of them was Mr. G_____. (He was the one who had paid for the trip with his American Express card.) They said that he was there but was sitting in his car and would need some help getting out and to get to the plane. I had not been informed that one of our passengers was handicapped. I wondered what kind of assistance he required.

"Does he need a wheelchair?" I asked.

They laughed and said, "No; just someone to steady him." I wondered what was funny about someone needing help, but didn't say anything.

The male passenger who had just come out of the FBO introduced himself and said, "I'll show you where Mr. G____ is." The other male passenger went with us as we walked around to the parking lot to the fifth passenger's Cadillac.

"Come on _____. The plane's here," one of them said loudly. The guy was sound asleep. I could see that he was hugging a half-empty whiskey bottle to his chest. Our lead (paying) passenger was drunk.

The guy standing beside me said as an explanation, "He's afraid to fly." I probably should have pulled the plug on the trip right then, but he had already paid for it and the other four seemed fine. His two buddies walked him to the plane and, by the time we finally got him on board and strapped into a seat, he was snoring again. The two women were excited and I suspected that they also had a few drinks under their belts. Their husbands (I guess) seemed to be sober as far as I could tell. This was a strange group. As we strapped in our seats, Johnny looked over at me.

I just shrugged and said, "Let's go to Ft. Lauderdale." (My real meaning was; "Let's get this over with.") It was getting dark over Alabama when one of the women came forward. There had been a lot of laughter and joking for the first forty-five minutes but it had quieted down in the back.

"Is there a seat up here where I can sit? I want to watch you guys. I think this is so cool," she said. (There was a jump seat which folded out into position just behind the pilots' seats.)

I answered, "There is, but it is not very comfortable."

"I don't care about that. I just want to watch you guys for a little while," she replied. Johnny helped her get the seat unfolded and fastened into place. After she had seated herself in the tight space, he handed her the seatbelt. It was dark now and Montgomery, Alabama was passing under our left wing. Suddenly I felt something on the inside of my right thigh. I looked down in the darkened cockpit. It was her left hand. I grabbed her hand and removed it from my leg.

"What's the matter? Don't you like that?" she said.

"Ma'am, you need to leave us alone," I replied. A couple of more minutes passed, and then I felt something on my left shoulder. When I looked, I saw that it was her foot.

"What the…," I exclaimed as I looked over toward Johnny. Her other foot was hooked over his right shoulder and I could see his face glowing bright red even in the darkened cockpit. He was staring straight ahead and not saying a word. I had no idea how she managed to get into a position to put her feet on our shoulders but I didn't turn to look at her to find out. I remembered that both women had been wearing very short skirts.

"Ma'am, you need to get your feet down and put them on the floor," I said.

"Why?" she said. "Don't you like me?"

Suddenly from the back of the airplane came a man's angry voice, "S____! Get your ass away from that cockpit and leave those pilots alone," he roared.

"Mind your own damn business," she said; "I'm not going anywhere."

"Yes, you are," he yelled. I felt the plane shift slightly as he quickly got out of his seat and came toward the cockpit.

"Leave me alone," she screamed as he grabbed her under the arms and dragged her over the back of the jump seat. I shielded myself and some cockpit switches from her kicking feet as Johnny did the same. I turned around as he sat her down and belted her tightly into her seat.

"Stay there," he said to her. Then he headed back toward the cockpit. I didn't know what was coming next.

He said, "Sorry guys, I guess she's had too much to drink. I won't let her bother you again."

"Yeah, thanks," was all I could think of to say. It was pretty quiet for the remainder of the flight to Ft. Lauderdale as our passengers all evidently went to sleep. As we shut down the engines four of them began stirring. The paying passenger had not moved from his position since we had strapped him in his seat in Memphis. (It was similar to the movie, "Weekend at Bernie's"; which came out about four years later; but this guy was still alive…I think.) The two guys got "Bernie" off the plane and into the limousine that was waiting. One of the women (you can guess which one) had not gotten off the plane by the time the rest of the passengers were in the car. I stuck my head in the door and looked toward the back.

"I'm too drunk to get off the plane. I guess you'll have to carry me," she giggled. I went to the limo and got the guy who had dragged her out of the cockpit. I relayed her message.

"I ought to leave her ass in there and have you guys take her back to Memphis," he said.

"That ain't gonna happen," I firmly replied.

Postscript: The next week I assigned someone else to take the flight to Ft. Lauderdale to retrieve them.

Jerry W. Cook

NOTHING TO GAIN

Little Rock Adams Field, AR, 1985

The owner of Little Rock Air Center had reached an agreement with Piper Aircraft to become a dealer for their new Cheyenne 400LS. It was a real hotrod twin engine turbo-prop that was reported to climb and cruise faster than some jets. It had been designed to compete with the popular Beechcraft King Air 200. A well-known gentleman who was famous for being the first man to fly faster than the speed of sound was acting as a spokesman in Piper Aircraft's Cheyenne 400LS marketing efforts. Of course he was very accustomed to hot aircraft and had recently set several time-to-climb records for its class in the Cheyenne. He had agreed to come to the Little Rock Air Center for the Cheyenne LS's introduction to the public in Little Rock.

Brigadier General (Retired) Charles "Chuck" Yeager was our passenger from Sacramento, California to Little Rock. The General's book, "Yeager: An Autobiography", had just been published. My boss had bought several boxes of the book and they were loaded in the luggage area behind the bench seat at the rear of the cabin. General Yeager had agreed to sign them during the flight back to Little Rock. They were to be available for the guests at the Air Center during the plane's introduction. I still have one of them in my collection.

The General lived at Grass Valley, California and the nearby Sacramento Airport was determined as the logical one to depart from. I was eager to meet him because like most Air Force pilots, I had closely followed his achievements in the air. He was a "fighter pilot's fighter pilot" and a test pilot extraordinaire. Additionally, he exhibited a propensity to speak his mind. One of his opinions that I wholeheartedly shared with the General was his attitude toward the early Astronauts, i.e. "Spam in a can".

The General was personable and, as you would expect, he came across as a very self-confident individual. During the flight, I removed the books from the luggage compartment and placed them near his seat ready for his signature. General Yeager sat quietly in the back of the plane and signed books most of the way. We were over central Oklahoma when my boss who was flying the plane turned around and asked the General if he had ever flown a Falcon 10. Yeager said that he had not. Then he asked Yeager if he would like to. The General jumped at the chance. The boss got out of the left seat and General Yeager strapped in. Then just like that, for the next few minutes, I was General Chuck Yeager's instructor. He sat and looked around the cockpit and asked a few questions. I briefed him on the speeds for descent, approach and landing. When we were about one hundred and twenty miles from Little Rock, I obtained a descent clearance from Ft. Worth Center.

General Yeager flew us to Little Rock and landed the little jet with no problem at all. I wasn't surprised. (I don't think it was my instruction skills.)

A lot of Arkansas citizens were thrilled to meet and talk to the famous gentleman and the 400LS's introduction seemed to be a success. Part of the time, he sat at a table signing and personalizing copies of his book. My boss served as his host and, during his stay at Little Rock, the General was a guest at the home of the Little Rock Air Center's owner.

After his visit in Little Rock, his next appearance was to be in Houston, Texas. He was scheduled to fly there in a Cheyenne 400LS with several Piper reps as his passengers. Just before he departed for Houston, I was talking to General Yeager and thought I would have a little fun by issuing a challenge. I told the General that I would like to bring a Phantom out to Reno, Nevada where he still flew Phantoms occasionally. I said that we could take off in formation from there and then; I wanted to fly a "one-v-one" air combat mission against him; "Because I've never kicked a legend's ass." The General's blue eyes twinkled and he laughed.

He said "Yes Colonel; I suppose some people might call me a legend, but you are not going to get a chance to try to 'kick my ass'. Besides, I'd have nothing to gain."

He had a point. He was expected to be able to kick my ass.

Postscript: Regarding "Spam in a can"; the original Mercury Seven astronaut selectees were picked not for their flying skills (of which they obviously had plenty) but for their expected ability to withstand the rigors of space flight that were predicted by the engineers and medical experts. Some additional requirements were; they could not be over five feet, eleven inches tall or over one hundred and eighty pounds. This was so they could fit in the Spam can referred to by General Yeager. Initially, the piloting of the capsule in which they were enclosed was not in their hands but in those of individuals on the ground who programed and controlled the capsules' flights. Later the astronauts asked for and finally received some manual re-entry controls. One thing that the astronauts obviously had in abundance was guts. To have the cojones to be strapped into a tiny container perched on the top of a giant skyrocket is not in my genetic makeup.

Additionally, the original astronauts selected were reported to be superb physical specimens with an IQ of at least the genius level. However, someone with a lower intelligence level, such as I, would think that a genius would know better than to allow himself to become part of a nosecone on a rocket!

Jerry W. Cook

TIME FOR A CHANGE

Little Rock Adams Field, AR; 1986

The call came from Monterey, California toward the end of the summer. It seemed that the owner of a private company with its headquarters in Sacramento, California had just purchased a Falcon 10. He had in operation a twin engine turbo-prop as his company aircraft but had recently decided that he needed a jet. His current pilot had no jet experience and the owner was looking for a pilot and a co-pilot to fly his plane temporarily while his pilot went to initial training on the Falcon 10. And when he completed training, their plan was to hire a co-pilot from the local area to fly with him. Little Rock Air Center had several Falcon 10 qualified pilots and it was an excellent opportunity for the company to profit from the pilot service fees that the gentleman was willing to pay.

I decided to go to California as the Captain and one of our co-pilots volunteered to go with me for the first few weeks. After we arrived in Monterey, we learned a few more of the details and the deal got even better. The plane would be based not in Sacramento, but at an FBO at the Monterey Peninsula Airport because the owner of the company lived in Pebble Beach. Although the company's main location was in Sacramento, he kept a small office with several employees in Monterey. His Falcon would be maintained by a company at the San Jose International Airport.

Another part of the company was located in Phoenix, Arizona and it operated a Beechcraft King Air, which was based at Phoenix Sky Harbor Airport. Evidently most of our flying would be between Monterey, Sacramento and Phoenix, but there would be longer trips and other destinations from time to time. The usual passengers would consist of the owner of the company and a few company executives. At times, his wife would also accompany him.

His Falcon 10 was a very nice plane and turned out to be the fastest 10 that I had flown. Likely that was because it did not have thrust reversers, which made it somewhat lighter. At first, I was a little concerned when I found out about the plane not having thrust reversers but, after a few flights, I really didn't miss them all that much. Its engines were evenly matched and someone had obviously taken very good care of the plane before this company purchased it.

As part of the pilot service agreement, the new owner paid all of our expenses. We were housed in nice hotels in Monterey when we were there, including the Sheraton and the Doubletree. He treated us well, the flights were usually short, and the weather was outstanding. It was an enjoyable experience but our temporary pilot contract period was quickly drawing to a close. One day I received a call from the owner's assistant. She said that he wanted me to come to his office. When I arrived, the owner invited me to sit down and then he got right to the point.

He said, "Jerry, I really like having you as my pilot. What would it take to get you to work for me full time as my Chief Pilot?" I had thought up to this point that his former pilot was going to take over as soon as he finished training. When I asked about him, the owner just said that he wouldn't be flying the Falcon. I had not expected this and I was rather caught off guard by his question. Although I loved Monterey, I told him of my hesitation to move to California and that I didn't think that I could afford to live there.

He replied, "Name your price." I thought about it while I drank the coffee that his assistant had just brought us. Although tempted I wasn't convinced that moving was what I needed to do at this time. Because of my position at the Little Rock Air Center, I knew what the going rate in the country for a Falcon 10 Chief Pilot was. I thought I would just add a substantial amount to that number and throw it at him. I presumed it would change his mind about wanting to hire me. I gave him the figure and waited for his reply. It didn't take him but a second and he didn't even blink. And his answer wasn't the one that I had expected.

"Done," he said and then; "When can you start?" and stuck out his hand.

"Well crap," I thought.

"What am I going to do now? I should have asked for more," were my next thoughts.

"I'll have to get back to you on that," I said.

"Okay. Try to make it as soon as possible because I've got several important trips coming up," he said. I couldn't believe that I had been handed this opportunity. I had suspected for some time that things in my life were about to change back in Arkansas. With twenty-six years in the military, I had begun to think about retirement. It wasn't easy to consider because I was really enjoying flying the F-4 and my present military position as the Assistant Adjutant General for Air for the state of Arkansas. However, recently I had sensed some subtle changes in the "atmosphere" at Little Rock Air Center and I was beginning to wonder about job stability there. I believe that perhaps I was extra sensitive in that area because of my awful experiences with Pan Am. (In March 1986, I had finally received a recall notice from Pan American. They were going to assign me to JFK International and wanted me to fly sideways as an engineer on a Boeing 727. That recall notice came a full ten years after they had last furloughed me. The final part of my answer to Pan Am had been; *"Not only you; but the horse that you rode in on!"* A good friend of mine went back to Pan Am with that recall and, in December 1991, the "World's Most Experienced" went bankrupt.)

When I returned to Little Rock I tendered my resignation with the Air National Guard. I then did the same at the Little Rock Air Center. Things were changing rapidly. Then in the middle of December and one of my last days at the Air Center a red-headed stranger in an expensive looking suit walked up to me in the parking lot and said; "Are you Jerry Cook?"

When I answered, "Yes I am," he slapped divorce papers in my hand. It wasn't exactly one of the changes that I had expected. In late December I headed for Monterey.

IF I CHANGE MY CALL SIGN TO DELTA 510CP?

Dallas Fort Worth International Airport, TX; 1987

They're not supposed to do it, or so I've been informed. But air traffic controllers sometimes give priority handling to airliners over corporate jets. They will inform the corporate pilot if he grumbles that he just doesn't have "the Big Picture". (Yeah; actually we do. So don't try to "blow smoke up our skirts".) I suppose they do it because of the difference in the numbers of passengers affected by any potential delays. I could perhaps agree with that reasoning to some extent; but if the traffic sequencing as a result is dangerous or excessive then it is not acceptable. The earlier story "Aspen Roulette" was an example of the former; this is an example of the latter.

My new boss had a business trip into the Dallas area. Although I tried to talk him into landing at Dallas Love or some other area airport besides DFW, he insisted on going there. At the time, the General Aviation area was a Frontier Airlines gate on the extreme north side of the terminal. In addition to the recurring heavy air traffic and resultant delays, the service for corporate aircraft was minimal. It was painfully obvious that they did not want us there. After a long wait, spent mostly at the aircraft, the boss finally returned. We started engines and called for our IFR clearance. After an extensive delay, it finally came through and we were ready to taxi. They were using runway 17R for departures and I was happy because it was only a short taxi from where we were parked to the runway. The ground controller gave us instructions to taxi via Zulu and hold short of taxiway Kilo for runway 17R.

I thought, "Yes, we'll be out of here in no time." I was also pleased that there were yet very few planes taxiing for takeoff. We must have caught a time between the airlines' "pushes" (when they all seem to try to come or go at the same time). I taxied quickly up to and held short of taxiway Kilo. There were two Delta jets taxing northbound on Kilo. I looked south toward the Delta Terminal ramp and saw several jets with their rotating beacons on. That meant that either their engines were already running or they were about to start. A few were obviously preparing to taxi. As of yet, none of them were moving and there were none on taxiway Kilo behind the two about to pass our position.

As the second Delta jet passed our position, my co-pilot called Ground Control and said, "Falcon N510CP holding short at Kilo."

"Falcon 510CP; I *know* you're holding short at Kilo. Now stay off the radio!" was the snotty reply from the ground controller. My co-pilot looked over at me, startled.

He said, "Man, what's up with that guy?" I looked toward the south again. There were still no other aircraft on the taxiway. Then we heard the same controller ask a Delta jet if he was ready yet. He was and the controller told him to taxi to Runway 17R via Kilo. It was another several minutes before that particular jet passed by our nose but the push had started. The controller was giving the Deltas taxi clearance as soon as they called and they were now filling up taxiway Kilo as they taxied past where we had been holding for many minutes. We sat there and waited as the ones still at their gates turned on their beacons as they prepared for pushback. We had already watched a lot of them start their engines, receive their clearance and taxi past us. By now I was fuming. Additionally, my boss repeatedly kept asking me what the delay was.

Then astonishingly, he said, "Maybe if you told them who your passenger is they would let us go."

Huh? I didn't know who he *thought* he was, but I finally just said, "I don't think that would help." (What I wanted to say was; "That would probably just make it worse.")

Finally I thought, "Enough is enough." I pushed the microphone button and said, "Ground, Falcon 510CP is still holding short."

The guy came right back at me with, "510CP, I told you to stay off the radio. *I'll call you when I'm ready!*"

I replied, "*Negative. I'm not going to do that. But if I change my call sign to 'Delta 510CP' will you let me taxi then?!*"

There was a long silence and then a new voice came on the radio, "Falcon 510CP, sir that won't be necessary. Do you see the Delta 1011 just south of your position?"

"Roger 510CP," I answered.

He said, "After he passes your position, follow the L-1011 to runway 17R. The Delta DC-9 behind him will hold for you."

I replied, "Roger, 510CP to follow the 1011 to runway 17R."

He then issued instructions for the DC-9 to, "Hold your position and then follow the Falcon to runway 17R." The DC-9 acknowledged.

After we turned onto taxiway Kilo, the new controller then said, "Sorry about that 510CP; contact tower for departure."

Now, tell me again that we don't have, "the Big Picture".

Toward The Evening Sky

YOU GOT TWO MORE THAN I DID

Monterey to Sacramento to Easton, MD; 1987

This was going to be a long day. We had the boss's wife aboard and we were enroute to Sacramento from Monterey. We had only climbed to fifteen thousand feet. My experience with Oakland Center on this short flight was that if you filed any higher you weren't going to get it anyway. I understood that it was because of all the crossing traffic into and out of the San Francisco Bay area. We were about halfway to Sacramento when the center cleared us to descend to eleven thousand feet. As we leveled at eleven, we were about one hundred feet above a solid white cloud deck that extended as far as we could see. We were commenting about how skimming along in close proximity to the clouds gave the sensation of high speed when suddenly, a big flock of ducks appeared dead ahead of us also skimming along just above the cloud deck. I quickly punched the autopilot disconnect button and yanked the Falcon's nose up. Unfortunately, that caused a startled shriek from the boss's wife. Fortunately, most of the big birds passed under us on our left side. We weren't sure if we'd hit any ducks, or if so how many, until after we landed. It turned out that we had missed all but two. One had impacted the left leading edge slat and the other had ended his final flight smeared on the bottom of the left wing just in front of the wheel well. None had gone into either engine.

We quickly cleaned off the remains and had an aircraft mechanic check over the plane. He declared it airworthy and we got it topped off with fuel just before the boss arrived at the airport. After briefing him about the incident and assuring him that the plane was okay to fly, we loaded his luggage into the Falcon. Twenty minutes later, we lifted off and headed for Coaldale, Nevada, the first point on our route toward the east. About seven hours later, including a quick fuel stop, we were landing at Easton/Newman Field Airport, Maryland.

We unloaded the boss's luggage which included a couple of shotgun cases. He had flown to Easton from California to hunt ducks and geese for two days with a client. His host was there waiting and we wished them luck. We then got busy and "put the Falcon to bed". Forty-five minutes later we checked into our hotel and were looking forward to a restful couple of days and some really good seafood. As hoped, we accomplished both goals and enjoyed the stay.

Two days later we were back at the airport with our flight plans filed, with the Falcon fueled and ready to head back to Monterey. Soon the boss came driving up to the plane.

As we pulled his luggage and guns out of the vehicle I asked him, "How did you do?"

He looked at me and frowned over his glasses; "Let's just put it this way; you guys got two more than I did."

Toward The Evening Sky

WELL! WHO *SHOULD* I HAVE TALKED TO?

Sacramento Executive Airport, CA; 1987

There was a big political gathering in Sacramento that evening and I assume, as his contribution, our boss had volunteered his jet to fly the guest politician and speaker from Sacramento to Los Angeles after the party. The politician was from a state in the northeast and his last name was famous and known worldwide. My boss discussed the trip with me and informed me that the passenger wanted to be dropped off at the Santa Monica airport. I told him that Santa Monica had a noise curfew and we would have to be in and out of there before eleven p.m. or we couldn't fly his trip early the next morning out of Sacramento. For us to do that, we would have to depart Sacramento no later than nine-thirty p.m. He assured me that he would inform our passenger of the required departure time. However, having flown several politicians in the past, I didn't have much confidence in our passenger being on time.

After dinner, Bob and I returned to Sacramento Executive airport by eight p.m. so we would be there in case the passenger showed up early…dream on. Nine-thirty came and went. At nine-forty five, I changed our flight plan destination to Los Angeles International Airport. It is located just eight miles south of Santa Monica. At this time of night, it would probably be just a ten or fifteen minute cab ride back to Santa Monica. Finally at about ten-thirty, the VIP showed up. As he introduced himself with his big politician's smile he said, "You guys are taking me into Santa Monica, right?"

I answered, "No sir. We're going to take you to Los Angeles International. It's only a quick fifteen minute cab ride to Santa Monica from there. We'll have one standing by for you when we land."

He said firmly, "I don't want to ride fifteen minutes to Santa Monica. I want you to fly me there. Your boss said that you would." He heavily emphasized the words *your* and *boss*.

"Then he also should have informed you that we had to takeoff no later than nine-thirty to do that," I said.

"I don't remember whether he did or not; but I want you to take me to Santa Monica," he said firmly. His fake smile had disappeared.

"You are too late. Their curfew starts in about twenty-five minutes and we wouldn't be able to take off again until seven o'clock tomorrow morning," I replied.

"*So…?*" was his slightly disdainful reply.

"*So…*; it's *not* going to happen," I said. He was persistent.

"So what would happen if you did take me into Santa Monica and then takeoff again tonight?" he asked.

"I would get fined and perhaps lose my license and like I said; it's *not* going to happen," I answered.

"Now…do you want us to take you to LAX or not?" I continued. He was not happy but he got on the plane.

After we landed at LAX, as he got off the plane he said, "I still don't understand. I talked to your boss about your taking me into Santa Monica and he didn't indicate that there would be any problem." Again he stressed the words *your* and *boss*. This was getting aggravating, it was late, and I had to get back to Sacramento for a seven a.m. takeoff the next morning.

I said, "Well I guess you talked to the wrong guy."

"*Well! Who should I have talked to?*" he replied rather huffily.

"*Me!*" was my answer. He didn't shake my hand before he got into the cab. That just broke my heart. (Because by now you know how much I like politicians.)

Toward The Evening Sky

MAR-MAYS AND NORDOS

Descending into Albuquerque International Sunport, NM; 1987

When you are starting out in a career associated with aviation, you have to be aware. Not necessarily of physical injury but aware of more experienced members in that field who like to take advantage of the newbie's lack of familiarity with the language of aviation. There are terms used every day in aviation that are completely foreign to those with more earth-based professions and to new members of the clan. Somewhat like medicine, aviation has developed a vocabulary of its own. One of the more common pranks is sending a newbie down to parts supply to get "jet wash" or "prop wash". Another lesser known one is to have them go to an aviation technician to borrow a "flight level". And sometimes the newcomer just sets himself up for you.

Bob was from Monterey, California and I had hired him to fly as my co-pilot on the company's Falcon 10. He had been flying for a while but did not have much jet time and was relatively low in flight experience. However, he was a very good pilot and eager to learn everything he could in as short a time as possible; certainly nothing wrong with that attitude. Consequently, he asked a lot of questions, perhaps sometimes before considering the possible answers himself.

We were returning from a several day trip to the east coast and had just begun our descent into Albuquerque for a fuel stop. Bob was looking at the airport diagram in our Jeppesen approach charts. He had not flown into the Albuquerque International Sunport before and wanted to familiarize himself with its layout. I was looking at Sandia Peak and the Albuquerque airport in the distance. We were still about fifty miles away and the Center had not yet switched us to the approach control radio frequency.

Bob had been staring intently at the airport diagram when he suddenly said, "What the heck is a Mar-May?"

I looked at him and said, "A what?"

"A Mar-May," he repeated.

"Let me see what you're looking at," I answered. He handed me the chart and pointed at the area on the chart that he was reading. There it was; "Use caution Mar-May heavy bird activity along the Rio Grande River." I bit my tongue to keep from chuckling and to keep a straight face.

After a moment I looked seriously at him and said, "Oh yeah. You know what a California Condor looks like don't you?"

"Sure," Bob said; "Why?"

"Well I've heard that some of these New Mexico Mar-Mays are as big as a Condor and that they frequent the Rio Grande River valley. Hitting one of them would sure ruin your day wouldn't it?"

"Man, it sure would," my newbie co-pilot replied.

"Help me watch out for them especially after we take off westbound over the river," I said with all the sincerity that I could muster.

"I sure will," Bob said as he earnestly searched the sky ahead. I wanted to continue the spoof until after we had taken off again and headed toward the river but we needed to tend to business. Besides I couldn't suppress my amusement any longer and started snickering.

Bob looked curiously at me and said, "What's so funny?"

I looked at him and replied, "'*Mar-May*'; as in March through May."

"What?" As he caught on he grinned and said, "Well crap. I knew I shouldn't have asked." Then he laughed as he reread the note on the airport diagram; "*Use caution Mar-May heavy bird activity along the Rio Grande River.*"

Then just a few days later we were approaching Sacramento Executive airport from the south. NORCAL (Northern California) approach control had just changed us to the Executive control tower.

They cleared us for a straight-in visual approach to runway 02 and added, "510CP be advised we have a Nordo five miles to the east of the field. We think he may be lining up to land on runway 30. We will issue your landing clearance after we see where he's going."

Bob hesitated and turned to me with a questioning look so I said, "Just tell them Roger, 510CP."

After telling them he said, "What is a Nordo?"

I answered, "Seriously? You don't know what a Nordo is?"

He said "No, what is it?"

"You've probably seen one. It's a French-built high-wing cargo plane with two really noisy turbo-prop engines," I said with a straight face.

"Oh yeah, I think I know what you're talking about," Bob answered.

"Well keep your eyes out for him in case he decides to land on 30," I cautioned.

"Will do," my co-pilot answered and peered intently toward our northeast.

"Falcon 510CP, the Nordo is no factor; you are cleared to land on runway 02," the tower said. We landed and taxied to the fixed base operator. A few minutes later I saw Bob talking to some other pilots. Just as I walked by I heard him describing to them what a Nordo was. I kept walking to a nearby chair and sat down with my coffee to watch. One of the other pilots was obviously questioning Bob's description. Bob looked at me and pointed. The other pilot grinned at me and just shook his head. Bob immediately "saluted" me. (You know what form it took.) No; I didn't blame him either. But he won't forget what a Nordo is. And he was okay after I bought him lunch. (NORDO Definition: "An aircraft with no radio.")

Postscript: There *is* a Nord 262 which fits the description I gave to Bob.

Toward The Evening Sky

TOO GOOD TO BE TRUE

Monterey, CA; Early 1989

What a beautiful place. Each morning I was in town, I would get up and look out of the apartment window. From there, I had a small view of Monterey Bay. And if I wasn't flying somewhere that day Linda and I would often head for the Monterey Tennis Center. There we could play tennis outdoors year round. We had made several friends who also played tennis and we could usually find a match. In the summer, the average temperature ranged in the high sixties. But even if the temperature was higher that day, we could still feel the cool breeze blowing in from the nearby bay. During the mild winter we could play in temperatures which averaged in the mid-fifties. Another characteristic of Monterey was that year round you needed a sweater or a jacket for the cool evenings; fifties in the summer and forties in winter. Adding to the ambiance, we could hear the sea lions barking down by the wharf just a few blocks away.

I would sometimes think; "This is too good to be true." And then unfortunately, one day…it was.

It was the boss's assistant on the phone. She said that he wanted me to come to his office. From the sound of her voice I knew it couldn't be good. Recently I had heard a rumor that he might be going to sell his business but I didn't know for sure how that would affect me. I knew that he loved having his plane and thought that perhaps he might keep it. At least that's what I hoped would happen if he sold his company. I was wrong.

My boss announced, "Jerry, I'm selling my company and we're going to have to get rid of the Falcon. Sorry, but we won't need you and Bob anymore. I will be staying with the company. Although I will still need to fly a lot, the new owner is a public company and their accountants want the corporate jet off the books." I asked him who the new owner was. I was surprised when he told me the firm's name because it was a Utilities Company that had recently made the news. The news was that they were going Chapter 11. (How do companies buy things when they've just gone bankrupt?) No wonder they wanted the jet off their books. To add to my disappointment he then said he was going to start using jet charter companies to do his flying. He said that he wasn't happy about that but the new owners had insisted on it even after he had informed them that the charters would end up costing more than keeping the Falcon. The purchasing company's bean-counters had told him it didn't matter. Even if it did cost more, they couldn't keep the jet on their books. There it was. The rumors had had a basis. Once again I was experiencing that all too familiar sick feeling in my stomach of not having a job. Although I would still be flying for a few more weeks, including the last flight to deliver the jet, I was effectively out on the street again.

I'd been working since I was fourteen. I was everything from a soda jerk in a drug store to a projectionist at a movie theater. At sixteen I had plowed wheat fields until three o'clock in the morning and bucked hay bales while standing on a sled behind a baling machine in the hot Oklahoma hayfields. Then, I began flying planes for a living when I was nineteen. However, I wasn't nineteen anymore. As my remaining days with the company started winding down, I began looking for a flying job in the local area and visited several flight departments to leave my resume'. I also applied to several airlines including Japan Airlines, Singapore Airlines and Southern Air Transport but had not as of yet heard anything back from them.

Here I was, a graying fifty-one year old Pan Am three-time loser, now out of work in the corporate flight world. Aviation wasn't working out that great for me, but I loved flying. My situation reminded me of the old story about the guy who was always complaining about his job shoveling elephant manure in the circus. When he was asked why he didn't just quit, he said "What? And leave show business!?" I guess aviation was my show business. But now what?

On the other end of the phone was the Chief Pilot for Stephens Incorporated, a well-known investment banking firm in Little Rock, Arkansas. I had applied to them for a pilot position several years before, but reportedly their Chief Pilot at that time had "round-filed" my application. The company was definitely aviation oriented and had operated corporate planes for many years. The Chief Pilot continued by saying that he'd been looking for me and that my son Jeff had given him my number. He stated that the Chairman of Stephens wanted to talk with me about possibly coming to work for them. He finished by saying that the company was looking for a highly experienced jet pilot and that my name had come up. I wasn't sure whether they knew that I was out of work, but suddenly my future in *show business* was looking much brighter.

Toward The Evening Sky

MR. JACK

Little Rock, AR; Spring 1989

Mr. Jack Stephens was sitting behind his big wooden desk in the Stephens' building then located on Capitol Avenue in Little Rock. My recently updated resume' that I had brought with me was on his desk. After first looking it over for several minutes he had been asking me questions about my flying and military experience. His last question to me had been, "Jerry, why do you want to fly for Stephens?"

I considered the question for a few seconds and replied, "Well Mr. Stephens, let me put it this way. I've flown for several companies who loved their airplanes; but it turned out that they couldn't afford them." When he realized I had finished my answer, Mr. Jack lowered his head and studied me over his glasses in complete silence. Smoke was curling up from the cigarette in his hand. I looked back at him across his big desk and waited.

He cleared his throat and quietly said; "I don't think you're going to have to be concerned about that here at Stephens. When can you start?"

(As luck would have it, not long after I had received the call from Stephens' Chief Pilot, Singapore Airlines notified me that they found me qualified to train and fly for them as an Airbus Captain. They had indicated in their message that, if I accepted the position, I would be based in Singapore. The time was running out for me to reply to them. I had just arrived at another fork in the road.)

I quickly made my decision; "How about next month sir?"

Mr. Jack stood up and said, "Fine." We shook hands on it. That gentleman was definitely a man of few words. Once again I would be heading from California to "Arkansas, The Land of Opportunity". For me, the state had definitely lived up to its slogan; twice.

Postscript: I don't know why they came from time to time but they did. The opportunities came; doors had opened. They came in various forms: telegrams; Air Force orders; conversations in a cockpit; phone calls; etc. And whenever they came, my life always seemed to change for the better. More often than not, they would arrive just when things weren't looking all that great for my aviation career. Whatever the source of these opportunities, I am grateful. And I am especially thankful for the one that landed me the job stability that had eluded me for all these years.

That phone call from the Chief Pilot of Stephens Incorporated was like handing a parachute to a free-falling man. Stephens had been operating corporate aircraft at least since the early 1960's and, as Mr. Jack had indicated during my interview, they could afford them. Equally important, their planes were used as vital business tools. They enabled Stephens to successfully compete in the many aspects of their business ventures. As I walked through the door of the Stephens Flight Department, I was beginning the final twenty-two year segment of my previously turbulent career in aviation. Here I was starting over again at fifty-one years of age, but I would need no more doors to open. At last I had arrived at a company which was being "piloted" with integrity and sound practical judgment by its President, Warren Stephens.

Toward The Evening Sky

WHAT DID HE SAY?

Little Rock Adams Field, AR; Early 1990s

The Falcon 10 was up for sale. We had just received two new Citation 5s a few weeks before so the "10" was not used very much while it was being marketed. It had been parked in the hangar. In fact on that day, the other pilot and I had not flown it for quite some time. However, by FAA regulations we were legal to fly it; but barely.

Usually our passengers at Stephens were middle and upper management types. That day, our two passengers were in that category and were fairly frequent fliers. However, one of them was not very fond of flying. He was a tremendous individual and a real "up and comer" at Stephens, but for some reason, he was a visibly nervous passenger. He asked about the weather as he always did before he got on the plane. He then went straight to the back of the cabin and sat down on the rear seat and fastened his seat belt tightly. The other passenger, who had quite the opposite attitude toward flying, had also gotten on and was preparing to get himself a cup of coffee as I shut the entry door. Ray the other pilot was already belted into the co-pilot seat and was carefully looking around the cockpit.

As I sat down in the pilot seat, the passenger by the door said, "Hey, this isn't a Citation." He had a Styrofoam coffee cup in his hand and was looking for the coffee pot.

"No, the Citation had a maintenance issue, so we're substituting the Falcon 10," I replied.

"Oh. Well no wonder I can't find anything," he laughed.

Ray from the co-pilot's seat loudly replied, "You think *you* can't find anything."

From the back seat of the airplane quickly came the anxious question, *"What did he say?"*

I knew the questioner could see and hear me so I mischievously decided to add to his consternation; I pointed to something on the instrument panel and said, "What in the Hell is that?"

"That's it! I'm out of here!" the rear seat passenger said loudly as he threw off his seat belt and stood up. Ray, the other passenger and I broke up laughing. It took us a few minutes to convince the nervous passenger that we actually knew where and what everything was and that we were only kidding. Although it took some persuading he finally decided that he would go with us.

Jerry W. Cook

GAGE PROBLEM

Little Rock Adams Field, AR; Early 1990s

In many corporate flight departments, especially smaller ones, the structure is somewhat informal. In these organizations the flight operations are governed by the Federal Aviation Regulations and little else. Because the FARs that regulate Part 91 operations (most corporate flight departments) do not require formalized and written Flight Operations Manuals, they sometimes do not exist. Where they do exist, they may not be all that comprehensive or are largely ignored. The organization of the departments is up to its manager, usually the Chief Pilot. The corporate flight departments where I had flown before had been basically one airplane and two pilot operations and I had not utilized a flight operations manual. In larger departments, the possibility for errors and omissions in ground and in-flight procedures grows exponentially.

Each pilot brings to an organization their own ideas based on the way they were trained and how they operated in previous flight organizations. With just two and perhaps even three pilots, these predispositions are comparatively easy to blend into an unwritten but relatively standardized way of operating. In a department with more than two or three pilots, the potential for mistakes increases substantially and the need for written and comprehensive standard operating procedures becomes essential for a safe operation. These standardized procedures basically outline who, what, and when; i.e., during any phase of a flight operation (including before and after flight) they outline *who* is responsible for doing *what* and *when* they should do it. One of these *whats* is getting the required fuel into the plane.

That day the other pilot and I arrived at the hangar at about the same time for the early morning flight. We only had one passenger. He was very high in the Stephens organization, a Senior Executive Vice-President. We were to proceed to Memphis, Tennessee and wait there for a couple of hours before taking him to New York. While we were getting coffee, I asked the other pilot what he wanted to do; file the flight plans and check the weather or get the plane ready to go? He said that he would get the plane ready. We decided on a fuel load and he said that he would take care of it. I checked the weather for Memphis and New York and enroute. It was good and both airports were fully operational, so I filed the flight plans. When I was finished, I got another cup of coffee and sat down to wait for our passenger. In a few minutes the other pilot came in and said the plane was ready. About ten minutes before our scheduled takeoff time, the passenger drove up and we all proceeded to the Citation 5 which sat waiting and *ready* to go.

After the passenger was seated and I had closed and latched the entry door, I stepped into the cockpit and sat down in the left seat. After I had fastened my seatbelt and shoulder harness, I reached over and turned on the battery switch. I then looked at the fuel gauges. They each read six hundred pounds. That meant that we had a total of twelve hundred pounds on board instead of the five thousand eight hundred that we had agreed on. I looked at the other pilot. He was staring at the fuel gauges.

I whispered, "Where's the fuel?"

He looked at me and very quietly replied, "I forgot it."

I turned off the battery switch and turned around to address our passenger; "Jon, we're going to be delayed for a few minutes. You will be more comfortable in the hangar office. I'll come and get you when we're ready."

He looked surprised and asked, "What's the matter with the plane?"

I replied, "We have a slight *gage* problem."

"Can it be fixed?" he continued.

"Oh, yes sir. It should only take about fifteen minutes and we'll be on our way," I assured him.

"Okay," he said and left the plane through the door that I had opened again. Now you're thinking that I lied but please, hear me out. I did not lie. Believe it or not, the other pilot's last name was *Gage*. And…he was the problem. (I'm not making this up.)

But Gage promptly *fixed* the gauge problem and we were soon on our way to Memphis. No harm, no foul, no problem.

Jerry W. Cook

THE BEST AND THE WORST

Wichita Mid-Continent Airport, KS; Early 1990s

Waymon Pearson was one of the finest individuals I ever met. About twenty years before, I had been a member of an Arkansas Air National Guard pilot selection board and Waymon was a candidate. During the interview he had come across to the board members including me as quiet, methodical and *very* slow talking. He had easily answered our questions but his manner left a mutual question in all of our minds. After the interview, we excused him to wait outside the conference room while we made the decision whether to hire him.

The question was: could he keep up with the supersonic and very unforgiving RF-101 Voodoo? His slow talking and deliberate ways had placed doubt in our minds about his ability to react quickly enough to the sometimes extremely challenging characteristics of the big jet fighter. I pointed out that he had graduated at the top of his pilot training class and that his last duty was as an instructor in the supersonic T-38 Talon jet trainer. I wanted to give him a chance. The rest of the board agreed subject to one condition: that I would be his instructor pilot for the Voodoo checkout. I agreed.

His was the easiest checkout I had ever instructed in a jet fighter. Waymon was a natural pilot. I would show him how to do something just one time and he could do it. And now twenty years later we were flying together again. He had been hired by Stephens about a year prior to me. He hadn't changed a bit. He was still slow talking and slow walking and still one of the best pilots with whom I had ever flown.

It was time for our Flight Safety Citation 5 recurrent training and Waymon and I were about halfway through the five day schedule. It was our second simulator ride and our young sim instructor appeared to be getting frustrated. He had been firing emergencies at us at a very rapid pace and we had been resolving them just as fast. Although simulators are notorious for being harder to fly than the actual planes, Waymon was doing a fantastic job in the left seat of flying and directing the action. He had just performed a single engine raw data ILS to minimums and landed after we had been given an engine fire and wing flap failure.

"All right, let's see how you do with this next one," the instructor announced. He sounded exasperated. I believe that for some reason he felt it would somehow be a feather in his cap if he could cause us to crash.

He electronically slewed the little Citation backwards down the runway to the takeoff end and said; "Okay Citation N1823S, you are cleared for takeoff. Maintain runway heading and climb to three thousand feet." I read back the clearance and we completed the "Before Takeoff" checklist. Waymon pushed the throttles up and released the brakes. I wondered what was coming next as we accelerated down the runway. I called "Rotate" and Waymon flew the jet into the air. Just at that moment the left thrust reverser deployed. I announced the failure. Waymon was solid as a rock and kept the jet level above the runway as I quickly reached for the stow switch. Just as I hit the "Left Emergency Stow" switch, the right thrust reverser deployed. The left one was still in the process of stowing. Waymon never flinched. I flipped the "Right Emergency Stow" switch as he called for it. He flew the Citation smoothly along nose high and wings level about three feet off the ground as the thrust reversers finally slammed into their normal positions. As they did so, the forward thrust returned and Waymon calmly called, "Gear Up."

He then instructed, "Tell tower we had a problem and need to return and land."

"Never mind," said the instructor; "I've seen enough."

He froze the simulator in position and said, "Let's go get some coffee."

After we sat down, the young instructor said, "Man that's the best I've ever seen. Hardly anyone has ever flown out of that scenario without crashing."

Then he said, "Now let me tell you about the worst."

He began, "They were from another country. It was one of those cultures where crew coordination means that the co-pilot keeps his mouth shut and does exactly what the Captain tells him to do, when he tells him to do it; nothing more and nothing less. The Captain is 'God' where the airplane is concerned." He said that the crew was on a simulator ride where some systems problems would be discussed and demonstrated. They were new to the Citation 5 and it had been obvious that neither of them had considered it necessary to study the aircraft systems very much. The instructor had the Captain put the simulated Citation on autopilot. They were at three thousand feet and he was giving them a landing gear problem. One of the main landing gear green "down and locked" lights was not on. When they were below 150 knots and with the instructor's prompting, the crew pulled the throttles back to check that there was no warning horn and light. Then he had them place the flaps to a landing position to check for safe landing gear in a second way. During these checks the co-pilot would not move anything at the instructor's directive. Instead, he would wait for the Captain to order it. After they had checked the gear by the two methods, the instructor told them the landing gear was confirmed down and locked.

Perhaps the Captain wished to demonstrate his authority and his knowledge of the Citation's warning system when he said, "No, I will check it further with the rotary test switch which will check the landing gear lights." The instructor told him that was not necessary but to go ahead if he wished. The Captain reached over to the left of his control yoke and located the rotary test switch. He turned the top of it one position to the right (*the engine fire warning light test position*). As designed, both engine fire warning lights lit up brightly.

The eager young co-pilot yelled, *"Captain. Both fire warning lights are illuminated!"*

While *holding* the rotatory test switch in the "Fire Warning" position, the Captain ordered; *"Shut down engines one and two!"*

The astonished instructor watched as the obedient co-pilot did exactly that.

They crashed.

Toward The Evening Sky

JUDGEMENT CALLS

Arkansas Skies; 1990s

There is an aviation maxim that in my view is exceptionally astute. It essentially states, "A superior pilot is one who uses his superior judgment to avoid situations requiring his superior skills."

Judgment Call #1: The passenger was a Senior Vice President who had been with his company for many years. His reputation was one of great success in the business world and that he expected the corporate jet to take him where he wanted to go and when he wanted to go there.

    The senior Captain on the Falcon 900 that day was a young but very talented pilot named Bill. He possessed a keen intellect coupled with a calm disposition, a great combination for a pilot. They had flown the high ranking company officer to Dallas for a meeting that afternoon and were scheduled to return him to Little Rock that evening. Before they departed Little Rock, the weather forecast had called for the possibility of thunderstorms in the vicinity upon their return but nothing more specific. However, while they waited for their passenger in Dallas, the forecast had been updated and the storms had begun to develop. Just before the passenger arrived, the new forecast and the FBO's weather radar indicated the return flight still looked possible. The Captain updated the passenger about the weather and he indicated that he still wished to go.

    Enroute over southwestern Arkansas as they looked at the aircraft's weather radar, it was obvious that the situation had worsened rapidly. Then, after the crew listened to the Little Rock Adams ATIS, they made their decision. They requested that the passenger come to the cockpit to brief him on the developments and to outline the pilots' plan of action. They told him that the weather was now such that they weren't going to proceed to Little Rock and informed the passenger that it should move out of the Little Rock area in a couple of hours. They then told him they were going to divert to Fort Smith, AR. They suggested that he might wish to have dinner there while they waited for the weather to move out.

    The passenger was not particularly happy and said, "Perhaps I should have taken the airline." He then suggested that the airline probably could have gotten him back into Little Rock. To their credit, the crew did not succumb to the Vice President's subtle pressure to proceed and attempt a landing at Little Rock.

    Instead, the Captain said, "I'll tell you what sir. We can fly you back to Dallas and you can get on the airline. They might *try* to get into Little Rock in that kind of weather."

The passenger hesitated a moment and then replied, "Dinner in Fort Smith sounds good." By the time they had finished dinner and gone back to the airport, the thunderstorms had moved out of the Little Rock area.

Judgment Call #2: Another Stephens pilot and I were flying the company King Air 90 on a summer day. We had flown to Fayetteville, AR in the nice smooth morning air. It was now mid-afternoon and the hot rising air was not so smooth anymore. We were about halfway to Little Rock and were winding our way between cumulus buildups with tops that were well above us. As soon as we arrived within radio range of Little Rock, we tuned in the ATIS. The information indicated that a very large thunderstorm had formed in the vicinity of Lake Maumelle and was moving toward the airport. Lake Maumelle is located a few miles to the northwest of the Little Rock airport. We were in the clear air between the widely scattered cumulus cells but could see the big storm both visually and on our radar.

Memphis Center turned us over to Little Rock Approach Control. After we checked in, Approach informed us that the thunderstorm was now approaching the northwestern edge of the airport and asked our intentions. After a very short discussion, we requested to hold in our present area until the storm moved away from the airport. Approach immediately issued holding instructions and told us that we were cleared to modify the holding pattern to stay in the clear if we wanted. We did. Then we informed our passengers and began the holding pattern. A few minutes later we heard an airliner check in with approach control. (I won't identify the airline but it was a large two engine jet.)

Little Rock Approach Control acknowledged the check-in and then advised the pilot of "Airliner 1" about the latest weather. It was not good; heavy rain with gusty winds and visibility just at minimums for the ILS to Runway 04. There were wind-shear alerts all around the airport. The controller asked the airline pilots' intentions. They replied that they wanted to execute the ILS RW04 and "take a look". The controller cleared them and in a few minutes approach control switched them over to the tower frequency. We continued holding in the clear air to the northwest and wondered how the airliner was doing.

Suddenly; "Little Rock Approach 'Airliner 1' missed the approach and is back with you. We're requesting holding until that storm gets out of the way." Approach gave the airliner holding instructions several miles to the southwest of the airport.

"Little Rock Approach, this is Airliner 2." It was a plane from a different airline. This time it was a turbo-prop commuter aircraft. The controller acknowledged, gave them the weather (which had not improved), told them that another airliner had just missed the approach and asked their intentions. Without any hesitation they requested the ILS RW04. I remember the other pilot looking at me and shaking his head. I knew exactly what he was thinking because so was I: *"Idiots."* A couple of minutes later we heard approach control give the airliner a right turn to 310 degrees and told them to maintain 2000 feet. The airline pilot acknowledged the instructions.

Suddenly, the call came from Little Rock Approach Control, "'Airliner 2'. Check your altitude." There was no answer.

Again came the anxious call from Approach Control; "'Airliner 2'. Check your altitude immediately." Still there was no answer.

I thought, "Oh no," and looked over at the other pilot.

"Little Rock Approach, 'Airliner 2' is back with you. Sorry I couldn't answer before now but we had our hands full. We evidently flew into a microburst. We pushed the power all the way up to maximum and couldn't stop our descent. We finally got it leveled at 1200 feet and are presently climbing back to 2000." He sounded amazingly calm.

"Roger Airliner Two. You had us worried."

"Roger approach," he replied. *"You should have been in here."*

Then he continued, "Request holding instructions away from the thunderstorm."

"A superior pilot is one who uses his superior judgement...."

Jerry W. Cook

CHARLESTON

Little Rock Adams Field, AR; Early 1990s

It was my day in the office. Before Stephens had a Scheduler to take information and set up the pilots and aircraft for trips, it was accomplished by a pilot who was not scheduled to fly on that day. This particular day, it was I who answered the phone when Jo Ann, Mr. Jack's assistant, called.

She said, "Jerry, about Mr. Stephen's trip tomorrow; if he leaves on time when should he be picked up at the Millionaire FBO?" I picked up his trip sheet for the next day and looked at it.

"Jo Ann, I don't think that there is a Millionaire FBO at Charlotte," I said.

She immediately replied, "Charlotte? He's not going to Charlotte. He's going to Charleston, South Carolina." I looked down at the trip sheet again and there it was in the destination box, KCLT. It should have been KCHS.

"Wow, I'm glad you called, Jo Ann. Someone had filled in the destination wrong. There *is* a Millionaire FBO at Charleston. He should arrive there at three p.m." Jo Anne thanked me, said she would notify the person meeting him and hung up the phone. As fate would have it, I was assigned to fly the trip the next day. We were at Flight Level 410 and I had just leaned forward and was looking down at the Atlanta Hartsfield Airport beyond the nose of the Falcon 900 when I heard Mr. Jack. He had just come into the cockpit.

"How much longer?" he said.

I turned toward him and replied, "Sir, we will have you on the ground at Charleston in thirty minutes."

He looked down at me over his glasses and said, "Charleston? I'm going to Charlotte." Then he went back and sat down.

Ray, the other pilot, looked over at me and said, "Well Captain, what are you going to do now?" I turned around and looked at Mr. Jack hoping to get some clue but nope. He had on his poker face and he just looked back at me. I thought about the phone call from Jo Ann the day before. I imagined her hanging up after talking to me and going in to tell Mr. Stephens about the mix-up in destinations. I turned around and looked at him again; still nothing. He just continued to look back at me.

"I'm taking him to Charleston," I said to Ray.

"What? You are?" he said surprised. The closer we got to Charleston the more I began to worry.

I thought, "What if I'm wrong? What if he wasn't just joking? What if he meant it?" I knew that he could see that we hadn't made a turn toward North Carolina. Surely he would have come up and asked why...or would he? I turned and looked at him once again. He just looked back at me with no expression. I began to wonder if this was to be my last flight for Stephens.

I thought, "I should have known better than to try to match wits with Mr. Jack. I'm an idiot. I should have changed our destination to Charlotte." But it was too late now. Charleston tower had just cleared us to land. As I parked the plane in front of the Millionaire FBO I looked for any vehicles on the ramp that might be picking him up; nothing. After shutting down the engines and without looking back at Mr. Stephens I rushed down the steps and up to the guy who had just put our wheel chocks in.
"Have you seen anyone here to pick up our passenger?" I said.

"No sir, I haven't," was the answer. I hurried into the FBO. There was no one inside except the lady behind the operations desk.

"Is there anyone here to pick up Mr. Stephens?" I asked; now almost desperate.

"Haven't seen anyone," was her cheerful reply. I saw my job flash before my eyes. Just then a door at the south side of the waiting area opened. A well-dressed gentleman came in and started walking toward the operations desk.

As he approached he asked the clerk, "Has Mr. Stephens' plane landed yet? I could have hugged the guy. Instead I just breathed a big sigh of relief. To this day I don't know whether I won or lost. All I know is; I kept my job. Mr. Jack never said a word about his little joke.

Jerry W. Cook

NOW WHERE DID I LEAVE THAT SOCKET?

Little Rock National Airport, Arkansas; Mid-1990s

The Falcon 900 from another company took off from the Washington D.C. area. After takeoff, there was loud air noise coming from the nose gear area but the landing gear indicated up. The crew elected to continue to their destination, Detroit, Michigan. When they arrived and attempted to lower their landing gear the nose gear would not extend and the aircraft eventually had to be landed with the nose landing gear still retracted. Dassault Falcon Jet, the manufacturer, found the cause to be low strut pressure in the nose gear causing the retracting gear to miss the nose gear door hooks during retraction. As a result, the nose gear strut rollers were above the nose gear door hooks. The nose gear would not extend in this configuration.

As a result, all Falcon 900s were required to be inspected and cleared for flight by the manufacturer. Because our company was located in Little Rock and so was the major American repair facility for Falcon Jets, it was a simple matter for us to have the inspection done and be quickly cleared for flight. All we had to do was tow our aircraft across the field to the maintenance facility for the inspection. Our 900 was found to be exactly as it should be and everything checked out, so we were good to go. Only one little item was going to prevent that. That little item was a wrench socket that was inadvertently left on the top of the nose gear strut by the inspectors. It sat completely out of sight where it encircled the Schrader valve. That valve is a point where the nose landing gear strut is serviced with nitrogen.

Bill and Johnny took off from Little Rock Adams Field and, as the nose gear retracted, it made a terrible noise as it jammed into the wheel well, very much like the one had after takeoff at Washington. And just as that 900, when they tried, the nose gear would not lower. For several hours Bill and Johnny flew around the area and conferred on the radio with the manufacturer's representatives. They tried various methods to get the nose gear down with no success. Bill finally brought the plane in for a very nice landing on Runway 04 with the nose gear still retracted. The aircraft sustained minimum damage.

The bizarre truth is that a beautiful aircraft in perfect condition now had a damage history clearly caused by an inspection that was meant to make sure that what happened didn't happen. During the inspection, the nose gear had been found to be exactly as it should have been; that is until the socket, which was accidently left behind, sheared off the top of the Schrader valve. That was what caused the nose gear to get stuck in the wheel well. I understand that some changes were made at the repair facility.

A tool inventory every time after maintenance is performed ain't a bad idea.

HE LANDED IT

Little Rock, AR to Augusta, GA; 1990s

It was one of those days that come along occasionally. The sky was clear just about everywhere in the country. However the wind was blowing hard and gusting just about everywhere in the country also. And it seemed especially so where we were and where we wanted to go. After they boarded the Falcon 900 I briefed Mr. Jack and his guests, the CEO of a national company and his wife, that it was going to be a very rough ride after takeoff until we were above about five thousand feet and then again below about five thousand feet on our descent and landing at Augusta, Georgia.

Mr. Jack looked at me over his glasses and said, "Are these winds going to last all day?"

I replied, "Yes sir, probably until after the sun goes down."

He thought for a moment and said, "Can you land in those winds?"

"Yes sir, it is right at the maximum demonstrated crosswind limit and it will be really bumpy and it may not be pretty, but I can land," I replied.

"Then let's go," he said. Even while we taxied toward the runway, we could hear and feel the Falcon being buffeted by the wind gusts. I briefed the other pilot that during takeoff I was going to stay on the nose wheel steering until at least one hundred knots. I also told him I would delay rotation by ten knots. I wanted to have some extra airspeed when we lifted off into the gusting winds above the runway.

As I had briefed the passengers as soon as we were airborne, the Falcon began trying to yaw and roll with the gusts. I was using a lot of aileron deflection to keep the wings as near level as possible. I kept the airspeed below two hundred knots so as to climb faster, and to somewhat soften the bumps. As we climbed out of about fifty-five hundred feet, it was as if someone turned off the rough air. The ride the rest of the way to our cruise altitude of forty-one thousand was smooth but we didn't turn off the seat belt sign until level-off, just in case. About forty minutes later as we approached the top of descent, the other pilot copied the Augusta Terminal Information. I listened carefully as the wind was announced. It had not improved. In fact it was worse because now the wind direction was swinging back and forth between west and north. It seemed to be favoring more from the west at the moment, so I told my co-pilot to request a visual approach to Runway 26. With six thousand feet of length, it was two thousand feet shorter than the other runway but there was less of a crosswind and it was more than adequate.

I flipped on the public address system switch and updated the passengers about the wind conditions. I requested that they put everything that was loose away and tighten their seat belts. I added that, because of the shifting wind directions, it was possible we might have to make a go-around and, if so, for them to not be alarmed. I was glad I did. As we descended out of six thousand feet, the turbulence began. It was worse than it had been after takeoff at Little Rock. The large corporate jet was being slammed around and the airspeed was swinging wildly at times. The wind was still favoring Runway 26 as I positioned the jet on a wide right base leg. We had set the landing speed indices for plus twenty knots over the Vref (normal approach speed). That was the maximum that could be added for wind gusts. We were now configured for landing and I was attempting to hold the airspeed at the computed 135 knots. The airspeed needle was bouncing at least ten to fifteen knots up and down. I was hitting the limits on the ailerons trying to keep the wings level. Suddenly, at about three hundred feet above the ground, the airspeed jumped to over 160 and it felt like we were going up in one of those elevators on the outside of a building. The runway was dropping away in front of us. I added power and we performed a go-around procedure. I climbed back to two thousand feet and we headed westbound still rocking and rolling.

The tower acknowledged our go-around and gave us the present winds. Now they were favoring landing to the north on Runway 35. We requested Runway 35 and I continued westbound for another two miles before turning south for a left downwind. Sweat was dripping off my hands making it hard to hold the control yoke. I had to keep wiping them dry on my pant legs. We turned a long final approach for the north runway and the winds were still blowing from the north to northwest. At their most northwestern point, the gust component was approaching the Falcon's maximum demonstrated crosswind limit. As we descended lower, the more aileron input I had to use until once again I was hitting the limits. At times, that wasn't enough to keep the wings level. The best words I can think of to describe the ride was bucking and jumping. My hands and feet were in constant motion and sweat was pouring off my forehead. Suddenly a loud crash came from the passenger area. A serving tray had been overlooked on the galley and it had gotten airborne and then landed upside down on the galley floor.

We had descended to about twenty feet above the runway when the gusts began causing the digitized voice of the Ground Proximity Warning System to start exclaiming loudly; *"DON'T SINK…DON'T SINK!"* repeatedly. I completely disagreed with the GPWS computer because we definitely needed to sink about another twenty feet, and soon. I lowered the nose still further while rapidly moving the ailerons and rudder to keep the Falcon near the center of the runway and the left wing down. The wind was trying very hard to weathervane the Falcon toward the left side of the runway. Implausibly, it was a very smooth touchdown. I quickly lowered the nose gear to the runway and grabbed the nose wheel steering. We were down. I felt that I had definitely earned my pay that day.

As I slowed the plane for the turnoff onto Taxiway Alpha, I heard the female guest exclaim loudly, *"Thank God."*

Then I heard Mr. Jack's completely unruffled reply to her, "You'd better thank Jerry. *He landed it."*

Jerry W. Cook

HE'S AN OLD FIGHTER PILOT; GIVE HIM HELL

Wichita Mid-Continent Airport, KS; 1996

The Stephens Chief Pilot had decided that he needed another Captain to fly the company's Citation 7. Consequently, I found myself in the Flight Safety International Initial Course leading to a Citation 7 type rating. As it turned out, my sim instructor was also a retired Air Force fighter pilot. He had flown F-104 Starfighters among other types and we found that we had several mutual friends from our Air Force fighter flying days. Since I was not attending the course with another Stephens' pilot, I had been teamed up for the simulator sessions with a pilot from another company, a young lady. It was her first type rating and, although noticeably nervous, she was doing well. She was very studious and it showed in her systems and procedures knowledge. I think she hoped that knowledge would serve to somewhat make up for her relative lack of flight experience and it probably did help. We progressed with no problems through the classroom and simulator training and it was now time for our type rating check ride in the simulator.

I had not met our designated flight examiner before and we were seated across the table from him in a small briefing room. It was the oral test before the simulator check and he was grilling us on the aircraft's systems and performance. We were doing just fine as he went back and forth between us with his questions.

It was toward the end of the allotted time and was my sim partner's turn to answer when he turned to her and said, "What kind of current does a vortex generator produce?" I glanced over at her and she looked absolutely stricken. The blood had drained from her face as she searched her mind for the answer from her studies. It was a trick question to which she obviously did not know the answer. The check airman seemed amused and just looked at her as she agonized over a possible answer. I felt sorry for her and I hoped that he would soon tell her that it was a trick question. I also hoped that he didn't ask me because, if I answered, it would make her feel even worse than she already did.

I finally spoke up, "Don't worry about it A___. It's just a trick question."

The flight examiner looked at me and said, "I guess that means you know the answer."

"Yeah, I've been around a lot longer than she has," I replied.

"What is the answer?" she insisted.

"It's going to make you angry when you hear it," I said.

"No it won't. Tell me," she pleaded.

I said, "Okay. Vortex generators don't generate any current. They affect airflow over the wing or other surface." As I had predicted, she looked angry. The instructor laughed. I shrugged. We took a quick break and were getting ready to go into the simulator for the check ride. Our sim instructor saw us and walked up to the table.

He patted our check pilot on the shoulder and said, "Watch out Jerry. This guy is a retired Army Aviator."

Then he did me absolutely no favor when he laughingly said to the check pilot, "Jerry's an old Air Force fighter pilot, give him Hell. He can handle it."

The retired Army pilot/check airman then looked at me and said, *"Oh really."* The way he said it made me think, "Well...crap."

My sim partner flew first and the check airman gave her a very straightforward evaluation. She did fine and after a short break it was my turn. The first indication that my evaluation would be somewhat different was during the "unusual attitude" recoveries.

As I held my head down with my eyes closed, I could feel the simulator rocking and rolling forcefully as the check pilot yanked and pulled the control yoke for an extended time before finally stating, "You've got it." I raised my head and looked at my flight instruments and quickly crosschecked the standby and co-pilot's attitude indicators with mine. They all agreed. We were going nearly straight up at about five thousand feet and virtually out of airspeed. I added full power as I rolled the simulator into a ninety degree bank and let the nose fall down through the nearest horizon until it was about thirty degrees below it. I then rolled the wings level and waited for the airspeed to build enough where I wouldn't get a secondary stall. Then I pulled the nose up to level off.

"Okay I've got it. Shut your eyes," the check pilot ordered. Once again I could feel the simulator being jerked and rolled all over the simulated sky.

"You've got it," he finally announced. I looked up. We were wings level but completely inverted with the nose about thirty degrees below the horizon and the airspeed up near the red-line. I simultaneously pulled the throttles to idle, "popped" the airbrakes and rapid-rolled the "7" simulator to wings level. As soon as the bank angle was less than ninety degrees, I added back pressure to start raising the nose. We missed the ground but not by that much. He had given me the controls at something less than three thousand feet. I heard my sim partner let out the breath that she'd evidently been holding. Sometimes it was easy to forget you were in a simulator. The check airman said nothing.

My check-ride then continued with very reasonable and rational in-flight situations until with fifteen minutes left in our sim period he said, "You're cleared to the Wichita VOR at five-thousand feet to hold as depicted." I'd already accomplished all of the required approaches so I was wondering what he had up his sleeve.

We proceeded to the VOR and my co-pilot called, "Citation 1828S entering holding." The examiner assigned us an expected approach clearance time just five minutes away. I asked for the present weather and he replied that the Wichita Mid-Continent weather was now zero ceiling with zero visibility and expected to remain that way. I glanced at our fuel gauges with the intent of diverting to some other airport with better weather. Both fuel gauges were dropping at a rapid rate.

I considered, "Could it be just the gauges?" But if not, there wasn't enough time to troubleshoot. I asked for the McConnell AFB weather.
The answer was, "Zero ceiling, and zero visibility."

I quickly said, *"N1828S is declaring a fuel emergency. We're leaving VOR holding and heading for the final approach fix. Request radar vectors for an immediate ILS to Mid-Continent Runway 1L."*

The examiner replied, "The airport is zero ceiling, zero visibility *and* it is *closed.*" I looked again at our fuel gauges as they continued their precipitous drop.

I said, "28S is heading for the outer marker and we are going to fly the ILS to Runway 1L."

He replied, *"I said the FAA has closed the airport."*

I countered firmly, *"I don't give a big red rat's ass what the FAA said. We're running out of fuel and we are going to land on 1L...period!"* We were down to three thousand feet now and slowing toward flap speed. I was staying in the "clean configuration" (no flaps, no landing gear, no speed brakes) as long as possible to save fuel. We were turning just over the outer marker. My co-pilot had not said a word since we left the VOR. As we "captured" the ILS localizer course, we were still fast.

At about three miles from the runway, I called, "Flaps to approach."

She replied "Flaps approach," and moved the handle. The flaps didn't move.

"I'll get out the Emergency Checklist," my co-pilot said.

"No. Put the landing gear down and start looking for the runway," I said.

She had already picked up the Emergency Checklist and she replied, "But our flaps won't lower. We need to do the checklist."

I reached over and slammed the landing gear handle down and ordered, "Throw the damned checklist on the floor and look for the runway." I heard a loud *"Humph"* from her and then the checklist hit the floor just as the landing gear locked into place. I took a quick look. The fuel gauges were now sitting on zero.

"To the left!" she exclaimed. I saw the approach lights flashing through the heavy fog. I banked left and then back to the right just before we touched down. We were rolling pretty fast but I didn't care. We still had about eight thousand feet of concrete remaining. Both engines flamed out as we neared the north end of the runway.

My co-pilot looked over at me and said, "Wow." Sweat was pouring off my forehead.

The check pilot finally spoke up, "No one has beaten that situation before. Congratulations."

"What usually happens?" I asked.

"They try to divert somewhere else when I tell them that the FAA has closed the field. They don't make it," he replied.

He then looked at the female pilot and said, "Well young lady, did you learn anything from that final scenario?"

"Wow," was all she said. I decided that when I saw the old F-104 pilot again, I was going to strangle him.

Jerry W. Cook

IS IT SAFE TO FLY?

Preface: Several times during my years of flying, I have had a potential passenger walk up to me while I was at the aircraft with the question; "Is it safe to fly?" I understand that the question is driven by a sense of anxiety and the questioner is looking for reassurance and a positive answer to their inquiry. However, what they would really like to have is a *guarantee* that nothing will go wrong during the flight. Very few situations generate such a sense of not being in control of one's destiny as does sitting in an aluminum tube while hurtling several hundred miles an hour at eight miles above the earth. Your tube is being guided at eight miles per minute by someone whom you may not know; whose pilot license you've likely not seen; and whose medical certificate was issued by a doctor that you've never heard of. And if that's not enough, your aluminum tube is being supported by an invisible force that you can't see as you stare out at the top of the wing. Is it safe to fly? Although I don't address the question directly in the following four accounts I trust that in them you might find at least an acceptable answer....

Teterboro Airport, NJ; 1998

The weather was really crappy, about 400 feet overcast with visibility in rain of one mile. Gene and I were flying the Citation 7 and had dead-headed to Teterboro to pick up three passengers. We were then to fly them to Nashville, Tennessee, about a one and one half hour flight. After waiting there for several hours, we would then return them to Teterboro. If there was enough time remaining in our duty day, we would head back to Little Rock and home. If not, we would get hotel rooms and stay in New Jersey that night. Gene flew the leg to Teterboro and landed from the ILS RW06. The weather had been as forecast and we had no problem getting in. We had refueled and were both back aboard the plane awaiting our passengers. A black sedan pulled up to the Citation. I opened the entry door and one man got out and rushed up the boarding steps. After short introductions, he said he needed to ask me some questions.

We sat down and he said, "Is it safe to fly today?"

I studied his face for a moment before I answered, "Yes sir. Of course it is. We just flew in here a few minutes ago."

Obviously my point was missed because then he said, "Well I just don't want to take off if it isn't safe."

I replied, "Sir, I don't either and I wouldn't take off if I didn't think it was safe."

Then I said, "I'm going to tell you something that perhaps you haven't thought about that may or may not make you feel better about going. I just met you and I haven't even met the other two passengers, but that makes absolutely no difference in my decision of whether it is safe to fly or not. It doesn't matter who my passengers are or even whether there are any passengers. Other pilots and I care about our own safety and that is our main concern when making our "go-no-go" decisions. It has nothing to do with you. Passenger safety is a direct result of the pilots' concerns for their own well-being." He had been staring at me while I talked and I wondered if I had made my point.

"Are you saying that, if the pilots don't say that we can't go, that means that they think it's safe," he said.

"That's right. For instance, just now when you got on the plane, I would have immediately told you we couldn't go and why. As a matter of fact, if I could have contacted you I would have told you not to come to the airport in the first place," I replied.

He thought about it and then said, "That makes sense. You certainly wouldn't takeoff if you thought it was unsafe for you." I nodded in the affirmative.

"Okay. Next I need to know if you can guarantee me that you can get me back into Teterboro tonight," he said.

"No sir, I can't guarantee it," I answered.

"If their weather is at or above the minimums, I can get you in. If it is not, I can't," I finished.

First he looked a little perturbed and then he said, "Okay; do you think that you can get us back in tonight?"

I replied, "Yes sir. Based on their latest forecast, I do."

"All right then, I'll get the other two," he said as he got up from his seat. While we were strapping into our cockpit seats, I had to smile as I heard him explaining to the other two passengers why he knew it was safe to fly today. Both flights went well and Teterboro's weather held above minimums all day and into that night. We got our passengers back home just fine. However, they were late getting back to the airport in Nashville and we would be flying past our maximum crew duty time if we headed back to Little Rock. Consequently, that evening Gene and I went for a big delicious steak instead of another flight. We had made another excellent go-no-go decision based on our own safety.

The delicious steak had nothing to do with it.

Fayetteville Drake Field, AR; 1990s

It was a beautiful clear day all the way from Little Rock to Fayetteville, Arkansas. There were some low altitude gusty winds but the air was smooth at cruise altitudes. We were to pick up three passengers and fly them back to Little Rock. As was forecast, the Citation 5 bounced around a little as we descended for our landing at Fayetteville but nothing worse than light turbulence was experienced. We could see our passengers waiting for us as we taxied onto the FBO ramp and parked the plane. We didn't need any services, so I had the lineman remove the chocks because we were going right back out. The male passengers nodded as they walked by and boarded the plane.

However, our young lady passenger walked up to me and said, "Is it safe to fly today?"

I probably shouldn't have done it but I had wanted to say it for years; "Hell no. I'm a dare-devil." Her eyes got big and she looked startled for a few seconds, then she started laughing.

She said, "I guess that was a stupid question, wasn't it?"

I smiled as I replied, "I think I've probably said enough."

Postscript #1 circa 1983: While I was still working for Little Rock Air Center, I was to fly a Falcon 10 charter customer to Dallas that afternoon for a meeting. After his meeting that evening, we were to return to Little Rock. He was a personable, well-known and very successful businessman but he had a reputation as being afraid to fly. He had shown that was likely true with his countless questions about the plane, the weather, turbulence, airport status, etc. before we departed from Little Rock. Of course it was his right to know and I briefed him thoroughly on everything that affected our flights that evening. The flight to Dallas Love Field was smooth and uneventful.

When he returned to the plane that evening, I gave him a complete update on the weather including the fact that a line of thunderstorms had developed in north central Oklahoma and it extended into the Fort Smith area of western Arkansas. He asked if it was still safe to go. I assured him that it was. We flew the Dallas departure and were at our assigned cruise flight level 290 as we approached Texarkana. The other pilot and I had been admiring the lightning display all up and down the line of storms which lay about two hundred miles to the north of our position. The thunderstorms looked like they ended about the Fort Smith area just as the radar at the FBO had indicated. I looked through the windscreen and the sky was so clear that I could already see the glow from the lights of Little Rock about one hundred and thirty miles dead ahead.

Suddenly the passenger appeared at the cockpit and tapped me on the arm. He said, "Where are we?"

I replied, "Right over Texarkana. There are the lights of Little Rock straight ahead."

He quickly said, "Do you see that lightning off to our left?"

I replied, "Yes sir, we were just admiring it."

He then said, "You're not going to go up there and fly through it are you?"

I turned and studied him for a moment and then I said, "I wasn't planning on it. Why, did you want to?"

He quickly answered, *"No. I sure don't! I just wanted to make sure that you guys didn't."*

Postscript #2 Circa 1990s: She was an officer of the company and had flown with us many times. That day we had flown her to Harrison, Arkansas and were waiting for her at the airport. Our weather was beautiful but, to the west of us in Oklahoma, a line of severe thunderstorms was developing and expected to spawn some tornados later in the evening. The line was moving east at twenty-five miles per hour. Later, when she arrived back at the airport, she asked me if I knew about the storms over in Oklahoma. I replied that I did.

She then said, "You're not planning to go over there and fly through them are you?"

Remember, we were in Harrison which is over one hundred miles north-northwest of Little Rock. The severe weather was one hundred and forty miles to the west of Harrison. Our destination was Little Rock, meaning we had to fly south-southeast to get there. Why in the world would we be planning to, "Go over there and fly through them?!"

Sometimes you have to wonder, "Just what do some passengers think we are; completely nuts?" And if so; *"Why in the world would they get on a plane with us?"*

Jerry W. Cook

CHANGE OF DIRECTION

Little Rock, AR; October 1998

I had planned to finish my aviation career just flying the line for Stephens. As I had hoped, this company had proven to be exactly what I had been told. It was solid, stable, and very successful. Warren Stephens, the talented younger son of Jack Stephens, was the CEO. Jack was the Chairman and the younger brother of the original founder, Witt Stephens. Stephens Incorporated believed in the importance of their corporate aircraft to the success of the company and they supported them accordingly. The Chief Pilot had decided to retire and I had been invited to the CEO's office for a meeting. As it turned out, the meeting was to offer me the position. I accepted and was immediately asked if I had any ideas for changes to the department. I did have a few suggestions and it was gratifying to see the genuine interest and support from the top. It was very obvious that Warren Stephens wanted the best corporate flight department possible.

Having flown for the military, a major airline, and several charter and corporate operators, I had experienced many different types of flight operations and therefore was in a position to compare. The Stephens Flight Department had a lot going for it with good pilots, new aircraft, excellent flight training and some of its own aircraft maintenance; but the best thing they had was the company's staunch support. Stephens' wanted and was willing to pay to have the best flight department; but it wasn't quite there yet.

One of my first goals was to reduce the number of aircraft types its pilots flew; particularly as a Captain. One type is perfect, two is okay, but any more is difficult for the pilot to maintain proficiency; i.e. "the fewer; the safer". This required more pilots, fewer aircraft types, or both. (When I retired the Stephens' pilots were flying a maximum of two types: the Falcon 900EXEasy and Falcon 50EXs.) Another goal was for increased in-house aircraft maintenance. This of course required more Aviation Technicians and more specialized tools. Now Stephens performs most of its own airframe, avionics and engine maintenance. This contributes to a dispatch rate of over ninety-nine percent. Some added benefits have been significantly less downtime (when aircraft are not available because of maintenance) and actual dollar savings in maintenance costs. These were just two examples of the many changes that were made during my tenure as the flight department manager.

But there was one thing that remained a constant. That was the outstanding support from the CEO, Warren Stephens. And now, largely due to that support, he has one of the best corporate flight departments in the world.

Toward The Evening Sky

"CAN'T GET HURT IN A SIMULATOR…RIGHT?"

Simuflite Building, DFW Airport, TX; Early 2000s

Another Stephens' pilot named Andy and I were attending recurrency training for our Falcon 900B. The ground training had progressed easily as both Andy and I had been flying the 900 for several years. Also it was almost like Old Home Week because our ground school instructor had flown for a company out of Little Rock for some years prior and another Simuflite instructor had once flown for Stephens. It was time for our second simulator period and we walked down to the "box" with our sim instructor who we had not met before yesterday's first session. He had just briefed us on today's training goals, one of which was windshear recognition and solutions.

This training had been instituted in flight school syllabuses as a result of the August 2, 1985 Delta L-1011 crash at DFW Airport. The National Transportation Safety Board listed as one of the causes "micro-burst induced windshear". The National Aeronautics and Space Administration had begun a study of the weather phenomena as a result. The extreme forces associated with these microbursts were not widely known and understood prior to this sequence of events.

But this day, we were going to be experiencing our micro-bursts in a simulator where it was safe. It was Andy's turn to fly the left seat and we progressed through most of the requirements for this session. And now it was time to accomplish the micro-burst training. Our instructor had placed the simulator in the visual mode and we could see terrain features including the airport. He gave us the existing weather which included thunderstorms in the area with gusting winds from varying directions; perfect for micro-burst generation. The runway was dead ahead at about five miles when we felt the first hints of turbulence. As Andy descended on the visual glide path all seemed normal with just a small bump now and then. Next the airspeed started jumping up and down making it difficult to hold our computed approach speed which included an addition for the reported gusts. Suddenly the speed increased drastically and the plane started upward. Andy lowered the nose somewhat to slow the upward vector but he knew not to pull the power back because we would likely lose the gained airspeed just as rapidly. He left the engine power levers where they were.

The airspeed indicator needles suddenly dived losing all of the knots they had gained and down into a range well below our "bugged" (computed) approach speed. It was now at bug minus thirty and, as Andy rammed the throttles full forward, the 900 started a sickening plunge toward the simulated ground just a few hundred feet below. He rotated the plane's nose skyward until he felt the stall warning shaker actuate in the control yoke. We were now very nose high and still sinking. Andy had done it right and all he could do at that point. Hopefully, there was room and time for the 900 to fly out of the micro-burst before we hit the ground. Only about one hundred feet of altitude was left below us but suddenly, we leveled off and started to climb. We'd finally flown out of the downward rushing air and the airspeed was increasing back toward normal.

SLAM..! BANG..! The simulator pitched violently up and then back down. The altimeters were wrapping upward at a tremendous rate and the vertical velocities were pegged at the maximum six thousand feet per minute climb. The 900's nose was still pitching up and down violently. BAM..! CRASH..! We heard the loud noises behind us and turned to look. All we could see was the bottoms of our instructor's shoes as he rocked back and forth on the floor in conjunction with the simulator's pitching motion. He had flown completely out of his seat and several feet toward the rear where he bounced off the simulator's entry door. The kick-out panel in the door was missing where his shoulder had hit it. The panel had made the crashing noise as it hit the concrete floor several feet below the simulator. Suddenly, the simulator stopped its pitching motion and then Andy returned it to level. We were at 41,000 feet. We had "bounced" eight miles straight up into the simulated sky. Andy said that the flight controls felt normal again. The instructor finally got to the red "stop motion" button and pushed it. He then stood up and brushed himself off and announced that he was not hurt. I asked him why he had "flown" out of his seat. He said that he had not fastened his seat belt because it was too tight. (He was a very big guy.)

We left the simulator with the sim maintenance guys after briefing them on what had just happened. At the door of the briefing room, the instructor said he was going to the restroom and would see us in a few minutes. While he was gone, I took the carrying straps off both of our Simuflite book bags and attached them to his briefing chair as a seat belt. When he returned, I don't think our instructor thought it was nearly as funny as Andy and I did.

Toward The Evening Sky

PROTOCOL

Little Rock Adams Field, AR; Early 2000s

He was one of the highest ranking foreign government officials in the world and we were going to fly him and several members of his entourage on our company's Falcon 900. Two other corporate jets would be joining with us on the trip, a Citation 560 and a Hawker 800. They would be carrying other members of the large group accompanying the VIP. After flying there that morning, all three of the jets were ready and waiting as the Vice-Premier and his large support staff pulled up to the planes at Orlando International Airport. There were a lot of bags and a lot of people in the several vehicles. As we began to load the luggage into the aircraft, I started to have my doubts about getting it all aboard. I remember thinking that maybe we needed another plane just to carry the suitcases. After a few tries, we finally got all of our passengers' bags into our luggage compartment. Just as the other 900 pilot and I were congratulating ourselves on a superb packing job, the captain of the Hawker 800 which was parked just to the right of us came walking up. He looked concerned. Just as we were, he was soaked with sweat from the bag loading.

"Jerry, I can't get all of our passengers' bags onboard. Can you take anymore?" he asked. I looked up into our baggage compartment and then squatted down to look under our 900 at what he had left sitting beside his plane.

I said, "Bring em over and we'll try." Then I climbed back up the ladder and we started shoving and lifting and shifting bags again. I wasn't sure how, but we finally got them in and closed the baggage door.

"You'd better stand back if you open this thing in Little Rock," I cautioned the other pilot. When we finally sat down in the cockpit, there wasn't a dry piece of clothing anywhere on either of us. One of the Vice-Premier's assistants came up to the cockpit and sat down in the jump seat behind the co-pilot. He announced that he had some instructions for us. I asked him what they were. He said that we needed to taxi and takeoff first and then we needed to land last. When I asked him why, he replied it was so the people on the other two jets could stand and wave at the Vice Premier when he left Orlando and then again when he arrived in Little Rock.

I looked back at him and managed not to smile as I said, "Oh, okay." I looked out of my cockpit window and sure enough all of the passengers from the other two jets were lining up out in front of us on both sides of our taxi route. I thought, "Well, all righty then." As we taxied between the furiously waving people I tried not to use very much power because none of them had on any ear protection. I wanted to look back and see if the VIP was waving back; but I didn't.

We took off first. Because both the Hawker and the Citation had slower cruise speeds than the Falcon, we changed our true airspeed at level-off so as to cruise at Mach .74. Our normal Mach was .80, about fifty miles per hour faster. We monitored the tower frequency and finally heard both of the other jets take off about fifteen minutes after we did. They weren't going to catch us even at their maximum cruise speed and with us slowed down to Mach .74.

"Memphis, Falcon _____, we have a request," I said later as we approached a point some fifty miles south of Memphis, Tennessee.

"Say your request Falcon _____," Memphis Center answered.

"Roger Memphis. We have a Hawker and a Citation several miles behind us and we need to land a few minutes after they do."

"You mean Hawker____ and Citation____?" he replied.

"Yes sir; that's them. We're requesting about a ninety degree turn in either direction and then to continue on that heading until both of those jets pass our six o'clock position. Then we'll be requesting direct to Little Rock," I said.

"Would a three-sixty heading work for you?" he replied.

"That'll do just fine," I said.

"Falcon _____, turn right to a heading of three six zero and maintain flight level 390," he instructed. We repeated his instructions as we turned to the three-sixty heading.

We had been heading north for several minutes when the Memphis controller said, "Falcon _____, the last of those two jets has passed your six' o'clock. You are now cleared direct to the Little Rock Adams Field." I began our left turn toward Little Rock. We thanked the Memphis controller for his help as he sent us over to another frequency. A few minutes, later we could hear the other two jets being turned over to the Little Rock Approach controller. Our timing delay was going to work just about right.

After landing, as we taxied into the parking area in front of the Stephens' hangar, my co-pilot said, "Say; don't those people waving at us look a lot like the ones we just left in Orlando?"

Toward The Evening Sky

HAVE YOU EVER SEEN A UFO?

J6 Airway/Flight Level 390; 2000s

We were westbound and had just made the slight right turn toward the HVQ (Charleston, WV) VOR when we heard the call to Washington Center. At first I thought the guy must have the wrong frequency because his voice was shaking like he was in a helicopter. But then I heard him identify himself as a Citation.

His call to the center was a question, "Washington, do you have any military air traffic in this area where we are?"

The Washington Center controller said, "No sir. I don't show anything in your area. Why, did you see another aircraft?"

The Citation pilot replied, "About two minutes ago something passed us northeast bound at our altitude like we were sitting still. It came so close it has taken me this long to get my voice back."

The controller said, "Stand by one minute and let me check with Navy Patuxent River to see if they have anything in that area."

In less than a minute he was back, "Citation N_____, Patuxent says they have nothing up at this time."

He then added, "Can you describe what passed you?"

"That's just it," said the Citation pilot. "We don't know how to describe it. It was big and it was green colored but we couldn't discern any particular shape to it."

The controller then said, "And you say it went by you very close?"

"Yes sir. It was on our right side and probably only a couple of wingspans away," he answered.

The controller said, "Sir, I've checked the other controllers and neither they nor I saw anything near you on our radar scopes."

"Do you want to file a near-miss report?" the controller asked.

The Citation pilot's voice had quit shaking somewhat as he answered, "I tell you what. Give me your phone number there and we'll give you a call after we land. We'll decide what to do then."

The controller gave him the number and then said, "It sounded like whatever it was scared you pretty bad."

The southern-sounding Citation pilot answered; "Son, scared ain't near a strong enough word. I'm still shaking."

Postscript: Over the years I've been asked many times if I have ever seen a UFO. Pilots are sometimes reluctant to talk about UFOs for fear someone will think that they are crazy if they admit to any such sightings. I will tell you that in my five decades of flying jets that, "Yes, I have seen several unidentified flying objects." However one must understand that almost every time, those same objects suddenly became identified flying objects as they got closer. Moreover, I suspect that those that didn't get close enough to identify were also easily explainable. It is also true that many of them were not even flying, but were a reflection from something on the ground.

Additionally, I have never chased a UFO but I have friends who have been assigned to do so. But for whatever reason, when they returned they would not talk about it. I have never had an experience like the Citation pilots in the above account but I have seen at least one UFO that made me uneasy. It was in the late 1970s over south Texas. We were in a Learjet and were northbound at 41,000 feet. It was midafternoon on a clear day. For some reason, I leaned forward and looked almost straight up through my windscreen. There was something there. I would estimate that it was many thousands of feet above us and it still looked huge. It appeared like a bright silver pulsating mass of some sort and its shape was not identifiable but seemed to keep changing continually. It reminded me of a huge silver jellyfish. I will admit that I felt very ill at ease. I told Bill the other pilot to look straight above us and tell me what he saw.

He leaned forward and looked up. "Jerry, what in the world is that thing?"

I replied, "I don't know but I'm going to call Houston Center."

Bill said, "It seems to be keeping pace with us."

"I noticed that but I wasn't sure," I replied. I called the Houston ARTCC and asked him what the air traffic was right above us.

He hesitated for a minute and said, "Lear N____, we don't show any air traffic above you."

I replied, "Well that's very interesting because we're looking at something several thousand feet above us."

"Just a minute, let me check again," he said.

After a couple of minutes he returned, "We don't show anything in your area on radar," he said.

"Is it still there?" he continued.

"It's still right above us," I said; "Several thousand feet up."

"Describe it to me and I'll fill out a report," the controller said. I continued looking up at the pulsating silver object as I described it and then just as I finished, it disappeared. One second it was there and the next it was gone.

"Do you see it anywhere?" I asked Bill.

"No, it just vanished," he said. I relayed the news to the controller.

"Did you see where it went?" he sounded somewhat concerned.

"No sir," I said; "I don't have a clue."

And I still don't.

Toward The Evening Sky

FROM ON HIGH?

Over Kentucky at FL390; 2000s

One can see a long way from thirty-nine thousand. Shane, my young co-pilot, and I were in one of our company's Citation jets. We had departed Teterboro Airport in New Jersey about an hour before and had just passed the Charleston, West Virginia VOR a few minutes ago. We were cruising along airway J6, the usual route assigned by Air Route Traffic Control. We had spent the night before at a hotel near the Meadowlands Sports Complex and had enjoyed a great steak at a favorite restaurant, "Charlie Brown's", also located near the Meadowlands. Flights into the New York area were a regular run for our company as it had many business relationships there. I had flown this trip a multitude of times and knew the route by memory. Today we had been lucky. Our departure time was early enough in the afternoon to avoid the usual crush of air traffic out of the New York area airports. Consequently, we had not been delayed waiting for our takeoff clearance. The weather at our cruising altitude was clear and the air was smooth. The sun was warm shining into the cockpit as we flew southwestward toward a broad expanse of cirrus clouds. Just a minute or two after we entered the clouds, I looked up and slightly to my left. I felt the small hairs on the back of my neck stand up as I stared at the sight before me.

I remember thinking; "Is this it?" I finally tore my eyes away and looked over at Shane. His mouth was open and his eyes were locked onto something above and to our left.

"Are you seeing what I'm seeing?" he finally said.

I turned to look again as I answered, "If you're seeing three crosses of light, I am." They were still there; three bright, perfectly formed crosses of light. The one in the middle was elevated above the other two. They formed a perfect equilateral triangle.

"Holy...," Shane didn't finish his exclamation.

"Holy something may be right," I replied. Then we sat there in silence staring at the phenomenon for several minutes. Finally, very slowly, the crosses of light began to fade. Then, they were gone. Several more minutes passed as we waited in silence, but they never reappeared. I finally looked over at Shane.

He said quietly, "Wow. I wondered there for a while if...."

I replied, "Yeah, I know; me too." In fifty-three years of flying jets all over the world, I never saw anything like it before that day; or since.

Like I said; "One can see a long way from thirty-nine thousand."

Postscript #1: One dark night as we flew along the same J6 airway, I saw another heavenly sight that I only saw a few times in all of my years of aviation. It was a beautiful clear night with no moon. The weather forecast and the radar had indicated no weather anywhere between the New York area and Little Rock. However, we were starting to see numerous flashes of lightning southwest of our position toward the Nashville, Tennessee area. We turned on the weather radar and searched the sky in that direction but there was nothing. As we drew closer to the vicinity, the lightning continued and got brighter. Our route took us just to the north of the area of lightning; close enough that we could see the lights on the ground beneath it and beyond it. There were no clouds whatsoever…just the lightning.

Postscript #2: Once again it was the usual route assigned by ATC; J6 to Little Rock. It was another dark night and we had begun to see lightning in the distance slightly south of our course. The difference was this time it had been forecast. There was an area of convective weather in Tennessee that ran southeast into Georgia. It would not affect our flight this evening except to give us an exceptional display of the electrostatic discharges. Most of the lightning was of the usual type associated with thunderstorms, that is cloud to cloud and cloud to ground. It was an almost constant light show as we sat at forty-three thousand feet and watched.

Suddenly a straight blue bolt discharged from the top of a large thunderstorm and shot straight up toward the stratosphere. It had lasted less than a second and the other pilot had missed it. It was the only one that I had ever seen. As it turned out; years later when I retired it was the only one that I ever saw.

Toward The Evening Sky

THE *FFA?*

Little Rock Adams Field, AR; 2003

I was sitting in the audience during the Little Rock Airport Commission's monthly meeting with a representative from a very successful FBO chain. I had been working on trying to interest his company in establishing a facility at Little Rock National airport for some time. I had begun a search for a competitor for our present fuel provider as a result of a marked difference of opinion over how much our company should be paying for jet fuel.

A possible solution which I had previously investigated was for our company to self-fuel our aircraft. The Executive Director of the Little Rock National Airport at the time had tried to impose some arbitrary guidelines that supposedly denied to us the right to purchase jet fuel elsewhere and then to fuel our own aircraft. I had hastened to point out the incorrect assertions by employing their own Little Rock National Airport Standards Manual and the FAA's Grant Assurances Program. (The Grant Assurances program happens to be how the airport gets a *very* large percentage of its funding.) One of its sections specifies the right of an aircraft owner or corporation to self-fuel. Because I was somewhat surprised by the apparent lack of knowledge or interest in the corporate aircraft operations area at the airport, I had begun to attend the airport commission meetings on a regular basis. It was enlightening to say the *least*. (Wow! And I had thought that the Executive Director was somewhat lacking in certain areas.) With the exception of one of the commission members who was a pilot, an apparent lack of operational knowledge about aviation was a considerable understatement.

The FBO representative sitting beside me was interested in building and operating a new facility at the airport and in fact it had progressed to the actual planning stage. Those plans included an artist's depiction of how the completed facility would look. The Commission had previously been presented with the proposal and it would be up to them to approve or disapprove the project. Understandably, the potential new fixed base operator was rapidly losing its enthusiasm for the project after experiencing the extensive delays and seemingly endless obstacles raised by the airport commission.

The Chairman of the Airport Commission was speaking. He was surmising what the Federal Aviation Administration would think about an unrelated project that the commission was considering that day. He kept referring to the administration as the *FFA!*

The third time he said it, the representative from the FBO chain leaned over to me and said, "Is he saying the *FFA?*"

"Why yes he is," I replied.

"What in the world do the Future Farmers of America have to do with it?"

"Not a damn thing!" I said; "But he also thinks Runway 18/36 is Runway *1863*."

The rep replied, "No wonder we're not getting anywhere on the project." A few weeks later the potential new FBO provider finally gave up and pulled out of the project. (I didn't blame them.) Reportedly they "had never seen anything like it". I don't have to wonder what that meant.

Postscript: Historically, some accounts have it that the Little Rock Airport Commission during the early 1970's was somewhat similar in its involvement with a new company known then as Federal Express. The company wanted its hub to be the Little Rock National Airport but, after dealing with the lack of support from the Airport Commission, it finally moved to Memphis International.

I don't know exactly why the commission members are chosen but, in my observation, it is likely not because of a requirement for any extensive knowledge in the field of aviation. But then again, I should not be so critical of the local airport commission when I consider this fact: *There have now been three heads of the entire Federal Aviation Administration who have not even been licensed pilots!* They too obviously were selected for reasons having little to do with any background in aviation. You don't suppose these folks' selection to these elevated positions had anything to do with politics do you?

But then who knows; perhaps they thought that they were presiding over the FFA!

Toward The Evening Sky

KINGS OF THE ADAMS FIELD

Little Rock Adams Field, AR; 2008

David, the younger of the two Falcon 50 pilots had just completed his post flight walk-around inspection, when the visibly upset man came walking across the ramp. He came up to David and engaged him in a conversation that was very critical of the way the Falcon crew had operated their aircraft prior to and during their landing. He said that he didn't appreciate being "jammed in" by the jet. David apologized to him if they had caused him any problems. Gene, the other pilot came down the Falcon's steps and, when likewise confronted, he stated that they had followed the Air Traffic Controller's instructions. The upset individual then agreed that was true but that the Falcon had originally been assigned Runway 22 instead of Runway 18. He then asked how much more trouble would it have been to accept that runway instead of jamming him in? Evidently he then informed them that the next time he would fly his normal speed on base and final and that the Falcon could adjust his approach to landing; that twice was enough. He also informed them that he was going to communicate what happened to the head of their company.

Gene came to me with the information about the incident in case I was contacted about it. I told Gene that it sounded like the guy was upset about something that he could have easily prevented himself. Then I told the two pilots not to worry about it and that they had done nothing wrong. But as Gene had suspected, it wasn't over. I received a copy of the communiqué that the guy had sent the boss. Indeed he wrote that he had been "jammed" by our planes twice in the last two or three weeks. Although he stated that at no time was safety of flight compromised, he then offered that it was "very bad form" and bordered on "abuse of privilege". He said it suggested that they are the "Kings of the Adams Field" and that everyone else should "give way". He recommended that in the "spirit of cooperation" in the future, our jets fly the extra five minutes to Runway 22 whenever there were smaller, slower and less expensive aircraft being flown by private pilots using Runway 18. He then suggested such consideration might raise us to a "higher level of professionalism".

After reading his statements I decided to try to answer his concerns and perhaps correct some misconceptions that he obviously held. I began by commending him for his honesty in admitting that at no time was flight safety compromised by our plane or his. One of his beliefs which I am sure added to his consternation was that our Falcons' final approach speed was "not much under" the maximum true airspeed of his plane which he stated was in the range of 150 knots. I investigated the computed approach speed of the Falcon in question that day and found it to be 107 knots. I forwarded that information along with the further fact that unlike his incorrect assumption that the "slowest controllable speed" of the Falcon was also not much under 150 knots, that it is actually 82.5 knots (almost 70 knots under his uninformed estimate).

Additionally, I addressed his suggestions that our pilots somehow were "abusing privilege" because they are trying to save five minutes of flying time by requesting a closer runway. I pointed out that his suggestion that we use Runway 22 would waste about 10,000 gallons of fuel per year. I then reminded him that, as the pilot in command of his plane, he had the right to decline the tower's request to modify his traffic pattern and to request a normal one. If he had done so, then different instructions for their approach and landing would have been issued to the Falcon pilots and they would have complied without question. I assured him that our flight department is one of the best in the world and our pilots fly in a safe, expeditious and professional manner and that would not change.

Based on the somewhat scathing reply that I received, I don't think the "jammed in" pilot appreciated my obviously unsuccessful attempt to correct some of his assumptions about the Falcon 50 and my pilots. It appears that some folks just don't want to be confronted by facts, so they respond with anger. Perhaps it embarrasses them because it exposes their ignorance about the subject. (Or; as my wise old Dad used to say, "Son, that's why there are more horses' asses than horses.")

However, in spite of his scolding, I did find something very amusing about the whole situation. It was obvious that he wanted to use Runway 18/36 exclusively (from any jets).

So remind me now; *who* was calling *whom*, "The Kings of the Adams Field"?

THE COCKPIT "JUNGLE"

Various Aircraft Cockpits; 1938-2011

The United States Government's oversight and control of air transportation began in 1938 with the Civil Aeronautics Act. Then in 1940, President Roosevelt split the Civil Aeronautics Authority into two entities, the Civil Aeronautics Administration (CAA) and the Civil Aeronautics Board (CAB). The CAA was responsible for air traffic control, safety programs and airway development. The CAB was for safety rule making, accident investigation and economic regulation of airlines. In 1958 came the Federal Aviation Act which created the Federal Aviation Agency (It later became the Federal Aviation Administration). It became solely responsible for a system of air transportation and air traffic control to be shared by both civilian and military aircraft.

The idea behind the government's involvement in aviation from its beginning in the 1930's had been a noble one, improved safety in the air. Their thought was that both pilots and aircraft should be government certified as being safe. This was and is an admirable goal and has been successful to a large degree. Unfortunately somewhere along the way, perhaps because of its sheer size, some of the FAA's safety initiatives have had some unfortunate omissions.

I believe that a majority of knowledgeable aviation experts would agree that most aviation accidents are at least partially attributable to pilot error. I certainly believe that to be so. However I suggest that in many cases, the pilots have a lot of help in committing many of those errors. They have been "set up" to make errors by non-standardization in aircraft cockpit layouts and by the undeniable fact that all humans including pilots sometimes make mistakes. It is the obvious goal of every pilot to make as few errors as possible. It should be a primary goal in cockpit design to help pilots in that quest. Aircraft manufacturers and their suppliers are required to meet FAA specifications in order for their products to be certified to fly in the United States. Airframes, engines, avionics, hydraulics, seats, tires, wheels…everything in an aircraft must pass muster before airworthiness certificates are issued.

In my opinion, the cockpit of an aircraft is the most important section and yet it is there, where pilots receive vital information and then effect inputs to the various aircraft systems so they can safely operate the plane, that the FAA has allowed the manufacturers and aircraft designers to *setup* pilots to commit potentially serious errors in the cockpit.

Obviously, sometime in the past, there was an effort to standardize the primary instrument flying group to assist pilots to fly their aircraft with more precision, especially in weather and at night. The attitude, airspeed, altitude, vertical velocity, and heading indicator locations are somewhat standardized in most aircraft. Usually they are arranged in basically the same order and in the same relative position from each other. Because of this, a pilot after a short familiarization can perform a primary instrument scan and find this vital information in just about any cockpit of an aircraft certified to fly in the United States.

However, leave this primary instrument group and the pilots enter a virtual cockpit jungle with seemingly at times no apparent rhyme nor reason for the locations of such things as: engine fire warning indicators, engine fire shutdown handles or switches, cabin fire warning indicators, baggage compartment fire warning indicators, door unlock warning lights, generator switches, battery switches, starter switches, trim control switches, landing gear handle or switch, landing gear position indicators, flap handle or switch, flap position indicators, speed/air brake handle or switch, speed/air brake position indicators, cockpit light switches, aircraft lighting switches, engine anti-ice switches, wing anti-ice switches, cabin pressure switches, hydraulic switches, hydraulic pressure gauges, hydraulic quantity gauges, windshield heat switches, windshield wiper switches, communication radio switches, navigation radio switches, weather radar switches, and the list goes on and on ad nauseam.

Aircraft manufacturers seem to place the above (and countless more) systems controls and indicators wherever it is convenient or perhaps wherever they wish. Consequently the same or similar item in different aircraft may be to the left, to the right, above your head, behind your head, in front of your knee, behind your elbow, over the windscreen, on the floor beside your seat, by the galley, in the toilet *(no...really!)* etc. Hopefully the point is clear. If a pilot is flying more than one kind of plane and an emergency or abnormal situation occurs, he has effectively been setup by the manufacturers (and the FAA) to make an error or at least to experience hesitation and stress while trying to recall where the switch or indication for an affected system may be located in that particular manufacturer's cockpit. To make matters even worse, the same manufacturers sometimes move things around in the cockpit of their own aircraft. One manufacturer even decided to swap the locations of the landing gear handle and the flap handle after they had been on the opposite sides for years. I don't know how many landing gear handles were placed in the up position while on the ground as a result, but I wager that there were more than a few. Why would they do that? Talk about a trap.

There is probably not a pilot flying, retired, or in his grave, who has not had an "Oh S___!" moment in his career caused by reaching for the wrong switch or handle (and sometimes actuating it) because it is located in a completely different place on another aircraft that he flies or has flown in the past. I would think that the National Transportation Safety Board and the

Civil Aeronautics Board before them would have had fewer accidents to investigate over the years if there had been some cockpit standardization requirements.

I can think of no valid reason why the FAA and the CAA before them did not require at least some standardization in the relative locations of all major systems controls and indications in every cockpit by every aircraft manufacturer who needs certification for his aircraft to operate in U. S. skies.

It's been 78 years since 1938. *Perhaps they could start!*

Jerry W. Cook

THE "BIG PICTURE"

Various Flight Operations; 1957-2011

Throughout at least the civilian parts of my flying career, I had always heard that some really important decisions that were constantly affecting my career, and at times my life and the lives of my passengers, were being made by someone called *"They"* because *"They"* were privy to something called *"The Big Picture"*. And me, I had been told more than once that I just couldn't see *The Big Picture*. *They* might have moved that room with *The Big Picture* in it but I've heard rumors that it may be somewhere in Virginia. However, I suspect that there may be an even *"Bigger Picture"* that some more important *"Theys"* have located somewhere even closer to or perhaps in Washington, D.C. It is a regret that I carry with me into retirement that I never could find out exactly who or where *"They"* were so I could go there and get into that room where *"They"* keep *The Big Picture*.

I wanted to see *The Big Picture* so that maybe I could better understand some things that occurred; because from my perspective in the cockpit, so many of *"They's"* decisions affecting me and my fellow pilots are beyond our understanding. (Of course we are just pilots and *"They"* would likely say that in itself may explain our lack of understanding.) The following accounts are examples of the expertise of *"They"*:

(1)…One of the busiest high altitude airways over our nation is J6. It proceeds from the far northeastern United States generally southwest until turning westbound over Little Rock, AR. From there it heads toward California, ending up at the Salinas, California VOR. Countless times other pilots and I have tried to file another routing when we leave the New York area to get away from the heavily used airway; but virtually every time we did, the FAA changed our route right back to J6. Understandably, many of the airliners had to utilize the VOR airway simply because VORs were the only long distance navigation equipment they possessed. Consequently, they *had* to bunch together and take turns flying down the VOR airways.

However in our case, the company jets had the latest long range equipment. We could navigate accurately to virtually any point on earth without using VORs; but that didn't seem to matter to the FAA. They continually required us to mix it up with the airliners on J6. And I do mean mix it up. More likely than not during climb out, particularly when we were departing from Teterboro, we would receive numerous turns for spacing. Some of these turns were up to 90 and sometimes even 180 degrees to get spacing behind and between airline traffic from the other area airports i.e., JFK, LaGuardia, and Newark.

During these detours back and forth, while looking out for the many other jets climbing out of the New York area, I would be wondering; "Why? Why won't they just give us our requested routes away from this mess?" (And I might add this danger!) I have had the above scenario happen even when the reason that I filed another route was convective (stormy) weather located along or near J6. The FAA would change it back to J6; and then inform me that there would be extensive takeoff delays because of weather along J6. Once, I had refiled for a routing over Cleveland because of the weather and, when I checked on for my clearance, the controller informed me that he had put me at the end of the line to receive a clearance, "Because I had messed up their system." Then when I finally did get my clearance, "*They*" had changed it back to J6 along with the instruction, "Do not start your engines due to extensive weather delays."

(2)…On still another day, and obviously far away from *The Big Picture,* there were planes sitting all over the ramp at Teterboro Airport awaiting our IFR clearances. The reason given by the FAA for holding all clearances was, "Weather to the southwest along the departure corridor." Interestingly enough, I was only trying to go out to Long Island's Republic Airport, normally a flight of about twenty-five minutes during good weather and light air traffic. Several other aircraft were trying to head north toward New England and Canada, not even close to southwesterly. The sun was shining so bright and hot at the airport that, if we been outside, we would have been getting sunburned. We waited and waited and then we waited some more.

I jokingly said to the other pilot, "You watch; our clearance will get here at the same time as the rain." An hour went by and then about fifteen minutes later we heard the thunder. The first sprinkles began to hit the windscreen. Then, after the rain had fully developed, our clearance arrived, along with clearances for the northbound aircraft also. I know it may be hard to believe but, we didn't get the clearance we had originally filed for that smooth twenty-five minute flight in the nice bright sunshine. "*They*" completely re-routed us because the weather was by now over us and between us and our destination on Long Island. Now it had become a forty-five to fifty minute very bumpy flight largely spent diverting back and forth between the weather cells. Additionally, all of those planes headed to the north also got weather re-routes for the same reason. Maddeningly, most of the aircraft could have been at their destination airport(s) long before the first raindrops ever hit the Teterboro Airport. Heck, in our case we could have already been checked into our hotel and getting ready to go to dinner by then.

Pilots, try explaining to your passengers why you sat waiting on the ramp in the sunshine for an hour and a half and then, when it starts raining and thundering, you go flying. Don't tell them that you needed some instrument flying time. They won't think it's funny. Instead, tell them that

"They" made you do it. Then of course we know what their next question will be, *"Who in the Hell are "They"?!"*

(3)...FARs (Federal Aviation Regulations) govern the actions of all civilian pilots flying in the USA and in many cases the military. In the late 1990s, the FAA announced some revised rules for obtaining and maintaining pilot night currency in jet aircraft. It was written with so much lawyerese that it could not be understood by mere pilots. After scratching our heads over it for a day or two, we printed a copy and took it to our local FAA Flight Standards District Office for an official explanation of the new FAR.

Their first response was an eye-opener i.e., "We don't know what you're talking about. *Where* did you get *this?*"

Our answer: "It's a printout from *your* FAA website." *Oops...!* They said they would look into it and give us their interpretation in a few days.

In a tad more than a few days, they got back to us with their *clarification*, "We don't know what it means either. We'll get you an answer from the Fort Worth Region Office."

"Okay fine," we said; "We just want you to know that we're trying to follow your new rules."

I thought, "At least we're not the only ones who don't understand it." A few weeks later when we still hadn't heard anything, an inquiry was made. Suffice it to say that the clarification never came but I did manage to get a look at the response that they did get back.

Basically the message was this; *"It is not our job to interpret the regulations for pilots. It is our job to prosecute them for failure to comply." (You just gotta love em'; don't yah?)*

Postscript #1: I still want to get into that room with *The Big Picture* if I ever figure out where it is. However I did find out where at least one of the *"Theys"* is. That *"They"* is in Fort Worth and that *"They"* wants to prosecute pilots for failure to comply.

And finally, there was such nationwide turmoil over the thoroughly convoluted new night currency rules, that they were subsequently re-revised. The result was somewhat less complicated than the original but it is still full of lawyerese. *(Just like all the rest of them.)* There's an old saying among pilots; "Federal Aviation Regulations are worded by the most stupid lawyers in Washington, or the most brilliant."

I personally believe it to be the latter. *No one could be that consistently stupid.*

Postscript #2: Reading the previous accounts one might think that I have nothing good to say about the Federal Aviation Administration and that is not the case. Since I began using the National Airspace in 1957, I have witnessed a multitude of changes and an almost unbelievable increase in the number of aircraft relying on FAA controllers for separation. Although I believe that, as in many other organizations, the "Peter Principal" and "Politics as Usual" are alive and well in the FAA, the actual troops in the trenches do a fantastic job of separating aircraft. That they accomplish this in spite of their often totally unqualified top leadership, political interference and antiquated equipment is especially impressive.

Unfortunately, there are too many members of the public who believe the politicians when they stand up and publicly censure air traffic controllers for errors or failure to stay alert during grueling tours of duty. But there are those, such as pilots and the controllers themselves, who know where the real problem lies. Serious understaffing and Washington's political games with FAA funding are huge factors when considering where blame should be placed. But you will likely never hear these matters mentioned by those grandstanding public critics. They likely could never do a controller's job even if their own lives depended on it; but they are the first to take the podium to condemn.

Often during my flying career, I have said to other pilots, "I don't know how the air traffic controllers do it. I don't think I could do their job."

One day a few years ago while I was flying at 41,000 feet, an air traffic controller told me to turn thirty degrees to the right for "noise abatement". My curiosity was aroused because I could not imagine my aircraft's noise disturbing anyone from such a high altitude.
I said, "N1829S is turning right thirty degrees. Can you clarify the noise that we will be abating?"

"Certainly sir," he said. "That would be the noise generated if you ran into that airplane that I'm turning you away from."

My hat is off to the men and women behind the scopes and in the control towers and to those who have retired from such duties. I thank you for your 54 years of "noise abatement" on my behalf.

Jerry W. Cook

20,000 HOURS…NEVER SCRATCHED A PLANE…NEVER BLEW A TIRE

Los Angeles to Little Rock…Falcon 50EX N1829S; April 2, 2011

It was toward the end of the last full week of March. It was less than a week until my retirement which was scheduled for Thursday March 31st. I did not have another flight scheduled before then. I had recently turned down as my last trip, a flight to Europe. The European aviation authorities had decided some time ago that if you were over sixty-five years of age, you were too old to fly as a Captain in their part of the world. Maybe it was because of pride or perhaps I was just tired of the bureaucratic bull____ involved in making international flights; but I had decided that I didn't want to go; even to fly my last flight in the "queen of our fleet", our beautiful Falcon 900EX EASy.

Bill Goff, soon to be my replacement as the Director of Aviation and Jim Martin, to be Bill's replacement as the Chief Pilot, had initially talked me into going but, after considering all of the walking I would have to do on an injured right foot, I opted out. The chronic pain when walking, coupled with the European authorities' affront to my seventy-three year old flying skills and abilities, tipped the scales to my not going. Instead it looked like I would probably have the last four days of March to wrap things up and clean out my office. I was thinking that perhaps I would fly an out and back day trip in one of our Falcon 50EX's before I retired. I did not want to retire without flying again. I wasn't quite ready to hang up my wings, not yet.

Marilyn was sitting at her desk in our beautiful new hangar with Jim Martin standing beside her. They were looking intently at the next week's schedule. They both looked toward me as I walked into the lobby area and I could tell that something was up.

"Jerry, could you possibly fly the trip that is leaving next Thursday the 24th? We are short of a pilot if I don't pull someone off a 'scheduled off' day; that is unless you will take it," Jim said.

"When is it coming back?" I asked, although I had seen the schedule earlier. I thought perhaps it had changed to a March return date.

"Friday, April 1st," Marilyn answered while smiling mischievously.

"Oh, so you need an old fool to fly on April Fools' Day," I replied.

She just smiled again, nodded and said, "That too."

"I'm going on the trip also," said Jim.

Then he continued, "Maybe you could postpone your retirement for a couple of days. It's an enjoyable trip, to southern California." It was going to be a nice trip. As I said, I had looked at it before but had disregarded it because of the return date.

"I'll check with Human Resources to see if I can extend my retirement. If they approve, I'll take it."

"Thank you," said Jim; "Let us know."

Human Resources basically said, "No problem," so I advised Marilyn. That's when I found out that it had just been changed to a Saturday April 2nd return. Oh well, now at least I wouldn't be flying my last flight on April Fools' Day. Somehow, that just didn't seem right; although perhaps appropriate. It really was a very pleasant trip. Several days spent near San Diego hanging out in a beautiful hotel on the southern California coast ain't all bad. Then after a twenty-five minute evening flight up to Los Angeles and a one night stay in another nice hotel, it would be time to fly my last flight.

I couldn't help having mixed emotions and lots of varying thoughts. I had spent nearly two and one half years of my life off the ground and flown about nine million miles. A recurring thought was that I had never put a scratch on an airplane or even blown a tire in fifty-four years of flying airplanes all over the world. I had mentioned that fact to my wife Linda just a few days before and she had quickly shushed me. She evidently was nervous about me making that statement before my final flight. I think that she was afraid that I might jinx it. Twenty thousand hours of flying does involve a lot of takeoffs and landings with their inherent risks. But I couldn't help thinking about the zero scratches a few times. Although a number of bad guys with big guns had blown some holes in, and some parts off my jet fighter during my two hundred plus missions in Vietnam and a wingman ran into my wingtip while he was screwing around stateside, I had never put a ding on an airplane myself. I was proud of that, especially since I had experienced quite a few opportunities to do so.

Indeed the few days turned out to be very enjoyable and relaxing and probably just about perfect for a last trip before retirement. I took advantage of the time between flights to get some sun, eat some good seafood and work on this manuscript. I was glad that I had opted out of the England flight and that this trip had been added to the schedule. It was very nice indeed.

Saturday morning April the 2nd at Los Angeles International Airport arrived and it was going to be a beautiful day. The airport was covered with the usual early morning maritime four hundred foot ceiling off the Pacific, which was just a couple of miles to the west of where I stood on the ramp. The visibility was good at six miles and a light breeze made it feel cooler than the sixty-one degrees. I stood watching a FedEx MD11 takeoff. The huge jet had a very long takeoff roll but it finally rotated, climbed into the cloud deck and disappeared from sight. It appeared as if he was only moving about twenty or thirty knots when he lifted off the runway. The optical illusion of very slow speeds by the larger jets when landing and taking off still fascinates me. They appear to be flying 130 to 140 knots slower that they actually are and about ready to fall out of the sky. It was obvious from his takeoff roll that he was very heavy. I assumed that he was probably heading somewhere in the western Pacific Rim with many long hours of flight before he landed again. I thought back to the late sixties when I was a Los Angeles based Pan Am crewmember and just heading out on Flight One "Around the World", some forty-three years before.

"Wow. Where did the time go and how did I get this damned old?" I thought as I walked toward my last takeoff. I briefed my two passengers about the upcoming flight. The forecasted weather for the trip to Little Rock was outstanding. It was to be clear all the way home after we topped the cloud deck at LAX and then we were to have a tailwind component of about fifty knots most of the way. The passengers had been on schedule so we lifted off runway 25R right on time. The Falcon felt good beneath my hands as we became airborne in the smooth morning air. I tracked the Holtz RNAV Departure and upon departing 620 feet headed for the first fix. The jet was solid and responsive as we popped out on top of the clouds in just a few seconds after liftoff. I had just made my final takeoff at the controls of a jet and in less than three hours I would be landing into retirement.

Falcon 50EX N1829S was our oldest plane. I had personally taken delivery of it in August of 2000. Somehow Stephens' oldest pilot flying their oldest jet on my last flight seemed very appropriate. And so did the gorgeous day that God had provided for me to do it. As had been advertised, there was not a cloud in the sky all the way to Little Rock.

My first clue that things were not normal was when the control tower operator answered Jim's call for landing instructions. Instead of referring to us as Falcon N1829S, the controller said, "Good afternoon Jerry, the wind is 140 at 6 knots. We are landing Runway 22R and Runway 18. Which one would you like?"

I said "We'll take 18."

He said, "Roger Jerry, you are cleared to land on Runway 18. I understand that this is your final flight before retirement." I replied that indeed it was.

He answered, "Congratulations sir on a great career." I thanked him and then concentrated on making my last landing a good one. There weren't going to be any more opportunities. It wasn't necessarily a "squeaker" but it was a good landing.

As we rolled down the runway the tower operator said, "Nice landing Jerry. Enjoy your retirement. Contact Ground Control on 121.9." I thanked him and continued slowing the jet as we rolled down runway 18. When we got about halfway down the runway I could see two fire trucks parked facing each other and waiting in front of our company hangar at the Supermarine Fixed Base Operations. I had just planned to land and then "walk quietly into the sunset" however, our hangar doors were open and it seemed to be full of people. I looked over at Jim and he just grinned. The ground controller added his congratulations and cleared us to taxi to the Stephens hangar.

I had talked to my son Jeff just that morning before I left Los Angeles. I had assumed that he was at his home in Florida. He is a Southwest Airlines pilot and I had asked him when he was flying next. He said that he had a trip later that day. I told him that I was getting ready to fly my last flight.

He said, "I know Dad. Congratulations on a wonderful career. I'm very proud of you." I thought about his words again as I turned off taxiway Alpha onto the ramp in front of our hangar. The fire trucks began spraying large arches of water for me to taxi Falcon 29S under. My passengers, Mrs. Stephens and Mrs. Erwin, had been in on the arrival plans and they began to applaud loudly as the water began spraying the plane. Suddenly I had to blink rapidly to see clearly.

"Who is that parking us?" Jim said from the right seat. Water from the fire trucks was still running down the windscreen and I looked again at the person guiding us into the chocks. It was my son Jeff. What a great surprise. He had flown in from Florida for my final landing. Now I was really having trouble seeing clearly. Jeff marshaled me in just as he had when he was working and taking flying lessons at the old Little Rock Air Center. He then gave the chocks-in signal as Reggie our head of line service chocked the front wheels.

As we finished the parking checklist Jim said, "Why don't you go ahead and see everyone and I'll finish this up." Mrs. Stephens and Mrs. Erwin offered their congratulations as I left the Falcon cockpit for the last time as a pilot. It was hard for me to believe that I had begun flying these wonderful Falcon jets in January 1982, over 29 years before.

I thought, "Where on earth did all the time go?" I blinked hard again and walked down the aircraft steps and tried not to limp on my injured foot. Everyone in the hangar was applauding loudly. I didn't know what else to do, so I stopped and took a bow. Fortunately it got the desired effect as everyone laughed and clapped louder. The rest is kind of blurred. It's hard to see when you have to blink back the tears. I remember hugging Jeff and expressing my surprise at seeing him because I thought that he was in Florida. He laughed and said that I had not asked him where he was. I saw my lovely wife Linda walking toward me with a congratulatory hug and kiss. Susan my stepdaughter and her husband John were there with big smiles and congratulations. Katherine and Eddie Creighton, two of our close friends from church also were there with smiles and applause.

I remember seeing lots of my employees and their families. Bill Goff was standing there grinning with Marty his wife; also known as my "Las Vegas Daughter". I had walked her down the aisle to Bill a couple of years before at a little Las Vegas wedding chapel and watched her and Bill be married by *"Elvis".* Bill had been responsible for a wonderful company retirement party for me early in March and here he was again, honoring me with still another event to mark the end of my long career in aviation. In addition to being an outstanding pilot, Bill had also been an exceptional assistant and Chief Pilot. I knew that he would do a great job as the new Stephens Director of Aviation.

Steve Austin and his wife Sheila were there. Steve was to become the new Assistant Chief Pilot. He had recently served an instrumental role during the planning and construction of the beautiful new hangar in which we now stood. Mary Hubbard, my dispatcher and all around Girl Friday, was there with her two sons and husband Greg. I had often told others that Mary was the real "boss" of the department. I can say with all certainty that my tenure first as a line pilot and then later as the Flight Department Manager was blessed by her dedication, hard work, and kind-hearted nature. Marilyn, our scheduler was there and she was laughing as usual. What a great addition she has been to the department.

Tim Cook, our perfectionist Chief of Maintenance was there and after offering his congratulations was all business again with his usual inquiry, "How's the airplane?" Several of the line pilots and their families were present as were members of the aircraft maintenance and line service teams. It was rewarding to see them all there. I tried to talk to each one of the well-wishers to tell them how much I appreciated them taking their time to come out on a Saturday and honor me with their presence. I hope that I made it around to all of them because I was sincerely moved and I wanted them to know it.

I remember telling the group in the hangar what Linda had said to my boss, Warren Stephens, when he had asked her at my pre-retirement party in March what she thought about me retiring.
She had smiled sweetly and said; "I think I'm going to have *twice* the husband and *half* the money." Warren had laughed that night and now everyone in the hangar was laughing too. It got a chuckle all right; but she spoke the truth.

I turned around and looked once more at the beautiful Falcon jet in which I had just made my last flight. It sat there gleaming in the afternoon sun. Some water that remained from the fire trucks' traditional pilot retirement ceremony was still slowly dripping from the wings' glistening leading edges. Once again I couldn't help but marvel at how fortunate I had been all of these years; 20,000 hours…never scratched a plane…never blew a tire. Fifty-three years of flying jets was a long stint and I didn't want it to end. However inside me I knew; *"Now it was time."*

Now I turned and walked slowly; *"No…scratch that."*
Now I turned and *limped* slowly; *"Toward the Evening Sky".*

GLOSSARY

Airlift International--A charter and freight airline based in Miami, Florida, now defunct.

Air Refueling Track--Airspace reserved for military aircraft to air-to-air refuel.

Angle of Attack--The angle of a reference line on an aircraft (usually a line from the leading edge to the trailing edge of the wing) relative to the air in which it is moving.

Angle of Attack Vane--A thin movable blade attached to an aircraft which when moved by the airflow measures the angle of attack and sends it to an instrument in the cockpit.

ATIS--Automatic Terminal Information System (Reports weather at airport)

ATP--Airline Transport Pilot. A term denoting the Federal Aviation Administration's highest ranked pilot license.

Base Leg--The portion of an aircraft landing pattern usually located 90 degrees from the runway.

Bird--Term commonly used by pilots to refer to an airplane.

Break--A steep-banked turn in a fighter aircraft used to evade an attacker. It is also the term used to describe the steep turn over the runway before landing.

BSX--Battle Staff Exercise

BUFF--"Big Ugly Fat Fellow"; the polite version of a nickname for the B-52 aircraft.

Bug--An indices set on a flight instrument as a reminder.

Bummed--Disappointed

Captured--During an instrument approach when an aircraft is established on the electronic centerline of the ILS.

Chase--The relative position of a plane flown by an instructor pilot or check pilot in relation to the plane of the pilot being instructed or tested. It is normally used in fighters or fighter-type aircraft.

Christmas Tree--The term referring to a large aircraft parking ramp which looks like the shape of a Christmas tree from the air.

Cocked--An aircraft that is fueled, pre-flighted and ready to takeoff at a moment's notice.

Combat Wing--The position flown by a second aircraft in relation to the lead aircraft during air combat maneuvering.

Cone of Confusion--The area directly above a VOR station where the navigational signal received by the cockpit instrument is changing too rapidly due to the aircraft's position and speed. As the aircraft proceeds away from the VOR the signal becomes steady again.

Course--Term used to describe the chosen direction to or from a navigational point or an airport runway.

Down in the weeds--Term meaning to fly extremely low.

Downwind--The portion of an aircraft landing pattern which is located at a distance from the side of the runway. At this point the aircraft is heading opposite to the landing runway direction.

DME--Distance measuring equipment.

Dragging--Refers to having the landing gear and/or the flaps extended before they are needed.

Dum Dum--The name of the main Calcutta, India airport until a few years ago. It has been renamed and is now referred to as Kolkata airport.

Easter Eggs--Refers to switches and levers/handles left in the wrong positon in a cockpit.

Element--Aircraft flying in formation; usually two.

En Masse--In one group or altogether.

FAA--Federal Aviation Administration.

FFA--Future Farmers of America.

Fighter Drag--Fighter aircraft flying in formation with air refueling tankers in order to refuel one or more times during extended flights.

Fingertip Formation--A formation of four aircraft. Their spacing resembles the fingertips of a hand.

First Officer--Co-pilot

Flown West--Term which refers to a pilot who has died.

Formation Lights--Lights added to the side of the nose and the wingtips of an aircraft to aid a pilot in maintaining the proper position as a wingman.

Form 5--U.S. Air force pilot flight records.

Furlough--Term used when pilots are laid off from an airline.

Ginza--Section of Tokyo, Japan known for its shopping.

G Load--The gravity forces pressing down on a pilot when turning his plane hard or pulling out of a dive.

Head Up and Locked--Unflattering expression used to describe a pilot who makes a stupid mistake.

Hidden Hilton--Refers to the facility where SAC crews stayed while on alert duty.

High-Angle Dive-bomb--When a fighter or attack plane is in a steep dive toward the target with the aim of dropping bombs; usually 45 degrees nose down or more.

High-Low-High--A flight profile involving a high altitude portion followed by a low altitude segment and then back to a high altitude.

High Wing Loading--An aircraft that has a high weight combined with a relatively small wing area. This increases the number of pounds per square inch supported by the wing. Although there is the potential for high speed, there is sacrifice of turning ability.

Holding Pattern--An area designated as a place for aircraft to circle in flight while waiting for clearance to approach and land at an airport or to proceed on course.

ILS--Instrument Landing System. Enables a pilot to approach and land utilizing instruments in the cockpit when visual approaches and landings are not possible.

In-country--Within South Vietnam.

Jink--High G turns or other aggressive flight maneuvers utilized to spoil a gunner's aim or a missile's guidance.

Kicker--The rest of the story as in, "What's the catch?"

KSFO--Official International Air Transportation Association identification code for San Francisco International Airport.

Localizer--An electronic signal sent from an ILS antenna to indicate the course to the runway. The cockpit instrument displays whether an aircraft is flying left, right or on the centerline of the course.

Localizer 16--Refers to an instrument approach to Runway 16 which utilizes only the localizer.

Main Gear--Refers to the wheels, tires and strut mechanisms which support most of the weight of an aircraft. They are usually attached to the bottom of the wings or fuselage near the midpoint of the longitudinal axis of the aircraft.

MARSA--"Military Accepts Responsibility for the Separation of Aircraft"

M-1 Maneuver--A method to help the body maintain vision and remain conscious during very high forces of gravity (Gs) encountered while flying high performance fighter aircraft. It is performed by contracting as many skeletal muscles as possible, closing off the airway behind the Adam's apple, and tightening stomach and chest muscles in short bursts to force air into the lungs. This helps retain the blood flow from the heart to the brain.

MiG--Slang term used to describe the aircraft designed by the Russian company Mikoyan-Gurevich Design Bureau. In this book it refers to the jet fighters of the North Vietnamese Air Force.

Military Power--The maximum engine power that is available without using the afterburner(s).

Mole Hole--An unofficial name to describe the building used by Strategic Air Command aircrews on alert.

O Club--Officers' Club

ORI--Operational Readiness Inspection. Tests an USAF organization's wartime capabilities.

O6--Officer rank level 6. Refers to a "full" colonel (Rank insignia is an eagle).

Pan Ops--Pan American Operations.

Parallel-type yaw damper--Early type system to keep the tail from moving side-to-side by utilizing automatic rudder inputs. It had to be turned off on early KC-135s prior to landing.

PCS--Permanent Change of Station. A military transfer for an extended period.

Phantom--Refers to the F-4 Phantom 2 fighter aircraft manufactured by McDonnell Aircraft.

Pitch-up--A rapid uncontrolled nose rise leading to out-of-control flight. Term used to describe this condition in the F/RF101 Voodoo aircraft.

PUP--Pilot Upgrade Program

RF-101--Reconnaissance fighter designed and produced by McDonnell Aircraft.

RF-101 business--Refers to the possession, operation and utilization of the aircraft by the U.S. Air Force.

RIF--Reduction in Force. When the military reduces the number of personnel in its ranks.

RMI--A cockpit instrument indicating heading and course. Used to assist navigation.

Round-filed--Thrown into the trash can.

RTU--Replacement Training Unit

Runway 09L--The leftmost of two parallel runways with their alignment being at or near a magnetic bearing of 090 degrees.

RW--Runway

SACumicision--Slang term referring to being forced into SAC.

SAM--Surface to Air Missile

Shiny switches--Pilot slang term meaning the cockpit switches that are used on a regular basis.

Sink-rate--The rate of descent of an aircraft. Term normally used just prior to landing.

Six o'clock--The area directly behind an aircraft.

Sled--A platform on skids hooked behind a hay baler.

Squawk--Term referring to transmitting an electronic identification code from an aircraft. Also a term used when referring to an aircraft discrepancy (i.e. an aircraft "squawk").

Stewardess--Most common term used in the past to mean a female flight attendant.

Stick--Refers to the control stick in a fighter or fighter type aircraft. Term is also used to indicate a pilot.

Suicide doors--An automobile door that is hinged at the rear edge and opens at the front.

Tac-Eval--Tactical Evaluation

Terrain masking--Flying at such a low altitude that radar cannot see the aircraft.

Third Officer--An additional co-pilot.

Touch and Go--When an aircraft does not stop after landing but immediately takes off again.

TWX--Teletypewriter network. A message delivered by TWX.

Vectored--Aircraft is given headings to fly by an air traffic controller who is normally utilizing radar.

V1--The speed during a multiengine jet's takeoff roll that either a stop on the remaining runway *or* a takeoff is possible with an engine failure at that point. It is also called "decision speed". If the engine failure occurs prior to this speed the takeoff should be aborted. At a speed higher than V1 the takeoff should normally be continued.

Vr--Rotate speed. When the pilot raises the nose of his aircraft for takeoff.

V2--Safety speed after an engine failure. Minimum aircraft speed required to clear a 35 foot obstacle at the end of the runway and to maintain a climb with one of the engines failed.

Voodoo--F/RF-101 aircraft.

Voodoo Dance--Term used to describe the flight maneuver sometimes used to achieve nose wheel retraction after takeoff in an F/RF-101.

VOR--Visual Omni Range. Ground based unit which transmits navigational information to an aircraft.

VORTAC--VOR combined with a TACAN (Tactical Air Navigation system. Used by the military. It provides a distance and bearing to a ground station).

VOQ--Visiting Officers' Quarters.

Water Augmentation--A system used to boost engine power by injecting water into it.

Jerry W. Cook

About the author

Brigadier General, Ret., Jerry W. Cook hung up his wings in 2011 at the age of seventy-three after piloting jets for fifty-three years. He flew in the United States Air Force for ten years before leaving to fly for the former Pan American World Airways. Cook also flew for the Air National Guard for sixteen years prior to his military retirement in 1986. Concurrently he became a corporate pilot actively flying various jets until his retirement from Stephens Inc. as their Director of Aviation. He has more than 20,000 flight hours, mostly in jets.

He is the author of the book, "Once a Fighter Pilot", first published in 1996.

Made in the USA
Charleston, SC
10 July 2016